A Rosellen Brown Reader

The Bread Loaf Series of Contemporary Writers

ROSELLEN BROWN

A Rosellen Brown
READER

SELECTED

POETRY AND PROSE

Middlebury College Press
Published by University Press of New England
Hanover and London

MIDDLEBURY COLLEGE PRESS
Published by University Press of New England,
Hanover, NH 03755
© 1992 by Rosellen Brown
All rights reserved
Acknowledgments appear on page 000
Printed in the United States of America   5   4   3   2   1

CIP data appear at the end of the book

FOR BOB PACK,
with gratitude and affection

Contents

Contents

A Bread Loaf Contemporary

A T A T I M E when the literary world is increasingly dominated by commercial formulas and concentrated financial power, there is a clear need to restore the simple pleasures of reading: the experience of opening a book by an author you know and being delighted by a completely new dimension of her or his art, the joy of seeing an author break free of any formula to reveal the power of the well written word. The best writing, many authors affirm, comes as a gift; the best reading comes when the author passes that gift to the reader, a gift the author could imagine only by taking risks in a variety of genres including short stories, poetry, and essays.

As editors of The Bread Loaf Series of Contemporary Writers we subscribe to no single viewpoint. Our singular goal is to publish writing that moves the reader: by the beauty and lucidity of its language, by its underlying argument, by its force of vision. These values are celebrated each summer at the Writers' Conference on Bread Loaf Mountain in Vermont and in each of these books.

We offer you the Bread Loaf Contemporary series and the treasures with which these authors have surprised us.

Robert Pack
Jay Parini

Author's Note

"Everybody got style—style ain't nothin' but keepin' the same idea from beginning to end." August Wilson gave that line to one of his characters in *Ma Rainey's Black Bottom*. It's an intriguing and self-confident statement but I've never been able to decide whether, put that way, it's a good thing or a bad one. Keepin' the same idea from beginning to end? If our careers are long enough we'd better hope to have more than one idea—more than one style, then, too. Yet the work had better not seem to belong to just anyone (or worse, to no one).

The earliest writing in this collection was published in 1965, the most recent in 1991.

Like a pilot flying low over the land, I've finally been able to study what my "central work," my novels, can't teach me—the general shape of my preoccupations across the years; the rises and declivities of skill, curiosity, casual engagement, and inescapable obsession. (Needless to say, I vacillate between satisfaction at what I see and shame at what I don't—the finite visible landscape I've wrought and the infinite invisible one I haven't dreamed, let alone created.)

Viewed from that distance, I wonder if others see it as contiguous. I wonder if Ma Rainey's vibrant creator, who makes it sound easy, would nod and say "Well, it ain't exactly all alike but yeah. Different ideas but they got your sound, they got your rhythm. You got some stuff on your mind all those years and it's in there everyplace you look." Wouldn't I like to hear "Don't sweat it, lady. Twenty-five years but I'd know your chops anywhere. . . ."

STORIES

The Wedding Week

N E X T Saturday night at this time I will be married. I am not afraid of that—it may be unfashionable but I haven't a doubt we are doing the right thing, we shall be at our best as husband and wife, if not in the old style then in the new.

To be blunt, what worries me is my father. How can I explain this?

How must he appear to the woman who is to be my wife? When she met the two of them it was, of course, my mother she remembered. My mother is small; she looks as though her very bones are dense; thrown into a pool of water she would surely sink like a stone, were she not so enterprising that she would raise the dead to come to her assistance. She wastes neither inches of flesh nor steps nor movements. They are, like all things, scarce, so they are only spent on work she fancies must be done, much of it scrub-work (into the dawn—God, from my bed I used to hear her harrowing the refrigerator's poor skin long past midnight) or cook-work to keep the holy fires stoked in our stomachs. She is the blower upon the one flame of life, digestion. This feisty little immigrant *balabuste* who started in Poland and continued in Hester Street en route to East New York— nonetheless she has a noisy dignity about her. I recognize that; she moves about, shapeless, in ugly shoes, haggling and bearing grudges at every street corner, but with a nun's certainty that she is doing God's work. (And more efficiently, too—with no thoughts wasted on God.) The old story. From the sight of my mother's print housedresses and shopping bags one could derive a view of my childhood that would have to be correct, as it is clichéd, in some if not all of its details.

What else, I asked my wife-to-be. What could she say about my father after a single meeting?

Kind. Frightened, she said. Of me?

Of the moon, I told her. The months. The mice. Start anywhere. The heat of his own mouth. All of it makes him hide. A gentle man, terrified of the command to breathe and keep on breathing. A rabbit on his way to the stew pot.

You have his arms, she says.

I do?

His legs probably. And more. Precisely. Down to the way the dark hairs lie. For all I can tell, you trade one pair of arms between you when I look away.

I am downcast and intrigued, hot and cold. What else do we share? I have a voice and I use it, though with little ease. I have shoulders he never dreamed of having, and in my muscles a history of basketball, of five-sewer stickball. Also, a will in which my mother's red blood runs hard. But I am so visibly his son. If he is a rabbit I am a lamb—his fears are my second-thoughts and third, his cringing has become my following. My wife and I will move into a house which would have been a palace to him on his wedding night. It will have a niche at the turning of the stairs in which we could place a statue—*The Winged Victory*—but will probably mock with a collage of beer cans or a giant mousetrap. If our doorway has a *mezuzah* tacked on with little nails, it will only be so that my father can visit us here. But I am going nowhere on my own, though I may punish myself for knowing it, with my second-generation self-consciousness. Updated vices. Each of us is just a shadow too helpless for whatever dreams we need.

I must assume he was a boy once. I ask him, he kicks himself for answer. Why do you want to know, he asks. Such memories no one needs. Think ahead. Think happy. I insist. His head goes into his shoulders. He could never wiggle his ears like some fathers but he could wrinkle his neck like an ancient turtle. He seems to think he deserved his past.

Always, apparently, the ground was frozen. (It will do you good to know? You need it for something, maybe a paper?) Summers he doesn't remember, nor any of the colors of summer. Maybe there were flowers, maybe not. Nor does he remember the pogroms, though Szeliezin suffered its necessary share. Mostly it was local hooligans, out with torches and jugs of foul local wine, nothing to be dignified with a word like pogrom. Good luck, who wants to remember?

4

But those days and nights, so weighted with flung stones, sank to the bottom of his memory and lie there now. He brims and brims with his ready tears that make me cringe. He had fur at the top of his boots—my father in boots! and a sort of Russian pea-coat with a fur collar, double-breasted—but holes at the bottom. The floor of his house was made of dirt, certainly. It had never occurred to me. Only the synagogue was whole and the houses of most of the goyim—out there, across a moat full of, what? drunks? rapists? assassins? A few of the Jews in the village had wooden floors—the *rebbe*, after all . . .

He swears he ran in the stiff stripped fields, he climbed, fought, made mischief. The youngest son always makes trouble, you know. Also he beat his breast in shul beside his father. He must have listened too well to the Yom Kippur chant of self-excoriation: *For the sin which we have committed before thee by the stretched-forth neck of pride; for the sin which we have committed before thee by levity; and for the sins for which we are liable to the penalty of forty stripes . . . to the penalty of excision and childlessness . . . to the penalty of death by the hand of heaven. . . .* He never met most of his brothers, nor did he replace them. Could it really be—while I, his child, climbed his steep sides, he was back inside his balding head, getting his firm foothold on a tree that still stands, leaning a long way down over the frozen river Szeliezin?

And then he woke up here? Was it like that? Yes, one long lurch of a crossing, boring, full of squabbling with strangers, and the smell of puke in your pores, a dream in which you suffered like cattle. Who has a new word for it—what should you say, you suffered like silkworms? No one ever said it was poetry. Cattle. *Shoyin*.

So the sidewalks here were frozen—worse than home in Szeliezin, at least he'd had those boots. But he didn't bring such things to the new world, *shmates*. So he was always cold. He lived on the ice. No matter how he sweated. All those shabbos candles, what did they ever melt? Not a heart, not a winter. Only his own heart dripped down in waxy tears, his mother covered her eyes and wept and prayed and wept. Never trust what's underfoot (his one long lesson to his only son—does it have anything to do with me, learned as he slid and tumbled down Delancey Street?). You slip, you slide, *greeneh*! You guess it all wrong, none of it's yours. *Go home, sheeny!* It's not for you to choose, this feast, this America—none of it's kosher—nobody said!—none of it's cheap. For fifty years you walk hunched forward ready to fall and break your skull, and never relax in the language.

What more do I know of him? I search him out like a father so long dead I never met him. All that's left to tell is this part that terrifies me. I go to her, my almost-wife, she holds my hand as though nothing is going to happen. She doesn't see.

I know, I think, when my father stopped his climbing games, when he closed the trapdoor over his head, when he learned the rabbit jerk and began to wait for the axe's shadow on the ice. It was this week in his life, the one I'm beginning today. Do you see? This week exactly. Listen.

He lived at home. He was the only child still with his parents, his sisters married, his brothers scattered, one even gone off somewhere without a trace, without a how-are-you. He brought his paycheck home from the shop and gave it to his mother whole. Finally he would bite off a corner of it, he had a girl, a possibility. He felt guilty about leaving them, he delayed the proposal that hung in the air until the girl made moves to break the whole thing off; she was wasting her time, she had obligations to her parents too, the first of which was marriage . . . That was my mother, of course, with long hair and a round face, my mother from the pictures at Bear Mountain wearing knickers, smiling in a tumult of fallen leaves. Everyone I know has pictures of their parents young at Bear Mountain, I have been to Bear Mountain myself with a camera around my neck . . . My father looks a foot taller in those pictures, his lips were full and his nose assertive, his eyes gave off complicated lights, refracted by evident laughter. He was a funny man, my mother has told me, more incredulous, even, than I. In Yiddish he would make word plays, jokes on people's names, nobody got away without being renamed. Really.

Then his father died. His father died on a Monday morning, coughing black blood.

It wasn't enough. His mother choked on the bone of that death and died—echo, obedient echo!—all in the week of his wedding. *He didn't intend to start his marriage sitting shiva.* The dancers in the mirrors stopped in their tracks, the looking glasses went dark, locked up what they had seen like memories behind blind eyes. It is forbidden to see yourself in mourning. *He didn't intend to lie down in the earth when he had a marriage-bed*, like a servant, a widow,

6

a dog. But the youngest son is sewed to his parents' bones with the strongest thread of their life.

Like a man whose hair goes gray in a single night, my father's life—can you see it?—drained down, to water their graves. They must have beanstalks on those graves, for all they took of his passion, for the little they left behind. There was a year that dragged like a terminal illness; then slowly, beginning again, my father remembered he had almost had a wife. So they were married.

Now, you see, whether I believe it or not—this is the week of my wedding. Deep winter coughs and chatters and washes down the air with killing cold. My father's bad eyes are clenched against an angel with better things to do (I say) than hang around for a chat where he's got no customer. The *malachamuviss* doesn't haggle. But my father, small as a boy, ducks under his 50 mg. of bottled sleep. He goes looking, shaking the bedclothes, beating the louvered closet doors, sniffing for the doom that slouches, still, just out of eyeshot.

I take his shoulders, in his old striped sweater that's buttoned wrong. Papa, the world is full of unlucky men! I swear he regrets he is not one, once and for all. His forehead is gray, the veins are lavender. I don't think he has pain in him, only aches. Not anger, just apology. The way my mother, all her life, has had not tragedies but "aggravations" . . .

I pull myself up, above him like a father: Will it make you happy, papa, you want a disaster? What would you like? You want me to say it, I will—here. The floor of your house, no matter what, will always, now and forever, be made of dirt.

Sonny, what do you want? What do you want from me. He shrugs, weakly, one shoulder, to get me off him.

He doesn't know. I am fighting for his life, for mine. I want him to marry my mother again, all of us together under the *chupa*, the arbor of good wishes. Begin again, start fresh, drink the wine of his children, be blessed with our hope against hope. I want him to have a honeymoon of lust and sun and wine prodigally spilled. *I want him to promise me, promise me like a man, not like a shivering rabbit, that he is not going to die.*

7

A Decent Period of Mourning

T H I S   W A S in the time of virgins, the time of marriage propos-
als. Men flew from coast to coast at holiday time to ask for unending
love, for a wedding in white. It was not so long ago.

There was the spicy taste of snow in the afternoon, snow ready-
ing, but none of it fell. She had walked downtown to do some final
shopping for the trip they were taking together—a flannel night-
gown, a parka, a gift for him that would contain more than a hint of
her implication in his life, enough so that she could not pretend she
hadn't meant it.

She accomplished her whole list in half the time she'd planned
on. The parka was navy wool, unprepossessing. It announced her
ordinariness to the world just at the instant when she was planning
to become secretly extraordinary, to jump off the edge of propri-
ety, a demon lover; it seemed a necessary protection. The nightgown
did the same—its demure granny neck, its undramatic pink-sprigged
flannel was meant as a sort of scoffing laugh at her past, a hypocriti-
cal salute to modesty meant to be stripped off in an instant, with a
cry of triumph.

Perhaps she was going to be decisive from now on, beginning with
this trip. She was full of beliefs that she had formed and practiced
alone, large and portentous, small and frivolous, and among them
was that marriage, the decision to marry, ought to promise comple-
tion, not alteration. She knew that completion when she saw it, she
was without a humbling doubt. Something heavy had closed behind
her and it left her steady, ballasted.

Or she'd thought it had. But what she felt, walking slowly back
home through the pre-Christmas crowds just as the light made its first
small modulation toward evening, was that everything was about to

be over for her. She was choosing happiness, and allowing herself to be chosen by it. The weight of it made her walk slowly, the burden made her eyes ache. She looked at the young men hurrying past and they seemed, all of them, to be possible suitors for her, alive with intriguing detail—willing, and in a dozen dissimilar ways, satisfying to the touch. The one who could sing a breathtaking counter tenor, the one who knew six dialects of Chinese, the one who was going to design a monument. And in the folds of their clothes they brought her the memory, not yet experienced, of so many places—Nantucket in January, opening a closed-up house, the smell of ashes flying out at them, and frozen apples. The stews of France and Germany and Puerto Rico; the sourness of horse stalls; the formal smell, high in the nostrils, of new leather seat covers in some improbable dazzling car. Sweat from a barn raising, from a morning of touch football, sand in her hair from a game of running bases on the beach. Newly laundered shirts. Cigarettes and cigarette kisses. All the men she passed spun like stars in the galaxy of her free will. She felt for them, strangers, an aching nostalgia as though they were the survivors of a half-remembered love. They came swimming around her silently, they did not meet her eyes, passing, cool as fish in a tank the size of the city, the water, like the air, just tainted gray.

In the evening, after dinner, she opened the door to another man who didn't know he had come to say goodbye. She saw no reason to tell him, she barely knew him. The evening passed slowly, typically, at an expensive entertainment, and she marvelled at how he was everything her mother would have wished for her: tall, prosperous, attractive, dutifully attentive. He was so perfect her hands went cold at the thought. She would spend a lifetime catching him out, pushing him in the direction of flaws like her own, hoping he would be caught by a limb and dragged under. What did he need to complete him but the perfect wife?

Although he didn't know her well he was anxious to press things to a close, he was getting ready to ask her to marry him, if not sooner, then later. Anyone could see that. He leaned to her that way, canted like a man who was trying out a position he would hold, or appear to hold, for a lifetime, buying a mattress that would have to give just the right way, yield and support, silently, reliably. Now that she had no need of it she could feel she had the power to make him want, if not need, her.

When, after the necessary applause and the slow navigation up the aisle with his hand on her shoulder to show she was his, they came back to her apartment, she gave over her will to him. Ordinarily she'd have resisted at this point in the evening, saving something for an important time, her whole self very far from the surface, inaccessible, waiting. But this is my very last kiss, she thought, reaching up to him, and tried to concentrate, to feel and taste it and in it feel and taste all the others she would never have now. She felt nothing, in return for her monumental longing; it was a kiss dry with abstractness. The urgent, particular hunger of this valedictory lover made him search her face to see how he had offended her into such remoteness. It was still a time when he would think he should not have pressed his need upon her—he was afraid he had been caught using her. She left him all alone except that her body was close to his, like flannel. She was listening for the dying fall of his voice as it climbed up her belly and breasts, over her head and out into the icy air.

Then she knelt, one knee on the blanket chest at the window, apologetic, watching the ground turn a milky white. Cars stood stubborn in their darkness as if they had been punched out of it and were not there. Or had the street disappeared around them? Losses, gains, presence, absence—it was like those figure/ground experiments she had done in college, she could not tell whether to look at what she had or what she did not have.

"Do planes land in snow?" she asked with her first real attention of the evening.

He supposed they did, or might. He had been left alone at a very bad time and was gathering up his dignity, half angry, half humiliated. But he did not ask her why she wanted to know about airplanes. He didn't really care. He thought he had decided she was not the one for him.

So she went to sleep, when he had gone, to wait. The man who was flying to her—he was really a boy but she couldn't know that yet— would be there in the morning. He would come to her door straight from the airport in a caul of snow, his head and shoulders chilled and caped. Cauls were lucky signs at birth. When he was there she would remember why she wanted him and not any of the others, but now it was hard to think of him. All she knew was that she would fall into his arms and weep with relief and delight and that same implacable sadness. After that, after a decent period of mourning, the duties of her joy would begin.

How Mrs. Fox
Married Again: A Story After Grimm

*... Then there arrived more foxes, one after another, each
with one more tail than the last, but they were all dismissed,
until there came one with nine tails like Old Mr. Fox ...*
—GRIMM, *Household Stories*

I T   W A S   generally conceded that when Senator Thomas V. Alexander, Jr. entered the sixth month of his illness, Mrs. Alexander, Lois, Loie, began her public search for a new husband. But the way it happened was nothing any of them knew.

He hated sentiment. (He said sentimentality, she said sentiment, any kind, warranted or not.) His father, Thomas Sr., had been a military officer and, unembarrassed by stereotypes, rather, proud of conforming to "the honorable few," he disbelieved in fantasy, the imagination, fear or even love. These were luxuries soldiers could never afford, he said without elaboration, as though their disastrous effects upon civilization were obvious. Instead, it was to ideas like honor, civility, loyalty, that he gave his passionate, often angry allegiance: all of them seemed to come surrounded by quotation marks. He cheated no one, was considerate of all creatures of two legs or four, was never seen literally or figuratively with his pants down, and if occasionally he used language his wife thought excessive, even that seemed to be done in a spirit of obligation: old soldiers cursed, they were expected to; surely their world had it coming.

The only interesting thing about General (Two Star) Alexander was that he couldn't trace his family back one decent generation (the standards of decency his) and he bore a tattoo of a snake crushing a globe, ineradicable, truly obscene, a detailed scaly map of anarchy, just above his right bicep. Certainly he had come on foot out of another life but he never said a single word about it, nor did he take the opportunity, as might some, to spin unverifiable tales of Horatio Alger tenacity or ancestral bad luck. Thomas Jr., already far gone into fantasy whether his father liked it or not, imagined a large poor family left behind, an ancient weeping mother kept alive by the hope that her son would some day reappear, and all of it to come clear one day, perhaps on his father's deathbed.

But General Alexander had no deathbed. He was leaning over a tee unsheathing his nine iron when something broke inside his head, dammed up memory or fantasy, perhaps, and spilled fatally out in an instant. Asked, during the period of decorous mourning and reminiscence, just what she knew of her husband's past, Thomas's mother claimed to know less than did her son: Thomas Senior was already a rising young officer when he met her at a foolish party and swept her dramatically out of the way of foolishness. No one had come to their wedding, no family, no old friends, it wasn't that sort of wedding but rather, sudden and exciting (like his tattoo: from a hidden life) and she found it irresistible. It was in fact the last sudden and exciting thing he had ever done.

So the anti-sentimental was a hybrid strain in the Senator, thus exceptionally strong. And he liked to play it, too, a little game for his own amusement, perhaps his homage to his father's mysterious ghost. Every time Lois found her eyes misting over at a movie, or at news of some distant tragedy or local pity, Thomas gave her a special look that said "Shame" and then, to show he meant no contempt, gave her a quick chuck under the chin as though, physically, to help her keep it up. She had never seen him in despair for more than two minutes at a time; then he was on the phone to do something about it or at least spread the alarm and come down on the right side for the record. She had never managed, to her naked eye or ear, to hurt him badly enough to slow him down in his even roll through his week, his year, his Senate term. In fact she had little reason to try to hurt him, except for the occasional need to know she could. But either, loving him, she'd lost the capacity to draw blood, or his veins had gone deeper under the daily callouses than she could hope to reach. It was frustrating, but he was what his father would have called "an exceptionally good man for the job," even if the job was only marriage. He was. He was. She didn't want to be ungrateful.

When he discovered he was dying, Lois observed (with the infinitesimal part of herself that remained capable of observing anything) that he was furious to be so inconvenienced, his schedule so irrevocably confounded. She had always given him the benefit of the considerable doubt: what was unavailable to her was instead available to his constituents, his staff, his colleagues; she was sure of that.

All that fast-wheeling energy he took along in his attaché case full of briefings and position papers. Sometimes it spilled over and she got some; otherwise she just admired it as it took him fast-footing it in the opposite direction like a cartoon character trailed by those emphatic horizontals denoting speed. She remembered that the most incendiary experience she had ever had in bed with him was on the approximate eve of his announcement that he was going to run (the thirteenth Democrat, bad luck and bad odds) in the New Hampshire primary. ("The next President of the United States would like to shake your hand, young lady," he had whispered with a small boy's gaiety, and once having seized her hand had appropriated it for the most unpolitical purposes.) He could travel to two cities in the morning: the breakfast speech, the ten-thirty meeting; be back on the Floor for a post-lunch vote; subdue fifteen other entries on his office calendar by dinner; have drinks with the visiting Ambassador of Abu Dhabi; come with her to dance at some diplomatic ball or private party; and still, catching *her* weary eye across the bedroom later, give her the charming and hopeful smile of the husband come home hungry. He took the fewest vacations he could until he dared not deny her "a couple of days on a bloody beach somewhere," getting sand in his notes and saltwater splashes on his peerless concentration. He made sure he was tired, bad company, irritable in all directions, so that, chastened, she would let him work; she licked the sweet cream off his attention. It was sufficiently filling.

In the hospital, bled and frightened after the first tests began coming in positive, he forbade her to stroke his hand. "Loie, don't get all melting, please, I can't use a pudding for a wife just now." His forehead was higher than he usually let it look but he hadn't troubled to comb the dark hair over.

"I'm trying to touch you, Thom, I'm not pouring tapioca in your palm," she defended herself. "Do you want to be alone?" and made a move to leave.

But he sank back, momentarily defeated.

She wanted to hurt him for that. "There'll be plenty of time to be alone, is that what you want to hear?"

And that did it, he wasn't so armored after all. "At four thirty-two in the afternoon, according to informed sources," she said, smiling bitterly, "tears appeared to spring to the Senator's eyes, although there has been no official confirmation of this. Is that better? Shall I sound like Herr General Alexander the First for you?"

He turned his head away, then boldly back toward her, eyes convex, huge with real tears, the first of his she'd ever seen. Then quietly, placatingly, "Lois, I'm sorry," which alarmed her far more than a bucket of tears could do. So she believed the doom those tedious tests promised, because apparently he believed it.

The first operation was officially represented as minor, everything about it benign because next year was an election year and you never could tell. Thom only smiled as his staff plotted its trail and reworded press statements and warded off discouragement. But who knew better than he what a complicated mixture of personal loyalty and the impersonal gratification of ambition he represented to his little office army? The young legislative assistants, the economist, the Nader-trained muckraker fresh from raking muck in Cambridge, all of them were as devoted as any wife could hope to be. They came to the hospital as regularly, then stood nearly in Lois's footsteps, melancholy, looking out the dead-black windows of the hospital lounge into the empty Maryland night.

The secretaries choked on tears—this after the second operation and the sudden deterioration in strength, when his squarish face began to lengthen and he took on an unsuspected resemblance to Mike Mansfield—when rumor began to nibble at the truth and finally swallowed it whole, only to spit it out on the six o'clock news. There was a committee chairmanship up and he was next in line; for the first time in his entire life he'd had to bow his head and step aside "for reasons of health and exhaustion." Waiting just beyond him to gather it in was one of his arch-enemies, who sent him a gigantic carnivorous-looking dracaena for consolation. "He didn't pick it out," Loie soothed, "don't be so paranoid. Do you think the florist follows the committee assignments?"

He was a big man in every way, the secretaries had always liked to say because it reflected so well on them; a man of genuine stature, "that rare thing, a truly serious Senator, and so thoughtful about little things," and he was wasting now. Even his vigorous dark hair, which had always seemed to have its own independent source of spirit, was wasting back to zero. It was (as all things are, only not so visibly) a question of time.

If his aides stood looking out at the landscape pondering their own futures somewhat more deeply than they pondered his, the Senator of all people understood: he would have done the same.

Self-preservation (in the name of specific ideals relating to national welfare) was the first requisite of political survival. It did not have to be ruthless. And sentiment was all that was left in the bottom of the bottle. It was distinctly a ladies' drink.

One Monday noon, after her morning visit with Thom in the hospital, one of the "average" visits according to her overloaded emotional seismograph, an hour or so spent with a man so involved with his newspapers and his correspondence it was like visiting him in his office during working hours, Lois went to have lunch in Georgetown with a friend.

It was clear from her first approaching step that Sandra was not altogether sure how to deal with Lois these days. Ordinarily she was a hard-drinking, hard-swearing, fast-moving woman devoted to obliterating every sign of what she called her A.D.C. background—Adorable Daughter of the Confederacy, that was—except that she kept her accent, which she liked to use as a form of entrapment, oozing out the sticky web and then snapping it back in holding some astonished stranger. But these were apparently not times in which to be cool around Loie Alexander; there was a protective, nearly pious tone her friends affected with her. It was easy to forget Loie wasn't the one sick, weak, exempt from strain.

"Oh Sandra," she said wearily when they were seated, turning a bun around in her hands more times than she realized, "tell me what you're up to, don't ask about me. I don't have any desire to think about me."

Sandra shrugged hugely; she was a big woman with quarterback shoulders and Harpo Marx hair, and even shrugging could sit queerly on her frame. She cultivated gossip the way some women tended roses, zealously, on any day of the week including Sunday (when people ought to lay off doing things that can be gossiped about, she complained, so she'd have a chance to catch up). Sandra, with a sigh of relief, told her some bits of cloakroom intrigue but even as she laughed she looked worried, and Lois could feel herself being turned to gossip then and there, her response, her lack of response, a live woman being coated with molten wax that would keep her approximate shape after she'd left. How often she'd been the beneficiary of such reports without giving more than an obligatory human grunt of commiseration.

There was a full calendar of social events, Sandra admitted reluctantly, that Lois was being spared: on the party calendars Senator and Mrs. Alexander were in a discreet holding pattern. "If you wanted to come to the Performing Arts business, Loie—the opening—it wouldn't be awkward. Or"—lamely added—"when Thom's home again."

Loie moved in her seat. "He's got this thing on his chest now, he wears it all snuggled up against his skin, that lets out the drugs very slowly, like a drip. Which is fine, he'll be home with it, it's very portable, but it *ticks*, Sandy. Like a time bomb, it just ticks away. Can't you hear it when the orchestra's playing? Or between movements? Somebody'll think he brought a metronome along to check up."

Sandra looked at her long and hard and, except for the immutable distance that was beyond her will now, openly. "What the hell are you going to do, Loie?"

So many clichés went rattling around through her head that Lois said nothing. They came to nothing anyway, different definitions of emptiness and want. She knew there were people, though none here in Washington, she meant secular, civilian people—who thought it strange for a man to be served as a senator is served: doors opened, phones answered; the correspondence staff, the speechwriting staff, somebody always going *before*. What a queer form of passivity, to be set free to do nothing but *appear* and speak your opinion into microphones and, presumably, think (although so many couldn't even remember how to do that, if they ever knew). Kings of no teritory; courtesans, the awful ones, in their vanity, with ladies in waiting and costume mistresses. And when he's gone, she thought (feeling traitorous, like one of his aides about to find himself out of a job), no castle, no homeland, all the power vanishes and nothing left to do. "I'll get a pension. I don't know. And a rocking chair." She swirled her coffee in her cup; it was gray with fake cream.

"And a lover. You're not exactly over the hill."

"Hey, take it easy there." She didn't want a lover, now or later. "Don't laugh, Sandy. A widow is a widow. I feel sixty."

"I can imagine," Sandy said. "Well, you'll see, they'll be beating down the door."

She shook her head. "Why? A senator's widow doesn't have a single thing they need. You can't keep the good will like some corner

grocery store that changes hands, you know. You lose your rank."
She picked at her lobster thermidor which looked, as so much looked
these days, as if it had been digested already.

Sandy made a face, half disdain, half grudging satisfaction. "What
do you mean? A good looking woman always has the single thing
they need. It's yours to keep, sweetheart." She leaned forward as if
there were something to confide. "It's the one thing he doesn't get to
take with him."

Lois closed her eyes, dizzy with the kind of motion sickness she
could stop by looking at nothing. But there she confronted a tangle
of images so terrifying that she opened them again to look at Sandy's
face. Her mind was full, at the slightest prompting, of Larry Hor-
witz, Thom's assistant, baring his lovely young chest before her, and
she saw her own cozy blond-skinned thighs, felt them the way they
used to look, at least; who even knew what they'd look like now to
a stranger? She saw Thom's hairline, retreating where it had given
up defending the line, and she saw his father behind him like a
shadow, gazing past her the way he always did, as though out of a
heavy frame.

"I'm afraid this conversation," she said to her friend, who was
touching up her lipstick, "is just brutal enough so that Thom would
be delighted with us. He'd like to think I'm replacing my heart with
something more—heavy duty."

"With balls, I dare say," said Sandy, and blotted her lips on her
napkin, a habit she indulged wantonly, like her language, because it
would appall all the ladies of Winston-Salem, if only they could see.
"But look where they got your husband."

"Sandy. They didn't get him there. I don't know what got him
there." Thom would be napping now, for the rest of the afternoon in
fact, still propped up till a nurse came by to lower him, his work all
around him, no quarter given.

"They didn't save him, did they? And they sure as hell won't make
a dent in saving you."

Lois, thereafter, was to remember this conversation with some
amusement because Sandy turned out to be as close to wrong as she
could be, given the prevailing limitations.

One evening, rather late, when he was at home in their own bed,
he said to his wife, "Lois, when I'm gone—"

"Thom, please—"

He brushed away the hypocritical delicacy and repeated more firmly, "When I'm gone, I trust you'll be prudent about your future attachments. It concerns me that—"

"*Please.*" She had been stripping the plastic cleaners' bags off a dozen crepe blouses. They hung before her like ghostly wraiths in her own form, turquoise, beige, and black, their cuffs neatly buttoned around air.

"Loie, would you like to make me happy?" He asked the question lightly, simply, and she turned, tricked, thinking he wanted some small comfort: juice, the *Wall Street Journal.* "I'd like to know what kind of hands you'll be in, you can understand that. I'm doing as much for my investments, you know. I'd like some assurance you'll be provided for. Financially, emotionally. Physically." He sketched arcs over his head, large areas to be filled in, the way he liked to lay out strategies. It was his grand voice that undid her, his full baritone with the resonance gone, no depth, no echo. "And I don't think a woman need wait, really, you know. This is going to be harder on you than you imagine, Lois."

"That is ghoulish," Lois told him, shocked, beginning to weep, the tears seeping suddenly not just from her eyes but it seemed from every pore. "That is a nasty—masochistic—humiliating—position to put yourself in, and I don't even want to talk about it."

He seemed genuinely surprised. Worse, he seemed wounded. She came and held his hand, which was dryer than a hand should be, papery, boneless. "Lois, love. I don't want to impose. Your private life will be your private life forever—with luck someone else will get to share it longer than I have." He touched her breast lightly with that paper hand, as though it wasn't his by right to touch, except in passing. "But think what a gift it would be for me to *know* who will have you, and get to give you my blessing. Who will inherit you. Treasure." Gently he kissed that breast, first through her lacy blouse, not hungrily but nostalgically, fruit of a garden he was banished from already; then, when in spite of her repugnance she opened the tiny buttons to him, fiercely, jealously. She stared over his bowed head dry-eyed, helpless, thinking, he wants to watch me, he wants to choose my lover and then watch. . . .

"Not to mention how unseemly it would be."

"Nonsense, you're a seemly woman, Lois. You can manage to be discreet when you choose to be, you could steal international secrets if you wanted to. Anyway, what good is seemliness to me?" He lowered his head to her again, embarrassed, she thought, at his instant of self-pity. After a while she took his face in her hands because he was hurting her.

He used his first veto on Larry Horwitz. When she dared to mention him timidly, blushing (because he had the dark eyes she most enjoyed, a gypsy audacity in a civilized face), he laughed. "But Lo, he's in knee pants. Really, I wouldn't have expected . . . I'll bet he's still waiting for the great descent of the family testicles." Which meant, as well, that he was fifteen years younger than she; that she'd better learn to protect herself against rebuff. After that she couldn't look at Larry without shame, for him, for herself.

Donal McLenahan, a good friend, had lost his wife the year before, which left him all alone. "Except for seven children," Thom reminded her. "He needs a den mother, dear. Have him to dinner if you wish but stay on the far side of the room, do me that favor. Stay in the library." There was a journalist who had always touched her shoulder with unpaternal affection; he was in suspicious odor, in view of a peculiar closeness to certain friends of the CIA. This Democrat was a shade too far to the left, irresponsible, sloppy about consequences; that most delightful old college friend, a bachelor, was essentially a Republican for all intents and purposes. "Well, a Tory then. If you cut him he'll bleed blue, Lois. And if you *bite* him, the Lord only knows what he might do." Businessmen were her least favorite species, academics his. Together they winnowed the lists of the eligible. Loie numbed to it after a while, their conversations on the subject began to take on the quality of a rainy-day sport, with an abstract purpose and an intangible score card—she had never had to confront an actual full-blooded man yet. Thom schemed obsessively and Lois modified his choices on the basis of her preferences, which he pretended to find astounding. But if Thom had been less self-absorbed he would have noticed the slightly condescending quality of her agreement to play the game, the gentle, patient indifference that bordered on pity. Perhaps he did notice, she thought, but went right on protecting her.

This particular morning, after a night of great pain (she had moved to the front guest room by now so that each could lie sleepless without disturbing the other), Thom called to her and made her sit beside him and look at him full face. "Lois, you need to have your hair done."

Her hand flew defensively to her hair, which was of course neglected, because what did it matter? "I still have to look at you, love," he admonished her and she thought with a shameful sinking in her chest, of course, of course, this disregard for herself must tell him it's too late to care what he sees: doom-ridden. He had never had to keep track of such nonsense for her. She had long since discovered it took perpetual attention on her part just to let him surrender to this thing with a little grace. She was exhausted. And even at that she'd slip up like this and give away the whole poor show.

Well then. "Can't I be depressed, Thom? I have reason not to want to go dancing, and you can't take that from me."

His movements had become minimal, every inch seemed to cut itself out of his nerves; by now they were notched with pain. "Go dancing, I wish you would. If I can't, you can." He gestured aimlessly with one hand that bent at the wrist like a chicken wing; each sight of it robbed her of her breath as if for the first time.

She shrugged. The room, everything in her line of vision, was washed gray, the color of water you've washed the floor with. Dancing.

Then, the way he'd have asked his administrative assistant about some strategic connection: "Are you following up on Ellery Woodson, by the way?" (E. P. Woodson this was, the current front-runner in their contest for her hand. He was an acquaintance they'd lost touch with, one of the editorial page men at the *Post*. He'd been divorced far longer than he'd ever been married.)

"Following up, Thom. How am I to follow up on him, just tell me. If I have occasion—"

"Please don't use that tone with me, Lois, I'm not your cleaning woman asking for the day off. I'll call him."

"Thom!" Her scalp prickled. "All right now. I've indulged this incredible whim of yours—"

He smiled his wincing smile. "Credible, if you will think about it for a moment—*credere*—Lois, means that which can be believed, and belief is an object of will. Or so I have always assumed. You will find incredible only those things you choose to."

Insofar as she understood what he was talking about—she tended to hear style and not content and what she heard was that Thomas Jr.

had begun to sound forbiddingly like Thomas Sr., post-tattoo—she did not agree that belief was a matter of will. But at this moment, content to believe anything that would placate her husband, "I'll call him," she said.

After that effort, he looked at her as though she stood at the flute end of an endless corridor. He had to narrow his eyes to see. But he watched her endlessly, ten minutes passed in total silence mutilated only by the sound of his breathing, and he kept her fixed the whole time. Possibly he was reviewing their twenty-five years together, the way drowning men did it in the movies, and aging boxers down for the count. He barely blinked. Such an effort would have anesthetized her.

Ellery Woodson came to dinner presumably expecting festivities flung in the face of grief; or at least a few quiet diners besides himself. He entered to find Lois Alexander, very pretty as usual with her pale winy-colored hair beautifully fresh, and a wan smile on her lips.

"Shall I get to see Thom a little, do you think, Lois?" he asked her, in the peculiar awkward way he had, words falling forward with some momentum from the slow start of his sentence like dominos tipping down: she'd always thought he sounded just like Jimmy Stewart. Now it seemed permissible to linger a bit on that impression, and on the attractive at-odds quality of a fairly young man whose hair was silver-white.

"Ellery—" and she spread her hands with an air of futility that was not exaggerated. She had thought and worried, decided and reversed herself: she'd have made a terrible senator. "He's terribly ill, Ellery, terribly. I suspect he won't have the chance to become much worse than he is." Looking down. Feeling how the blood that, months ago, had seemed to gush from her heart at such a possibility was now a poor defeated trickle.

Ellery thought she wanted to talk about Thom's illness, so they walked around it decorously, discussing private nurses and other impersonal parts of the whole. Afraid to offend, he turned it a bit with his well-shined shoe.

But after a properly respectful space of time and a second drink, Lois told him why he was here. "Ellery, don't even be embarrassed, please, will you promise me that? Before I begin? Because this is a sort of charade I want to ask you to be in, for Thom's sake entirely, and if you feel yourself under any pressure—" And so she went on, extremely agitated, heart beating so hard and so fast she thought she would need to lie down.

Her guest listened calmly, lacing his fine hands together, lighting a small cigar, crossing and uncrossing his long ankles. He smiled vaguely all the way through her recitation. If he were vain enough, pray God, he would simply embrace the compliment of having been chosen for such a task—the king is dead, long live the king—and not think she was perverse, or worse. Ellery chewed on brazil nuts with his mouth closed: muffled footsteps, a spiny swallow. The house was so quiet she was sure she could hear Thom turning upstairs; face to the wall, listening; then, failing to hear, relinquishing himself cell by cell to the heavy drug-soaked air.

After a dinner which they ate in a silence both remote and intimate, still thinking, Lois suggested they go upstairs to see Thom. To show themselves.

He was asleep but he stirred quickly when they stood beside him. "Ellery!" Thom murmured. Perhaps he really was surprised that Lois had done as she'd promised. Or perhaps in his sleep he'd been farther away than either of them could venture.

Ellery came three times that week, and once on Sunday, very late, after work. Each time Lois served a very formal dinner at the long table that could hold twenty. He looked like a knight in some medieval hall, served by a maiden. There should have been an echo. He was right to think she would never have entertained him quite so frostily under ordinary (or were there any "ordinary"?) circumstances. Nor did they dream of going elsewhere; this was a drama to be played under the Senator's own roof, for his edification. At one point she considered having some other friends come over: wouldn't Thom like to think there was the seal of public acknowledgement on this little amour? It would be convincing. . . .

But the night she was planning to consult with Ellery about it, just as they were moving towards the broad staircase to go up to visit Thom, Ellery touched her from behind as she hadn't been touched, she realized—and something tore away inside her and floated off like an enormous chunk of ice—forever and ever. She turned to him like a young girl, half astounded, under obligation to scold, and half relieved; then she clung to him, shivering, while he practiced her name, over and over again, consolingly. If she let herself dissolve she would surely disappear. The gray watery atmosphere still waited to drown her, and the dulling silence of the cavernous house.

They climbed the stairs almost stealthily, hand in hand. Like Thom, Ellery was large, her fingers hid in his hand.

"Thom?" Her heart thumped again. One day he wouldn't answer.

It took longer to rouse him each time. Then he blinked at them, impossibly small under more blankets than ought to be bearable in June.

"Do you have something to tell me?" he asked them. It was a well in which he seemed to lie these days, curled at the bottom, looking up at the tiny hole in the darkness that must have been the light in which they stood. "Tell me, do." Otherwise, he seemed to be saying, why have you bothered me?

She wanted to say "Forgive me." She wanted to reach across— incredible?—fact into memory and watch his bare white shoulders above hers, rising, lowering, so many times it must have been, right against that very pillow there, the one his head rested on now without rest, without weight, chewed nearly beyond recognition.

"Kiss her," he commanded Ellery in a whisper. "Do let me see you kiss her now."

The chunk of ice that had cut free loomed and thrust against her stomach wall; she froze around it. But Ellery nodded, not watching Thom; watching her.

They stood at the foot of the Senator's bed, hands joined, and kissed chastely at first, only their faces touching.

"Please, Ellery," she whispered, terrified, feeling Thom slipping away, disappearing into the past like a man under quicksand. She wanted to break from this stranger and go to him, comfort him, keep him.

She twisted a little out of Ellery's grasp, just sufficiently to see Thom smiling, or nearly so. As much as he could smile.

"Listen to me, Lois, *don't*," Ellery said. "Turn to me."

And she obeyed.

A Good Deal

M Y F A T H E R does not live in what I would call a "home." We'd never have considered anything that even resembled the word, with its hypocrisy built right into its name (home cooking, comforts of home). I like to think he is in a sort of benign arm of the Catskills out on Long Island, a brightly decorated and well-kept hotel complete with live entertainment and a built-in synagogue a few blocks from the ocean. The air outside his hotel has that sharp salty extra dimension that makes you realize you are standing in something nourishing, almost tangible, not transparent, nonexistent, like most air. He won't go out in it because for him the extra dimension he anticipates (besides mugging or murder) is germs—a cold, bronchitis, pneumonia: who wants to smell *air*? Not at his age.

When we visit, we take him walking once around the building as if "outside" were a destination in itself. He's got his hat—a pale yellow golf hat for our summer visit, a formal fedora for the winter, the kind the FBI used to wear before they started passing as hippies and stoned collegians. "Come on, let's go for a walk," I suggest as soon as I see my wife and the kids sinking into torpor on his roommate's bed in the room on the fourth floor.

This time we have brought him a little radio with earphones because the roommate complains about noise, any and all, after 8:30 and the management will not "mix in," either out of scrupulous fairness or their (correct) suspicion that reason is destined for defeat here among the elderly with their habits that have turned to stone. Jane has correctly predicted his reaction again—she maintains that my father is the only person she knows who has never said an unexpected thing. He is, for some reason I can't fathom, bewildered by the radio dials and I can see that it will go unused, he will leave it in its little blue box on his half of the closet shelf, another failed toy alongside the hearing aid and the electric razor. Inertia overpowers energy, impossible as it sounds. Entropy makes promises; someday I suppose I'll know what it is saying.

He has embraced his grandsons, offered them small dusty-looking cookies that he's saved from lunch in a napkin. They are touched, Timmy especially (he is the little one), at a sign of awareness that they were coming, that they might have needs or pleasures he could gratify. They don't ask or expect much—some rudimentary consciousness, a sign. They take one cookie apiece and chew it carefully, as if they are thinking hard. I ask more, although I don't get it. Well, I am his son, the remoteness of the third generation has not made me forgiving.

So we troop downstairs, Jane ahead of us, wearing her glorious red hair that made my father, when he first saw her, call her a Yankee; the two boys trying ceremoniously not to step on each other's heels, giving off, though, with every gesture the suppressed air of kittens in a sack, all frisky irresistible quenched movement. The elevator is one machine Pop seems to have mastered; not only does he hold the door, assured, while we file in, but he smiles and keeps his hand on the OPEN button for another tenant of his floor, a short, vividly-muumuued woman who hobbles on slowly inside a walker. As we move down the floors, sinking so hard our stomachs rise up into our chests and Josh says "Gulp" out loud, she looks at us, smiling, and then, apologetically at her aluminum contraption and shakes her head. "Don't get old, *kinder*, that's all I can say."

After she's gone—we politely wait for her to drag herself out and disappear around the elevators toward the gift shop—my father says "So who asked her? We need her opinion on anything, we'll remember to ask her."

Jane opens her mouth and closes it; so do I. We are going to berate him for his lack of generosity but instead we berate ourselves: the same impatience that bit her into speech bit him into anger. The hotel is fine, we assure ourselves, it is age that's depressing.

But no. I watch my father walk toward the door slowly but securely. It is mostly women who are seated, watching, in the purple and yellow leather chairs on both sides of the aisle, because life seems for the most part to be a widowing. He has very few real complaints, considering what a man his age can expect—even the Bible would agree. It is all that has never changed that rankles: he is the same father I've always had, lacking a few appurtenances (teeth, hearing, hair, a wife) but otherwise stock still the same. "Kill me!" he pleaded after my mother died. "It's a mistake, how could such a mistake happen! I was always going to go first." I don't know how much losing her cost him. But he was terrified to face his life alone without a mother, that I know. He was bewildered, and he's still bewildered—how could it be that he has come through eighty-two years intact when strong men, men twice his size and a hundred times more vigorous and full of will, have died and left these women?

Timmy pushes on the hotel door with all his weight and the live air opens to us, edgy with salt, the sky bright blue as pure deep water. "Oy," my father says, turning his face back toward the building. "I'm climbing into my grave out here. What are you doing, Joey, punishing me with this cold?"

I wish I could find a sin in my father's past. I thought this once when I was embroiled in an episode of, what shall I call it, a brief unsanctioned lust—Janie never did find out, no harm was done—because I was caught in a paradox. My father didn't drink (a little schnapps on *shabbos*, gone in a blink) and neither did I; he was a dutiful breadwinner, earnest in his work, and so was I, give or take the moments of insolvency any writer is heir to. His shortcomings were all of omission, never of commission. He and my mother, however they had begun, had endured a marriage of convention and dependency. They mocked and quibbled, demanded and berated, my father thrust his neck out to be shamed and my mother enthusiastically did her best to shame him, and how they had me is hard to envision. As a teen-ager (like all teenagers who have everyone experimentally in bed with everyone else, their teachers, their friends' mothers, the President) I could never manage to imagine them so much as acknowledging each other in the Murphy bed they pulled down from the living room closet. (It was a tiny apartment; their son got the bedroom for his more hallowed activities.) But just as people unquestioningly needed marriages in those days, so did those marriages need children. I suppose I was a duty and they did me.

But then, as I said, the moment presented itself when I was less than dutiful and I found myself gathering up the odd ingredients for a great stew of justifications. I found myself thinking, I am not my father repeated once down the line. Even though you could confuse us in the dark by the shape of our bodies, the nap of our hair, he is a man in whom the blood beats weakly, whom the traces bind. Admirable and not admirable, those things. I didn't know just where I stood on virtue just then. It seemed to me, but only in flashes, as if there were a blinking sign at the corner of my vision, that virtue was only safety and safety was timidity. Cowering. Then that sign would blink again and I wasn't so sure. I saw Janie's face, innocent of worry (though I tried to see it anywhere but in the bedroom) and I saw the blond, thoroughly gentile, slim-hipped woman (a student of mine, not, to be honest, as innocent as my wife) who wanted me enough to put a lot of foregone conclusions in danger, hers and mine; and it was my father who seemed, or at least ought, I thought, to be begging me to *do* it, leave the strait and narrow, seize the hour and be bad.

I was bad; I could achieve badness with the best of them (only perhaps not as a recidivist). As it happened, I didn't enjoy it much, either in anticipation or in retrospect, only in the single blinding instant, gone as quickly as that ritual fire-in-the-throat whiskey after *kiddush*, that drives all of us every time, in the dark, on the sly, the animal instant that slaughters reason. And perhaps I enjoyed this colloquy too: Pop, I thought, a man has to dare to dare. Then I would ask myself why. To be able to say he dared? Say it to whom? I wasn't telling *him*. If my father, who was too simple and decent to lie or even give short-weight, wasn't good, only frightened, what was a good man? Sometimes he seemed to me, all of a sudden, not so naive as I had thought: telling me about a gangster neighbor, a philandering cousin, his aunt who took in boarders and then took off with one. He had noticed there was a world out there. But his own record, I thought, that was clean enough to be an incitement. In retrospect I see I was averaging my guilt over two generations. In my own way I was a coward too.

A few months ago, the night before we were to make our biennial trip to the city to see him, he called me. A call up here to Providence—"the country," he calls it—is a long-distance affair, very daunting. He hazards it rarely and only in emergencies. His voice had broken through distance to me, quavering, when he went into the hospital with pneumonia a few years ago, and once when his brother Abie died in Miami, to weep for twenty minutes while he cursed himself for the bill he was running up. This time, hearing his voice saying "Joey?" as if he doubted it was really me, I was alarmed.

"What's the matter, Pop? Are you okay?" Our suitcases were already out on the bed waiting for our New York City clothes.

"I'm okay, a little cold, I cough, but I'm okay," he told me and his equivocal voice seemed to wait there for me to tell him why he had called.

"Listen, sonny," he said finally, "I got to ask you something."

"Couldn't it wait? We're—"

"I wouldn't bother you without a reason. I don't need a phone call on my bill, you know."

"Well—" I hadn't intended to be so uninviting. It was all to the good when he made himself push against the world; using the telephone was the challenge to him that climbing up a sheer rockface would be to me. I could see him pacing while he held the phone; I do that too.

"Listen. What do you think if—I want you should tell me if you think this is such a good idea."

"Right. Okay." I imagined he was going to ask to change rooms and be done with his roommate's *mishugas* once and for all. Play the TV till midnight. Sing in the shower.

"What?" he asked.

"All right, go ahead."

"What head?"

"Nothing. Tell me what you want to tell me." Janie and the kids sometimes come running when they don't know I'm on the phone with him. "Who are you shouting at?" they ask. He must hear me as if we had one of those ancient undersea connections. "Pop. What idea?"

"I'm thinking I might get married, Joey. But I'm not so sure."

I bit my lips closed to keep from laughing. Then, guilty, I made my voice approximate simple interest and possibly even approval. "Married," I yelled. "Married?" The world was an astounding place; maybe if I leaped out the bedroom window I could fly.

"I don't want you should think this has to do with Mommy,"

29

he began, and I listened speechless while he explained. Then I went downstairs and told Jane he had finally said something surprising.

And so we were ready to meet Frieda the next day. "Is Frieda grandpa's fiancée?" Timmy asked, saying the words as if he were holding a fishbone by its repulsive tip. I said I didn't know. My father had asked my advice but I hadn't given any.

Usually he was seated just inside the front door of the hotel so that he could jump up anxiously at the sight of every clump of people who approached. This time, confirming my understanding that all his routines had changed, there was no one waiting for us.

The woman at the desk rang his room; no one answered. (His roommate, he had told me incidentally, was in the hospital for tests— "He was falling down"—and, although such an intimation of mortality had always frightened and depressed him before, not for the roommate's sake but for his own, this time he was too distracted by his own changing fortunes to take much notice.)

The receptionist suggested we try the card room where they were having their daily bingo. "He's in there a lot," she told us amiably. "And *she's* a hot one at games," she added indiscreetly. "Let me tell you, she wins real money!" We were dealing with common knowledge, then. The boys giggled and Jane looked grim.

We walked down the long hall that had the mildly antiseptic, beige, asensual ambience of a Holiday Inn. The door to the card room was open and I could see him from the hall, seated next to the cage in which the bingo pieces flopped and fluttered like lottery tickets, so that he could hear the caller with his better ear. Which one was Frieda, then?

On one side of him sat a dishevelled woman with hair twice as red as Jane's but slightly purple at the roots, as if it were emerging from a wound. She had the look of someone on loan from a back ward. On his other side sat a *ketselah*, a little cat, smaller, under what looked like a real lace shawl: my mother would have called her quality. She had a good hairdresser for her dry sherry curls (or was it a wig?) and a vaguely European tinge of irony, or tolerance, to her smile. Everyone here was European, of course, but I don't mean Poland, I don't mean Odessa, I mean, say, middle-class Prague or Vienna. *Cafe mit schlag.*

And she was raking in the chips. "Good Lord," Janie breathed at my side. She was thinking, I know it, of my mother's orthopedic shoes, the plastic flounce and flowers that spread like a rash to cover every undefended piece in the now-dispersed apartment, the Decline of Rome wall decorations, all pillars and crumbling temples, or Gainsborough ladies in gilt frames. She was thinking of the little piece of paper we had found in my mother's coat pocket when we were going through her "effects," the rain check from Waldbaum's for a 39¢ cauliflower. This Frieda, you could tell from a hundred yards, knew her antiques, her armoires, her netsukes; a hundred to one she kept sachet in her bureau drawers.

Pop introduced us but not until he had pulled everybody into the hall so that we wouldn't impede the next bingo round. "You look as if you've won enough for one day," I said to Frieda as pleasantly as I could. "You must have talent."

She laughed and shrugged self-deprecatingly. Even her teeth were a cut above the hotel average. Her winnings had gone into a delicate purse that closed with a businesslike snap of finality.

What had they agreed to? I couldn't tell—on the phone my father had simply said she had "asked him" and he was "thinking about it." She had been widowed fairly recently and was lonely living alone, and so she had (admirably? shamelessly?) come to see whom she could meet here. To make a deal. She had her own money and apartment and didn't need his, her own children and grandchildren ditto. On the phone that had made sense: a frightened little woman, permanent immigrant-class like Pop, toward whom, not on purpose, I had been—I and my generation, I mean—condescending since we were children.

But this Frieda was something else again. She entertained us. I had suggested we do something besides the usual tour around the shabby block and she suggested a nice little restaurant, "strictly Kosher"—with a calculating smile at Pop that would have passed, in his book, for "consideration." It was nearby, her daughter had found it and they'd gone there for brunch just last week. "It has privacy," she promised. "Booths. Nice. Upholstered."

The boys were ostentatiously enjoying all this. I could see they liked this new wrinkle in the dull fabric of their grandfather's life. She looked like the kind of grandmother who could reach into her purse or her pockets—not that she'd done so yet—and produce charming surprises, more interesting than plain butter cookies. At very least she was an impressive gambler. Or maybe it was relief at the chance to do something besides sit in the blank air of a dozen old people with their canes and cataracts and forced cheerful Happy-to-meet-yous and their self-absorption.

As I say, she knew she was charming and so she entertained us. She told stories, in a firm quiet voice, about her father who had been a scholar in Cracow (therefore a pauper here, untrained to do a days-work). Her husband, continuing the tradition of useless luxury—a philistine she was, but honest—had been a violist. Whatever are you doing *here*, I wanted to ask her. What do you want of my poor father? He will make a woman like you more lonely still.

Well, the violist had dreamed of music, as it happened, but worked in "clucks"—that's cloaks and suits—like the rest of his *landsmen*. A cutter, then a presser at Waranow Togs on 35th Street. An unhappy man, unreconciled. For forty years, music on the side.

And that was how she had met my father, all those years ago. Some kind of garment workers' union picnic, wives invited. A rare Sunday in a park on Staten Island. An unforgettable day.

"How you met my father?" I echoed stupidly. Pop was eating a bagel, trying to negotiate it in spite of his insecure teeth. He looked at me shyly, blinking.

"He didn't tell you? Sam—" She lay one wrinkled but manicured hand on his bare arm. She was a woman who made disappointment into a charming pretext for flirtation. How my mother would have laughed. "Sam! A *tschotskele!*" she'd have said. A little trinket. But Frieda turned her widened eyes on all of us with innocent enthusiasm. "Yes—he didn't tell you we knew each other in the old old days? So when I met him here, what a surprise. A shock! Children—" and she fixed them, unfairly I thought, in her softening gaze and put one hand helpless on her chest as if to still her heart's persistent amazement. "Can you imagine, this old tired lonely lady comes out here to a strange place, she doesn't know a single soul—but, you know, my daughter, my son thought it would be good for me to get out from my apartment, they said it wasn't healthy to be all the time alone. And they were right, now I can see that!" The boys were attentive to her gaiety even if it was the kind of love story that only brought forth from them retching noises when it concerned the young and the beautiful. "And who do I meet the very first day, I'm sitting next to him at supper, they put me there, you know, just like that, and they bring the soup and I look at him—"

My father is embarrassed. He struggles with the cream cheese, which will not spread evenly on his bagel. Timmy reaches across unsmiling and does it for him. "Thanks, sonny," Pop says, shamefaced. Do you know you will be a nursemaid? I want to ask this stranger. Do you know he gets lost on his way to the bathroom? He lived with us for a year after my mother died, and there wasn't a day I came home not expecting the house to have burned down because he'd left the gas on again, long after the kettle had gone dry.

I wasn't used to complex and contradictory feelings in my father's presence, I have to admit that—except for the contradiction of loving someone you don't respect. About myself and the way I live my life, he is impossibly ignorant, try as I might to enlighten him: beginning back when I first refused to put on my galoshes for the rain, that old story, I have been a confusing rebellious undutiful son whom he has loved, as I love him, in spite of all. (Had I been lovable on his terms I'd have killed myself long ago.) That I should have become (happy or not) an impecunious writer instead of a doctor or, at worse, a businessman, has been an unforgivable affront to his dreams for me. My working wife, the dishevelment of our house—no bedroom set, no wall-to-wall—have only been corroborations. He is a straightforward little man desperate for solvency, invisibility, silence. Tit for tat, I failed him, he failed me.

Now what am I to think?

Why does this woman want him? He is a live male, in better shape than most—two eyes, however cloudy; two ears, however shot; vestiges of a sense of humor, though that was better when he could hear. No stick to lean on, no apparent illnesses. Perhaps that makes him a prize. Is he flattered? Does he want to get out of this hotel because, comfortable as it is, you live in public here? Does he see her as a woman? What would he *do* with a woman besides hand her his dirty socks, his underwear?

We do not talk marriage; or, that is, we talk around it by admiring her proferred proofs of ownership: pictures of her Sheryl, a teacher; her Arthur, a podiatrist with blow-dried hair and stunning practice; their children; a polaroid of her living room, which is not so different, actually, from my mother's: Italian Renaissance chairs, pseudo, only no plastic to protect them from the depredations of use. It is not so much her dowry as the bride-price, I am thinking, studying the stubborn hairs that sprout like weeds from my father's nearest ear.

Later, when we'd left her—awkwardly—in the lobby of the hotel where she claimed she had some business with a friend but hoped she'd see us again soon (were we off to Providence immediately or would we take advantage of the wonderful city, the shops, the shows?) I went up to my father's room alone with him. He looked deflated, though for a man who hasn't much wind in his small sails to begin with, that's a matter of conjecture. "You like her, Joe?" he asked me, afraid to meet my eyes.

"She's—fine, Pop. A lovely woman. Very well-preserved." I hated to say that, it always made me think of embalming, on the one hand, and a feat against great odds on the other. But I sometimes found myself purposely blunt with him, if not downright cruel. Partly it was to fulfill his disappointment in me, to rub his nose in it since he'd think it anyway. But also I think I did it out of disrespect, as if I knew his hide was so thick nothing I said could penetrate to sting him. How could I ask what she saw in him? I made it a question about calculation which he, ever the paranoid, could appreciate.

"What she wants? I don't know, Joey, but it's true. Living alone is no way. Especially a woman, all the way out there on Ocean Parkway by herself. . . ." He left the meaningful details to my imagination. "She's a good woman. Not selfish. Anyway, she's got her own."

"A little—fancy, maybe—in her habits? Do you think?"

He shrugged. "You know, I told her she wouldn't get much from me in the—you know—that department." He raised his eyebrows on "that," which made it sound like what my mother had darkly referred to as "*dorten*"—"down *there*," that island that was to be isolated from thought, speech, and, most important, touch. "Not like before."

I assumed the "before" was his marriage. "Well, there are lots of ways men and women can be friends," I said, and wondered if that sounded as pious as it felt. "She's probably not interested in—she just sounds lonely."

"Before she was always very—she's a modest woman, considering she's what you would call attractive."

The conversation was getting deeper than I tended to expect with my father. "Before she was modest? Pop, what do you mean, before?"

"*Before.*"

"When you met her on that picnic, you mean?"

His eyes lit for just an instant with a warmth I had myself seen often before I was, say, twelve.

"You met her—more than at that picnic? You got to know her?"

He shrugged again, this time not for vagueness but for its opposite: detailed memory he did not care to discuss. I sat down gingerly on his roommate's bright blue bedspread and clasped my hands between my knees. "A lot of things I wouldn't tell you, sonny. A father wouldn't tell his son certain things. You shouldn't be mad—"

"You knew her—well? For very long?"

He was looking out the window, though the blinds were three-quarters closed. "Oy, sonny," he said the way he did when something hurt him. "What can I say? Not long enough."

"Did—" I couldn't ask if my mother knew about it. "It" was not so very horrible, considering the facts of their marriage, or not even considering: my marriage is perfectly fine. But I had no memory in forty years of having addressed a single sentence to my father's back.

"Nobody knew it, Mommy never, you never. Not even Harry either."

"Harry."

"Her husband, Harry Abrahams. He was a nice man. He had some temper but when he wasn't mad. . . . Not what you call a hard worker but a nice man." He twirled the string of the blinds in his hand. "We only wanted nobody should get hurt." He looked at me briefly, to check my face. All I knew about my face was that it felt very red, hot, inflamed with confusion.

"What happened, then?" I managed to ask. I think I was stuck somewhere between laughter and a huge chest-clearing shout, a massive bleating beyond good or bad taste, beyond a son's discretion. "What?!" I wanted to yell. "What?!" like Archie's father in the comic strip.

"Once we almost—people were asking a lot of questions. So we couldn't take no more chances."

"Pop," I said from where I sat. I wanted to touch him, comfort both of us, but he was very calm, very distant from this tumult in my chest. "Were you glad? Did it—" I looked down, embarrassed. "Were you happy?"

"Happy? With her?" He hadn't mentioned her name once. He

laughed. "I was all the time looking over my shoulder Mommy shouldn't find out. I don't know if that was so happy." He ran his hands hard along the sides of his head, where the remaining fringes of his gray stubble grew; it was not a gesture I recognized, probably something he did when he had a full head of hair. "So anyway, Joey, you children with your happy, all the time happy this and not-so-happy that—how do you know what this happy feels like?"

It was the thing that had separated us, really: my choice to be happy in my life, not simply "comfortable." "You'd have known," I said with a bitterness I thought nervy but couldn't take back. "Well, then, why did you do it? Why would you take such a chance?" If it wasn't for joy, I meant, if it wasn't for ecstasy. I saw him trudging up from the subway with the *Journal-American* under his arm, and sometimes the *Daily News* or the *Post* if he had found one abandoned on the train, summer, winter, all the time except the slack season when there was no work. I couldn't imagine the mechanics of an affair in the life of a man of such regular habits. Did he really go to union meetings when he said he did? Or to play pinochle?

"Why?" he echoed. He had sat down facing me, in his familiar defeated slouch. All his life my father has looked as if the chairs and mattresses he sat on were too soft. "Why?" He shook his head. "She was a nice woman, I told you. Very lively. A good talker. She dressed good, it was a pleasure to sit by her." He looked to see if I understood. "And miserable, all the time he made her sad. I don't know about his problem, what it was. Maybe the music. He thought he was a genius, a Heifetz, the world should see it, so all the time he was taking it out on her. How she suffered by him! I don't know what it was."

No matter what kind of English a man spoke he could be an adulterer, I thought. The word seemed hollow, as if its meaning had spilled out of it, leaving a dry pod with no mischief in it. I still felt as if I'd fallen hard on my stomach, though, the way I used to when I was a kid. And he was not apologizing. I was impressed.

"So are you going to marry her? Have you been dreaming of this every since you were—"

He shrugged and looked into his baggy lap. "I don't know, sonny, it's not the same thing now. After all. Then I was, you know. . . . A man. Now." My father pulling his clothes off in a frenzy, not taking the bills and coins out of his pockets, his glasses, his comb, not laying his slacks scrupulously over the back of the fat brown armchair with the clawfoot legs to keep the crease, not putting on the pajamas my mother had ironed, striped or figured with one of those aimless silly patterns, green or gray. I used to run the drawstring through with a pin when it came out in the wash. No, my father locking the door, approaching her, this Frieda, slowly, to draw out the pleasure a little longer. I knew the dream ritual too in which everything moves incredibly fast and incredibly slowly, both. It is forbidden pleasure that leaves a scar. Memory heals ragged when it isn't repeated a thousand times. He would know, if I said that, he would recognize the crater where the shame and jeopardy lay, and the sharp ridge of healing. Everything in me heaved once, the feeling in the elevator that had made my son say "Gulp" and press his palm to his stomach.

"Well, think about it, then. You don't have to decide right now." I stood up as if this had been a routine conversation. I was glad to find my knees steady. "See how it feels to think about it. Waking up with somebody there besides old Morris." I hit Morris's bedspread with my hand.

"I don't know, Joe. Ocean Parkway, what am I going to do all the way out there?" Being with Frieda didn't seem to loom large in this proposal.

"What do you do here?" You can sit in a chair anywhere, I thought. You can wrap your *tfillin*, eat your poached egg, huddle out of the wind.

"If she could drive a car. I got my doctors' appointments, and the *shul* maybe isn't so close. Here it's convenient under one roof." He was teetering. A shove either way could do it. I embraced him, showed him how to work the radio one more time, went down to the lobby by the stairs two at a time, agitated, while he stood bewildered beside the elevator whose button he had pushed for me hospitably, the way a host watches till the car departs, taking you with it.

We began the drive toward the city in silence. Jane asked me what was wrong and I snapped at her. "Why are you angry?" she said, though I swore I wasn't angry. My father rising from the warm rumpled bed and pulling on his rough layers of clothing, shrugging on his coat, his muffler, his gloves, and coming home to the Bronx, to me and to my mother standing over the endlessly steaming *tup* of soup. Steam coming out of his mouth as he turned the corner from the hilly avenue and headed toward me where I sat in front of the apartment house, on its two wide brick steps, in exactly the same place every day, even, preposterously (and to my mother's irritation) in the dead heart of winter. It was my challenge to myself, my hardship, my fifty-pound weights, my four-minute mile, my swan dive, to sit with my corduroy knees drawn up in the three-quarter dark, tears of cold in my eyes, my gloveless hands jammed in my pockets, waiting for him, knowing it was only my secret endurance that made him come.

Bed

I T W A S N I C E of them to offer it but, gift or not, I refuse to
sleep in their bed. I'll tell you why: they hate each other.

They think it's love, and that makes it worse. They have an out-
dated, dangerous, maudlin conception of love that consists of abuse
and abject apology—abject forgiveness, too—and I will not, my dar-
ling love, put my head on a pillow so often soaked with tears, or lay
my bare body next to yours in a space that smells—I'm sure it does,
deep in—of rancor and regret and the terror of letting go. Bad karma
is not something you want in your bed with you.

I watched Nat pour a beer in Eva's lap yesterday. She yelled so
loud, and tried to tear at his hair and strangle him with his tie, that
he ran for the phone and called the police. Since they never arrived I
assume he was bluffing, but it was enough to quiet her down. Then
he tore out of the house and drove away as abruptly as a Hell's Angel
on his bike, only his big slow dusty car had to grind and lurch out
of the driveway and down Bottom Street and run the stop sign for
effect.

They hadn't cared that I was gawking—hadn't noticed. Or maybe
they had and it stimulated their penchant for outrageousness. One
way or another I said to her Enough. Really, Eva, isn't that enough
for you? He's crazy and he's going to hurt you one of these days.
What do you know? she said. You and your gentle *boys*. She made
gentleness into a far more contemptible quality than murderous self-
indulgent rage. I forced myself to walk out of there and leave her to
her fury, her hard exhausted breathing that sounded as if they'd just
made love.

I walked toward town—we needed some supplies if we were plan-
ning on eating dinner (I suspected she wasn't but I wasn't going

hungry for her, let alone for him)—and first I thought about her, or her and him—them—and then I thought about you. Eva says it is all her fault, all of it, always. If I didn't irritate him, she begins, or, What can you expect, I knew he liked this or couldn't abide that. She will cram herself into the wrong, no matter what contortions she has to get into to fit, and so she's all melted down and soaked with effort by the time he comes back needy and remorseful. Then I hear him—I've had to listen to all this sometimes, the apartment's not that big— apologize. But I haven't heard him tell her it's not his fault, he only says he's sorry it happened. Well, so am I, and so are the neighbors.

Once she thought he had a gun—a Nice Boy from Long Island this is, who'd just finished a thesis called "A Marxist Solution to the Foreign Debt"—not a thug, not a rough character from a nasty neighborhood. He loved watching her cringe, or if he didn't love it he needed it. Why is it I have the terrible feeling that a part of her is enjoying the unlikeliness of it all, saying to herself, So this is what it's like to have no self-respect, to be one of those women, a moll, a Mafia wife, a soprano singing, "He's my fella and I love him," in a dark melodrama that isn't quite real. It's grown-up. It's sordid. When people write stories about scars on the psyche they're called "uncompromising" and "relentlessly honest" and the *Village Voice* annoints them with many column inches of awed approval. It puts her in touch with a whole subclass of sufferers she never gets to confront while she does her research in the graduate school library.

I've told you about the abortion, after which she rewarded herself with a recuperative trip to Montego Bay, so that it seemed she had only exchanged an incipient child for a good buttery tan without strapmarks. I've told you how she got a Mustang for her twenty-first birthday. She's generous with it and lets me drive it casually, without making me feel self-consciously grateful, but (perversely; I guess I have my own perversities) her very ease with this cool expensive hunk of machinery only tends to rub in our differences. She would regret it if she knew that.

So. Now she says we get along so well because you're there and I'm here and three thousand miles of empty air separate us. She stood at the mirror this morning brushing her hair a thousand times (because the secret of all her behavior is that she is a carefully-raised, finicky, well but not seriously educated middle-class daughter who still does half the things her mother taught her, from arranging frail

petals of toilet paper on public toilet seats to never putting a milk
carton or a jar of mayonnaise on the table, and then tries to can-
cel them out with behavior that would put her mother in a coma if
she knew about it). So, as she brushed her straight reddish hair into
a wild electrical halo, she damned us to a lifetime of decency and
frustration.

You intend to be faithful, she said to me, an accusation.

Well, I should hope so. What's the sense of getting married if—

You see. You don't know anything about it, do you. You think
marriage is about *facts*, about what you *do*.

And it's not? (This should not make me sound humble; I really
was trying to challenge her.)

It's an attitude, Monica. Really. It's a long-range commitment to
a shared existential commonality. A preparation not to be alone in
the universe at the hour of your death.

She hissed out "universe" as if it were a hell we can all expect to
be consigned to in the bitter end.

Really, I repeated. Is that why you were fighting about his week-
end with Debra Flaherty, isn't that the name I heard? The one with
the short hair and the *bust*? The chem T.A.? (I stood my ground for
both of us, my sweet, I swear I did, with my hands on my hips.) Last
night, I went on, you sounded like the hour of your death was upon
you already, and if you weren't going to be alone in the universe it
was because you were going out together. Murder and suicide. Or
maybe murder and murder. *Really*.

She flipped her hair. Moments like this I wonder why I'm in gradu-
ate school, living with fools with big vocabularies. I want to work
in a greenhouse, clean work, silent, big, born-yesterday flowerheads
nodding at me, expressive as music and just as remote from a life of
too many syllables.

Anyway, I'm writing to say that in her plans for this marriage of
theirs, which seem to progress with the stubbornness of a disease no
matter what is thrown in their way, she has offered us most of the bat-
tered old furniture in the apartment, which was her grandmother's.
(The Orientals, however worn, their edges ragged, go with her. We'll
find someplace to put them, she says wearily, sounding, I'm sure, like
her mother, put-upon by the tedium of so much ownership.)

I don't mind the charity aspect of taking the scuffed dressers and
the many-times painted kitchen table, which we can strip down to

its original mystery wood—at this point it looks like one of those scratch-paintings on which children pick with a pin through layers of black crayon to the colors underneath. It's not like borrowing her car, which smacks of noblesse oblige. But, darling, the bed . . .

If they are speaking to each other on their wedding day, I will be a cheerful maid of honor. By the time we stand up and do our vowing, she will have been transformed into a "matron" of honor. What knowledge will separate the maid from the matron by then? Did you know that often in the late nineteenth century a woman didn't have her bridal portrait taken until well after the wedding, sometimes as late as a year later? It was, I suppose, her state, not herself, that was being recorded. Imagine the secrets she'd have borne to the photographer's studio! I hope for Eva's sake that she won't bring to our wedding the malign probabilities I see right now: Nat more careless of her feelings than he is right now, and she more desperate to please, more oblivious to her own instincts, and more convinced of the inescapability of it all.

As for us. One of the feelings I've been most astounded by is my desire to spare you pain: I feel as if, every time a blow is thrown (and they're thrown rarely enough) I want to run to receive it for you. Nonsense, Eva says. Everyone in a relationship wants power and you might as well not pretend otherwise. Nat thinks that, too. You have to fight for a balance, he tells her: it's Darwinian. What kind of boxer would you make? Do you dare draw blood, go for the kill?

The kill?

Watch out, kids, Nat warns, and I want to shove his condescension down his throat. (Yes, I can draw blood but my victim won't be someone I love.) You have, he says, too many illusions, and they're the heartbreakers. He means, I suppose, that *they*, the prudent ones, have nowhere to fall from: he's already felt her flesh between his fingers when he's pinched, and had her vomit up her disgust with his taunting. (She found him on the porch at someone's party, sweet-talking a new graduate student, a tall thin girl with a sluice of slick hair like water down her back, leaning against her, a certain familiar look in his eye, "the tumescent look," Eva calls it, "swollen irises, a direct correspondence." She went into the john and got sick so that someone would call him. He came in and saw her kneeling over the toilet bowl and said, Jesus, Eva, when did you take up praying? Whereupon instead of laughing or kicking him in his nearest shin, or worse, she passed out and he carried her into the bedroom and woke her by crawling in on top of her, between the coats and purses of the party-goers. She woke crying Rape! and he nearly suffocated her with a striped school-colors scarf to get her to shut up. But she told me all this the next morning, proudly, I'd swear, as if they were Bacall and Bogie, and their daring indecencies sealed them in a kind of intimacy.)

Am I expecting too much, love? I feel very young beside my room-mate, this woman who wants to suffer as if it's the natural next phase, just the way little girls are desperate to grow into the adult discomforts of periods and hairy armpits and pinching bras. You feel very young to me beside her Marxist-with-annuities lover with his kick-ass glamour and the crushed Camels he's always removing, with a resigned sigh, from his back pocket, with the look of someone who's seen yet another climber fall to his death, or another horse collapse under his load. Eva likes to say, I love him for his ass, his little tiny ass, it fits right into my hands. Such bemusement. Can you really talk like that and simultaneously register your silver pattern at Lord & Taylor so that all your chaste-mouthed aunts can call forth pickle forks and gravy boats in your name?

Her father, an artist-with-annuities, was a bad boy in the Village in his time, which was the twenties. Or so she likes to say. The adjectives I associate with him (whom I never met, his liver long since tattered to lace) are "falling-down drunk" and "quick on the draw." The kind of man who, a century earlier, would have died in a duel. I suppose she's just being his little girl, maintaining the family honor. Artists eat the people they live with, she assures me cheerfully, in her mother's name.

As for me—if I love you I'll prove it by taking anything you want to dish out. If I think this assumption is primitive, she makes it sound like honor. I've begun to have trouble breathing when I'm with her. I see these two dreadful unfamiliar people who wear our clothes and have our faces, hulking behind us like shadows, ready to eat us up without chewing.

And are there no exemptions? I ask, pretending to be ready to sit at her feet.

Through innocence to experience and out again, that's what I was taught. Nobody just gets away with purity. She shrugs when she says this kind of thing. She sizes me up like someone she's just met, who's applied to her for something she can generously bestow if she thinks I deserve it. What makes you so damn virtuous?

Nothing. I'm not virtuous, not particularly. What makes you so eager to catch us out?

Reality, babes. I want you to face the truth.

Let the truth come and get me. (That wasn't easy to say but I said it anyway and thought I sounded frighteningly like her.)

It will, don't worry. Don't even try to imagine. He'll shock you sometime. Or you'll shock him.

This is too theoretical for me, Eva. I don't live in the abstract.

Hand in the till, all right? Hand in somebody's underwear. Cowardice in the line of fire, some kind of fire, at work probably, I don't know. Moral corner-cutting, maybe.

Jesus, you're twenty-two years old. What's the matter with you?

A little daily arsenic, hon, and you'll never get poisoned, all right? Life's too complicated for that round-eyed stare of yours. You dumb angels. I want to see you when you give up your Good Housekeeping seal.

She smiled at me as if it were a blessing. I can't believe we've lived together for two years, with our high ceilings and our unkillable philodendrons. If you're lucky, she says, sometime between now and later you might even get interesting.

Come to my rescue. Please. Tell me she's crude, not adult. Disillusioned, not unillusioned. Why does the negative get through, though, I do want to know that, the dirty secret, the bad fairy godmother? I remember when I played the piano the mistakes were the first things my fingers memorized and the last things they gave up.

Assure me, can you, that I'm right to tell her to give the boxspring and mattress to Goodwill, where just the promise of two—man and wife or lovers, any sex—side by side might be a comfort against aloneness. As long as they don't know her and bring down her blessing on their heads. Write or call me, sweet, but tell me I'm not crazy and, however generously offered, we don't have to take this bed we haven't made and lie in it.

ESSAYS

On Not Writing a Novel

THERE IS nothing most of us would rather hear than stories about the difficulties—plural and specific, not the singular and generic Difficulty—of getting a poem or story to "work." Is it that writing, a sedentary sport, needs to be made to seem dangerous? (How I navigated these tricky narrative waters! How I made the eleventh hour choice between first person and third, and how that has made all the difference!) Or is it simply that the books or stories we admire, met with whole, seem in spite of our own experience to have been born perfectly formed, felicitously edited, and therefore invulnerable?

Readers who have liked the book seem to like to hear, for example, how I came within an inch of throwing the half-typed manuscript of my first novel, *The Autobiography of My Mother*, into the fire—but, like the suicide who wants to be saved, cried out for help by announcing my intentions and by taking my time approaching the fire. That the book didn't exist always in its authoritative final form complete with extravagant jacket blurbs astonishes some readers, to whom my uncertainties seem very nearly perverse.

What we rarely hear about, of course, are the works that don't survive their birth traumas, although there may be as much to be learned—chiefly about choices and how quickly they become irrevocable—from the "failures" as from the "successes."

I want to deliver this memorial to a book that will never be written. Needless to say, since not a single word of this novel has been committed to the finitude of ink on paper, I can be sure it would have been my favorite. At the same time I reluctantly admit it gave me infinitely more pleasure in the instant of my laying it to rest than ever it did in the working out.

The idea had been with me for a very long time. About five years

47

ago, waiting in the library for a friend, I stood absently flipping through a book on the new acquisitions shelf, a collection of stories told about their own lives by Nigerian women, and in the introduction I had come upon a brief reference to an Englishwoman, late Victorian, named Mary Kingsley. She had angered the queen, apparently, for differing with British colonial policy in Africa, this book said, using her as an example of *what* I can't precisely remember, and the queen (Victoria), whom one provoked at one's considerable risk, had sent her off to a plague spot to die—which Kingsley most conveniently did.

There were no details about the woman and no way to know what a profound and delightful person she would turn out to be, nor to guess how engaging were her own books on the subject of her travels to West Africa. (As it would turn out, in fact, the better her books appeared to me, the less likely I felt I would be able to improve on them—but more about that later.) Why, I ask myself now, did I respond to this single sentence about Mary Kingsley? Although I have been interested in politics and have written sometimes from what seems like documentable reality, it has been a strictly domestic, American, contemporary reality: hard enough to do that well. And, though I have subsequently been asked over and over again why I was writing about this woman dead in the year 1900, all the answers are, to be honest, after the fact.

They recount a biography that is patently interesting and they draw parallels with contemporary concerns, especially with a search for genuine unselfconscious heroines, that are perhaps valid but they no more explain or account for the initial half-blind attraction than one can usually make comprehensible an initial sexual attraction. There are as many kinds of chemistry at work between writers and their subjects as there are between potential lovers: some of them are rational, based on a solid sense of who one is, what kinds of experience and capability one has; some are based more on hope and dream, on *as if* and *if only*, and perhaps on the smallest bit of perversity, a pleasure in the very unlikeliness of the match. Sometimes, as in "real life," we attach ourselves to impossible objects which turn out to be just that; other times we stretch ourselves, learn the new skills we need and try new styles. If those revisions of our natural style don't take, don't convince, don't win us this demanding love, then we have at least learned who we cannot be, and thus perhaps a bit about who we are. It's a dare, and like all dares that are not basically self-destructive, it is probably worth the gamble.

Mary Kingsley was born in England in 1862, niece of Charles Kingsley who was, and perhaps still is here and there, famous as a theologian and as the author of *Westward Ho!* (which I remember as it was enshrined in Classic Comics) and *The Water Babies*, starring Mrs. Doasyouwouldbedoneby and other earnest didactic types.

Her father was a dashing, infuriating man who was a sort of society doctor, on retainer to dukes and earls (one at a time), thus keeping the better part of his energy free to travel around the world with them, while giving the impression that he was gainfully employed. After a time he dropped that pretense and simply traveled, and his life came to be perceived by his daughter very much, I think, as Isak Dinesen's father's did. If you happen to know anything of the biography of that other great Victorian who went out to Africa you will recognize this pattern: both fathers ran among Indians in the United States, fooled around in the South Seas, in Newfoundland, Japan, New Zealand. The major difference seems to be that Dinesen's father's wanderings yielded up little that we can judge except his own obscurely motivated suicide, while George Kingsley, making the most of an odd combination of Victorian impulses, on the one hand transcended ambition, if that is not too generous a word, and gratified his every whim while his wife stayed at home and, more and more of an invalid in protest, raised their two children alone.

On the other hand, he produced a number of books: *à propos* of nothing, a version of Chaucer and other middle English texts; a book about his travels with an earl; and he did a great deal of serious gentlemanly scholarship on the subject of the primitive religions and customs he came upon in his travels. Perhaps this educated Victorian doodling was the tithe he paid to conscience. In any event, the women at home suffered his absence the way so many women of their time bore other kinds of male absence, sexual, emotional, intellectual, as a matter of course. Mary thought her father "the noble, perfect English gentleman . . . who never did a mean act or thought a mean thought, and never felt fear," which virtues she did her best to emulate when the time came, and only occasionally berated him for having, in large measure, broken her mother's life and stifled her health and energy.

Her own education, except for that which she cadged on her own, was sketchy. Virginia Woolf, in *Three Guineas*, quotes her as a fellow sufferer of the common female affliction of the day, a thoroughly skimped-on home education: "I don't know if I ever revealed to you that being allowed to learn German was all the paid-for education I ever had. Two thousand pounds was spent on my brother's, I still hope not in vain." (I must add that the German was bought for her so that she could assist her father in his translations; and yes, by almost any standard of measure, her brother's Cambridge education was of apparent use to no one, least of all to himself.)

Mary Kingsley did as close to nothing as a lively young woman could do: she read the books in the family library, often surreptitiously; she raised fighting cocks, though of course not to fight; she tended to her sick mother dutifully; and directed the servant and gardener, which appears to have taken nearly as much out of her as tending a house unaided does nowadays. She was not socially at ease, she travelled nowhere, and planned little for herself. Later she was to say "My life can be written in very few lines . . . it arises from my having no personal individuality of my own whatsoever. I have always lived in the lives of other people, whose work was heavy for them. . . . It never occurs to me that I have any right to do anything more than now and then sit and warm myself at the fires of real human beings. There is not one of them who has ever cared for me apart from my services . . ." Then, when she was thirty-two years old, within five weeks of each other her parents died, and in the truest sense of the word, Mary Kingsley was born.

There are two ways of looking at the step she took next. It was so thoroughly discontinuous with her previous life that her friends worried about her sanity. If you have ever entertained the admittedly simpleminded theory that psychology often proceeds along lines analogous to physics, you will see how perfectly logical it was that the spring that had been more and more tightly coiled down for thirty-two years might conceivably snap in a single exorbitant burst of energy; on its trajectory this spring bore Mary Kingsley to equatorial West Africa because, she said simply, it was one of the few places where her father had never been. She was prepared to get on with his work, she said, still marginally dutiful, making a study of what she called fetish, which we might call religious customs, and bearing with her a modest, because unsubsidized, set of preserving materials in which to pickle some unfamiliar fish to bring home to the British Museum.

She set forth in a long black skirt, white blouse, a little beaver hat; she took with her a pair of her brother's trousers which she submitted to wearing only to keep the leeches off her legs when she went wading in mangrove swamps, though never instead of her skirts— only underneath where no one but the leeches in question might have to confront them because "one would never want to go about Africa in a way that would embarrass one to be seen in Picadilly."

In fact Mary Kingsley did not, when she was at home in England, approve of bicycles, which seemed to her unsafe, or of omnibuses, which seemed indecent. Nonetheless, with infinitely greater ease than Katherine Hepburn's Rosie in *The African Queen* she settled in with the traders who shared her steamer on its slow way from Liverpool to Sierra Leone, she bore their cursing and their drinking in good spirit, and began what would be the most enduring of her friendships because she saw the commercial traders as the only other foreigners in sight whose motives, like hers, did not demand, as did the colonial governors', the suppression of native custom or, as did the missionaries', the yielding up of native soul.

Mary Kingsley began, then, in 1893, a remarkable career which consisted, to begin with, of a succession of astonishing acts of courage involving crocodiles, cannibals, previously unnavigated waters and unclimbed mountains, leopards confronted alone at midnight, traps fallen into and avoided, unimaginably fierce epidemics that consumed foreigners without regard to age or moral intention. Suffice it to say that Africa is for many of us, and quite understandably, still the heart of darkness, the unplumbable depths of danger and unpredictability (and judging from the reaction I've had to discussions of my projected book, it is). One can imagine; then, what it was like more than seventy-five years ago when even England, where Mary Kingsley began, would seem to us barely civilized in the matter of "common amenities."

But Mary Kingsley's true courage lay only in part in her brazen confrontation with physical danger. What she became, unintentionally, was a voice raised on behalf of the native tribes whose ability to legislate their own lives was continuously and fatally under attack by English, French, Belgian, German, and other (she was, of course, primarily concerned with the British) colonial administrations. It would be anachronistic to pretend that she was not an imperialist; she was a woman of her time and believed Africa needed the rule of Empire, and its technological salvation; and that Empire needed Africa. What she took vigorous and articulate exception to was the way the monarchy misunderstood the intricacies of tribal self-rule, its own subtle interdependencies, its ability, in spite of institutions like cannibalism and polygamy, to deal justly, if not in the precise manner of parliament, with its own laws and lawbreakers. Africans were not, she insisted, pathetic, underdeveloped white men, deficient Europeans.

Mary Kingsley went back to England twice, once because—obeying without overt objection her old dutiful mandates as sister and servant—her brother needed her to keep house for him between his own voyages; and once to rest, to attempt to bring some influence to bear on colonial policies, to write a book that would articulate her ideas. She wrote two extraordinary, interesting, witty books (*West African Studies* and *Travels in West Africa*), pursued her beliefs modestly but with force, and became an incandescent public speaker who attracted huge audiences everywhere she went; became in short a pest, an embarrassment, an enemy of a queen who did not take kindly to opposition. Finally, when the Boer War began, Mary Kingsley volunteered, as an old Africa hand, to be of what service she could; was rebuffed; had to argue her way in, at the end; and finally she was asked—clearly challenged—to promise she would go anywhere they chose to send her. Anywhere? Yes, by now irritated, she affirmed, yes, anywhere. And so she was sent off to Simonstown where an outbreak of virulent fever was murdering many more than the Boers ever could; and after serving a hospital full of dying prisoners with a selflessness long familiar to her, in a situation that sounds as bad as Scutari before Florence Nightingale arrived, Mary Kingsley caught this plague called enteric fever, died without much ceremony at the age of thirty-eight, was deeply mourned, and was buried at sea—in freedom again, not in oppressive England but in the waters off her beloved west coast of Africa.*

* Mobil produced a television series, text and pictures also available in book form, called *Ten Who Dared*, which featured Mary Kingsley as the only woman explorer among a fairly predictable bunch of men. They had little to say about her origins and not a single word about her political problems or her death, an omission which may

Now to the part I fancied for myself in all this. Having been intro-
duced to Mary Kingsley via that final episode—the "and so she was
sent to die and die she did" sort of thing—I believe I began with that
scene in my head.

You have to understand that my writing has always suffered (if
that is the word) from an absence, or at least a minimum, of plot.
"Here," I thought, "imagine: There sits Queen Victoria, squat and
stubborn in her power; here Mary Kingsley stands, frail, righteous,
selfless, but perhaps a little ambivalent about her position as an oppo-
nent of Empire, ready to dare and challenge but perhaps to allow
herself to be punished . . . Talk about plot. Intricate motive. Power
of the state, power of the person . . ." I began to spin out the friend-
ships Mary Kingsley might have had, could have had, given the dates
of her life: her correspondence with Beatrice Webb or Alice James
or . . . What I had in mind was not biography, not even fact, any
more than, say, Doctorow gave us the real situation of Emma Gold-
man and J. P. Morgan in *Ragtime*. I would play fast and loose with
history and try to do a semibiographical, seminovelistic portrait of a
strong and complicated woman in her age. Once upon a time I was
as good a graduate student as the next, I knew how to do research;
I looked forward to the kind of focusing of attention that makes
everything suddenly relevant, germane to period or place: you walk
past Memorial Hall at Harvard, that great Victorian monstrosity,
and allow yourself to study the architecture. You come across the
1885 edition of the Sears and Roebuck catalog, and seek out the exact
style of blouse that Mary Kingsley once gave a dozen of to a Fang
tribesman who was making threatening overtures; you imagine what
he looked like, pleased with himself, wearing one of these blouses
and not another thing. For a Calvinist like me who loves to feel she is
accomplishing something every minute, I can't think of a better state
to be in than research, unless it is pregnancy.

But. And here begins the long list of Buts.

To begin with, though I was once a graduate student as good
as the next, I was considerably more miserable than most and quit

---

have come about because the researchers, more uncurious than timid, seem not to
have pursued her far beyond the confines of her own books. But the foreshortening
of her life skimps on its real drama and makes her courage a more routine matter of
meeting animals and natives face-to-face and not shuddering, as most women would
presumably have done.

graduate school because I wanted to write, *now*, and I was endlessly frustrated by the passivity of research. And so, confronting my deskful of books that were to bring me close enough to Mary Kingsley to be able, perhaps, to speak in a voice indistinguishable from hers, half the books about the late Victorians, the other half about West Africa, I began to see that it would be an age before I could begin to write, feeling solidly placed. And writing, getting something down on the page, is a gratification that, like a child faced with a candy bar and an empty stomach, I have trouble postponing. Yet if there has been a constant in all my work, it has been an obsession with place, with the specifics of where my characters are. I have gone from Mississippi to Brooklyn to New Hampshire in my writing; I was going to have to know a hell of a lot about London, Cambridge, Libreville, and a series of villages called M'fetta, Egaga, and N'dorko to be satisfied. All right, I said, and began making plans to go to all those places which, praise the Guggenheim Foundation, I could even afford to do. But none of it was writing. Adventure, bound to be stimulating, surely necessary. Just to see how the sun sets over Mt. Cameroon!— but not until after the rainy season, that long wet pause in the African year—and even then, not writing.

A small noisy part of me, all this time, was pleased with that qualification: it set up a racket in my head. You have been writing and not much besides that for years, cravenly staying at home contemplating the QWERTYUIOP on your typewriter keys. Now it may be time to "put poor words away and be content to live" as an old Irish obsessive said one time. But research is not necessarily living and a month in another town, even if it's a jungle town, may turn out to be expensive tourism. The question was going to remain: with my strong reliance on place and detail not only for texture but for substance, was I likely to be satisfied with what I could learn second hand, from books and a quick junket?

The subject herself, fine feisty Mary—it was clear to me that I liked her so much precisely because she was many things I am not, and promised some relief from my self as well as from my study. She was physically courageous, indefatigable, morally determined, selfless in her commitments and—whatever the complicated cause and effect that underlay it—not even minimally introspective.

That is an old fascination of mine because I have met others like Mary Kingsley, as opposed to the 1,001 armchair contemplatives like myself, who have made me wonder if there is such a thing as a person who is intelligent, sensitive, thoughtful about the functional aspects of this or that subject, but who has no "inner life"? All of her writing is anecdotal, brisk, self-mocking, and minimally personal. Add to this the testimony of those who knew her, of the accessibility and remoteness that made her a loyal friend but never, say, a lover, nor even a truly intimate friend, and, though you have a marvelous subject for biography, do you in fact have one for a novel? Or rather, do I, for my novel? And here is where I finally come up against it.

Those who can write adventure stories would have a fine time with Mary Kingsley's adventures, but even they would have to take a good look at the fact that just about everything we know about her comes out of her own two 800-page books, and they are so lively and so full of a sense of her person, that the act of fiction has surely been supplanted.

On the other hand, to furnish her with what I am calling, for short, an "inner life"—doubts at 3 o'clock in the morning in the dark night of the soul, longings to be somehow different or somewhere different, the probings of one's motives as though they mattered—some of these issues are, to begin with, anachronistic; they are the searchings and struggles, perhaps, of today's men and women. And the others are simply unauthorized creations of a writer with a confirmed interest in certain kinds of introspection. Mary Kingsley was real, not a function of my imagination, however much I'd like to have brought my inventiveness to bear on her. As such, *pace* Doctorow, I felt I owed her a kind of debt—not of strict truth to fact or perfect verisimilitude—but I owed her a respect for the very essence of life that had first attracted me: that it was active, that it was *not* innately self-regarding. There is, for example, what a reader might call no "love interest" in Mary Kingsley's life. This absence engages me: how instructive a life for today's readers who are so hungry, many of them, for examples of how that can be done: so-called masculine work accomplished with not even a suppressed hope that her coworkers be good looking or otherwise "eligible." Fine or not for Mary Kingsley, but there is one fewer emotional complication to write about. Again: for the biographer such dryness may be grist for a thousand speculations. For the novelist, it is another blank, a lost opportunity for intensity. When you are not writing *about* a person, as biographers do, but trying to evoke one more impressionistically, as fiction writers must, you need a sort of emotional foothold; and both the resolved soul and the adventurer, both of which Mary Kingsley was, have sheer straight sides with very few declivities in which to sink your toes. Biography is not an intimate form, however intimate its revelations: it is analytic, it judges, it speculates, it is an approach to character from without. One can write chapters about what aspects of personality aren't there. But for the novelist, speculative distance can be a trap, while the live subject goes roaming at large.

Well then, said I, feeling brash and daring in Mary Kingsley's uncharacteristic territory, I'll have to invent a new way. Maybe discuss the problems as I go? Diane Johnson's book called *Lesser Lives*, which is about Mary Ellen Peacock Meredith, Mrs. George Meredith, is a unique biography for looking squarely at the limitations of its own form as it proceeds. I will forge the structure that can transform the absence of inner complication into some other kind of complexity. Possibly I could have done that, but I know myself at least well enough by now to realize that in all of my writing it is shape that comes last, or at least late. I go through many many opening pages until I have the only perspective that will show what I want to see, or rather hear, no more, no less, and trying to pin myself down before those first pages are written is useless. I don't take it seriously.

Then how, in Mary Kingsley's case, could I spend all this time reading, chasing down the rivers she crossed in her dugout canoes, and not know what I was going to need to know? Biographers may have to find similar perspectives, let me not minimize their difficulties, but they are at least certain their *subject* exists. My subject, in her new life as quasi-invented character, did not yet exist, nor would she until I felt ready to make her. Catch-22. And trapped between the visible life she had so beautifully recorded, and the invisible life I doubted I ought to create for her out of whole cloth—there I stayed for a good long while, working arduously, falling asleep over my books every day after lunch. In a graduate student's slump of inactivity, living off the work of those published others, I saw Mary Kingsley's strong chin and wonderfully inappropriate travelling hat in black and white on my wall, amid my maps showing the 1898 boundaries of West Africa, so real and yet so lost to me—and the questions I was thrown back upon were so basic as to appall me and sap whatever remaining energy I had left.

Just because the novel is a capacious form—baggy, flexible, merely, as it's been called, "a fiction of some length that has something wrong with it"—being large, is it really the *best* shape to swallow any mouse or elephant that happens along? If the novelist feels that her subject is in need of significant revision to make it amenable, why not start somewhere else altogether; with fiction, for example, where invention, not revision, can go on unashamed, with debts owed to no ghosts. Even poetry could better contain Mary Kingsley, I think now. Consider Margaret Atwood's *Journals of Susannah Moodie* or Ruth Whitman's Tamsen Donner poems, *A Woman's Journey*. Both these writers were willing to be content with a series of short meditations which isolated a few characteristics of their subjects that could stand for the whole, thus make felt their impact against a vaguely sketched-in background. The characters hang somewhere halfway between fact and metaphor, between what is known and recorded, and what their chroniclers chose to see in the cracks and shadows. But they do not, by way of the large assertions of the novel, and the thousand exact details by which it proceeds, try to replicate real life or pretend to tell the whole story. Nor would any reader take the poems for such. Poetry can make a series of simplified gestures; the novel, especially one that plays across two continents, takes simple gestures and pulls the strands apart, unbraids the whole action into component parts, and they proliferate. One needs to realize that it takes at least three hands to hold together the stuff of any novel when it's on the work table.

I'm certainly not speaking against experiments in subject matter and form: none of us would grow beyond our adolescent writing if we didn't dare them. My own writing has been very different from one book to the next. But what I needed to understand about my work, and for a long time refused to, is that the way I have made most of my characters has been to start from life—a face, a stance, a real friend's or acquaintance's situation—and to narrow my eyes until all the real details disappear in a blur. What enters my line of vision then is all invented. Filling in the empty form. It is fiction as a means of completion, the ending of the sentence that begins: "What if . . . Say someone were . . ." I can very well understand why it is that the composers of the best *lieder* tended most often to set mediocre poetry, poetry that needed their music to join and enlarge it. So I think what I need, and what many others do, is not so much strong subject matter, vivid plots, and fascinating personae, as subjects that could never live without the breath I give them. And Mary Kingsley, as I can now see, having her own extraordinary but alien integrity, did perfectly well without assistance. What she didn't have that I made for her *I* needed, and she didn't.

Therefore I am leaving her life intact, its mysteries—or nonmysteries—unprobed. None of this process was a waste of a minute of my time, I ought to add. But finally, turning back now to my own ideas I think this must be the same feeling a baseball player has when he swings five bats so that the one he takes to the plate will feel like a toothpick—planning that begins and ends in my own head feels like the easiest, freest kind of work I've ever done.

Displaced Persons

W H E N people ask me where I come from I tell them nowhere.

Someone who introduced me at a reading recently told the audience that I grew up in Philadelphia, which was a fair enough assumption, based on the information on some book jacket or vita that I was born in Philadelphia—Pennsylvania, not Mississippi—but he was entirely wrong. I lived in Philadelphia for ten weeks. At the end of ten years of not much belonging there, my parents, who were New Yorkers, were obviously waiting with their bags packed for me to be born, so that we could take off to what turned out to be a series of other places in which they also never felt at home.

Our vagabondage was not particularly exciting. We weren't natural gypsies who chose the next town over the hill because it looked inviting; nor was my father a circuit-riding preacher or a military man, as many are quick to suggest. He was following a job or two to this or that unlikely outpost and was indifferent to the charm or charmlessness of our living arrangements. These days, "quality of life," as it's quaintly called, is being written up in studies that tell us we should try to live in Palo Alto, California, but not, at any cost, in Haverhill, Massachusetts. This was not always an active concept. My father went to work as a typist for a railroad company at thirteen, having had a few desultory months of business school, and my mother, though she also missed out on high school, worked hard at transcending the tenements in which she grew up as a Russian immigrant. I assume that for them, dutiful and loving parents, once having ascertained that we lived, as the ads say, near schools and shopping, a good job was a lot more potent an attraction than a graceful skyline or a dozen lakes scattered across the horizon. As for family, in that kind of vertical move family is necessarily left behind; or if it does not disappear, it hangs on the way my grandmother did, barnaclelike, once her own household had dispersed, moving as we moved for want of anyone else to live with or anywhere else to go.

In any event, until I was a teenager the longest I lived in one place was four years, which I spent in a town in Westchester County outside of New York City. Now we all know that "where you come from," where you grew up, is a matter for the imagination. The date on a questionnaire doesn't begin to approach the significant center of one's experience. The town I lived in from ages five through nine was called Mount Vernon: it was a short and, to me, wondrous commuter-train ride away from Manhattan, which we made on many a Thursday night (when the department stores stayed open late) or Saturday afternoon for shopping or a concert. But when people say to me, "You grew up in New York then," I have to demur—there are so many fine distinctions. From time to time I borrowed its vigor and its cultural endowments, but the city (by which people mean Manhattan, whether they realize it or not) wasn't mine. I was not that kind of natural New Yorker.

Although reason tells me that every year of those four that I lived in Mount Vernon consisted of the requisite four seasons, and even though I can recall plenty of winter and summer scenes if I try, still for whatever entirely subterranean reason, when I remember what I think of as the central years of my childhood—the others having trickled away a year or two at a time in places that left no particular residue—it is always fall and I am kicking up noisy leathery leaves in a particular stretch of woods within sight of the solid-stone castlelike bridges that cross the old winding highways of Westchester County. I don't know why this is the abiding image I have taken from the full years of my childhood. Nothing special happened there, either ecstatic or traumatic, I have no whole picture that tells me whether I played there once or twice or a hundred times, and I don't remember who I played with. I must have felt some heart-centered, solitary, sensual delight, some essence of childhood freedom otherwise denied me, in that place. I remember that certain grim sunlight that precedes winter-in-earnest, and the kind of temperature in which you keep your jacket open because it's not quite cold, but yet your ears hurt with the hinted beginning of serious weather.

But this is very nearly all. The rest of my memories from childhood, I should say, though they are numerous, are not continuous. They yield less than they ought to of pattern and ritual, and of rich pictures of neighbors in their characteristic places, of townspeople whose behavior became, after years, predictable to a concentrating child, and whose family laughs about this one or that, or shakes its collective head in disapproval at the dinner table. I did not have the repetition of year-in year-out expectation that comes of belonging in a community. The only advantage to this kind of random childhood, I ought to say, is that when I want to date something in my mind I can think, ah yes, I must have done such and such in 1948 because that was the year, the only year, we lived in Los Angeles. There is a backdrop for the memories and it is always recognizable because it changes so distinctly with each move. So, while those of you who lived in a single place may see a blur of years, I have them all too neatly separated and captioned, like photographs, according to city and setting.

It goes without saying that I missed a great deal in our peripatetic life. Though my parents were wonderfully adequate to the tasks of parenthood, a stable address is the only detail of nurturing they didn't bother to provide, and I think they suffered considerable loneliness themselves for the lack of a single place we could call home. (Even that character was luckier than we who came, according to Flannery O'Connor, "not even from a place, just from near a place.") Mainly, I think, the bit of geography on which you grow up, with which you identify yourself before you even think about such things—the world to which you first belong—acts in your life much the way your parents do: it becomes that immutable *fact* in your existence which, when you come to consciousness, you either embrace or resist. You are defined by it, your vision made by it, though no one ever asked your opinion of the matter; and so eventually you will either love your hometown, your neighborhood, your house, or you will struggle against it, you will dream of the bus station or the college admission that will set you free, or the simple year of majority after which no one can force you to stay and continue your childhood past the time when it is seemly to be "Sue Anne's girl" or "Junior" to your father, or the exfootball star or prom queen. Or you will love and hate it in unpredictable alternation.

Edgar Z. Friedenberg in *The Vanishing Adolescent*, a good book popular in the early 1960s, talks about the problems of adolescents who grow up without resistance from their permissive parents, without boundaries against which to hone themselves, to sharpen and define their differences, to discover who they are not and, consequently, who they are or may want to become. I think that I, lacking a hometown to spurn, lacked a starting point from which to move away, toward which I might one day have decided to move back, in a sweet reconciling return.

But let me not sound too forlorn: one lives with one's biography, whatever it may bring, and in my case, it is starting nowhere, having no sense of place, that has been by bedrock reality. I have scraped up against *that* to make my world on the page. My subject has turned out to be exile; turned out to be place, which, unpossessed or forfeited—the obverse of home—can be just as obsessive a preoccupation.

(And, parenthetically, I should say that I began writing as an antidote to the loneliness of exile. I can of course place the memory against a particular backdrop: it was in the lee of yet another move, from one coast to another, that I found myself at nine bereft of friends. I would go off to school clutching to my—nonexistent—bosom a secretarial notebook in which I wrote stories of perfect girls who possessed perfect horses, and *they* kept me company. I looked busy while all the old friends stood around in comfortable groups to which I had no invitation, and in my book—out of words—I made new friends far more dazzling than those who were merely real.)

So, as it's happened, I have immersed myself in a rather unwieldy number of borrowed terrains in my writing: three, so far. In a block in Brooklyn inhabited by blacks, whites, Puerto Ricans, the poor, and the middle class that became my book of stories, *Street Games*. And in New Hampshire, where I've set one novel, *Tender Mercies*, and *Cora Fry*, which is a kind of novel in the form of eighty-four short poems, a presumptuous ventriloqual act in which I speak as a New Hampshire country woman born and persevering right down the road from where she began. (She flees to Boston and comes gratefully home again, quite clear, if conflicted, about the virtues and drawbacks of intimacy and anonymity. I didn't have to be a psychoanalyst to grasp that I wrote *Cora Fry* as the obverse of my preoccupation with not-belonging: Cora knows as little about exile as I know about living on native ground, and I got to live in her skin for a while and ponder the implications.)

Then there was Mississippi, in my first book of poems, *Some Deaths in the Delta*, and my most recent work, exhausting to write and, I've been told, to read—*Civil Wars*. Although I lived in New Hampshire for more than eleven years—it is my children's one original home as no place was mine (though that's complicated by their parents' pervasive outsider-hood)—and Mississippi for only three, I want to talk about my discovery of the South, and how it's worked in my books. I apologize for taking on the inadvertently aggrandizing tone of the critic, by the way, whose work is to justify her interest in an author by making the books sound *very* important and worthy of a reader's time. I don't necessarily think of them that way, but I do think their obsession with place and my own discovery of my shifting, searching, essentially unmoored self may illuminate something for the fixed and the well-moored.

New England and the South are among the very few parts of the country that still have real distinctiveness, though of course it is fast being levelled. Even now—I live in Houston—I know that it was the southernness of Houston that pulled me to it, not the westernness: the heavy-laden feel of the air, and the hanging moss. It was the familiar long-missed look of the chipped-paint shacks leaning exhaustedly against each other like nothing in the north; the live oaks, and the modest bungalows with no foundation, the smalltown shops with their metal awnings only half an hour from the Astrodome. It was the bayous and the violent late afternoon summer showers that drew me to Texas, not its oil money and certainly not Houston's beautiful brittle glass skyline.

The first time I left my teenage home, which was a characterless part of Queens, New York—very few people who live outside of New York or occasionally visit Manhattan realize the astounding aesthetic bleakness that prevails for most New Yorkers at home, the darkness of ancient apartments and the industrial clutter of the boroughs—when I left that home to which physical memories have trouble sticking as if it were too smooth a surface, it was for New England. I discovered that there were places with a visible history, with an indigenous feel to them, characteristic textures, colors, climate, and that people in small towns took an intimate interest in each other's affairs. Without having partaken of the pleasures of the rich or the impacted intimacies of the poor, I had the middle-class New Yorker's anomie with relation to our neighbors; one went unimpeded, on our street, by much curiosity or concern. Good and bad in equal parts, this freedom again left a void I hadn't even known I possessed. Once I got a glimpse through a crack in the door, I longed for the life of the New Englander, to be lived under an afghan on a high antique four-poster bed in the imagined company of Emily Dickinson, who had lived hers that way. This was an ideal of quaint specificity I wished for but couldn't have.

After New England I lived in San Francisco, which was a different sort of picturesque, an ideal that I loved but didn't want—it seemed to me a diet of lotos and civic self-congratulation.

I came to Mississippi in 1965 half-mature at best, as a grownup in any case whose childhood book was closed on many empty pages, and that is where I learned that if one could not be born again a native of a place, it was at least possible to bring to it the cultivated virtues of curiosity and freshness of vision—of entranced concentration—so that no one could ever be thoroughly barred from writing about *anything* if one found it interesting enough. "Write about what you know," we writing teachers are reputed to tell our students, but I don't necessarily tell them that at all. Because "many events casually called experiences"—I am quoting here from the critic Denis Donohue—"are merely happenings. The test of an experience is that it alters the structure of our feeling; if it doesn't, it has been merely a circumstance, it hasn't entered our lives in any radical sense." And of course—this is me again—the converse is just as true: a writer who finds him or herself profoundly affected by a circumstance or by a place can, by a kind of exaggeratedly focussed attention, render that scene. It has become an experience in Donohue's terms; it has counted on the pulses, it has taken its place in the circuitry of the brain. But, of course, with a difference.

It would have taken nerve I didn't have to write about Mississippi as if I were a native. The skills I have are different from those of someone writing from memory: one is not so much a historian as a sociologist crossed with an anthropologist, both of whom are passionate outsiders, and an inventor rather than a preserver. The question of perspective always looms for a writer—who speaks, and with what authority? The care with which one chooses the distance at which the narrator will plant his or her feet (or its—sometimes the narrator has no gender) is exaggerated when the writer is, like me, a newcomer, a native of nowhere; Flannery O'Connor might say, a displaced person. Writers can be carpetbaggers if they're not careful,

or colonialists, if you will, immodestly appropriating that which is
not theirs. Sometimes they ought to dare if they can pull it off. But if
they can't, such appropriation ends up looking like a moral failing,
like lying or the crime of theft; petty larceny.

The first thing I wrote about Mississippi was a poem. It was the
summer of 1964. The poem was called "Landing in Jackson" and it
begins my first book, *Some Deaths in the Delta*.

> I wear my fear like wool against the skin,
> walking from corner to corner of this graceless city,
> squinting down doorways, warily at faces.
> For a familiar token I take the sky,
> stretched taut between the tent-poles of my sight—
> that northern sky that bore me up for hours,
> then set me down in this ungentle place.
>
> What shame may be here keeps its uneven heartbeat
> under the breast-pocket, the clean white hanky;
> if any danger passes, it keeps its eyes
> turned in like something hidden in the palm.
> I sniff from corner to corner, guilelessly,
> skulking for welcome.

This is, of course, a poem about being a stranger in a strange land.
An experience—Denis Donohue might even agree—can be some-
thing you create for yourself without benefit of the occurence; the
real event may be the least important ingredient. Which is to say,
I wrote the poem on my back porch in Brookline Village, Massa-
chusetts, in terrified anticipation, before I'd ever set foot in Jackson,
Mississippi. (I should add that since life is more complex than I knew
at the time, it turns out that working-class Irish Brookline Village,
Massachusetts, to judge by the behavior of similar Boston neighbor-
hoods, probably harbored—covertly—as viciously racist a climate
as anyone might find on the continent. Only its particular history
and the publicly civil behavior of its leaders had kept that such a
surreptitious reality in 1964 that I really thought I had to go some-
place else, by airplane—some mysteriously evil city surrounded by
alien woods, in a different time zone—to find racial brutality and
the indignities of segregation.)
Eventually I was to write half a book of poems about Mississippi,
not didactic but, I would say, elegiac and often angry. Even though

one can fudge a thousand details in poetry—this is how, later, I dared to write in the voice of a New Hampshire woman—I was sufficiently daunted by what I still thought of as the otherness of the South that I wrote as an outsider. Thinking of Jackson again, the selfappointed "crossroads of the South," I saw myself accosted by a woman amidst the "alien corn":

> Blonde as the grass in January,
> walking with legs padlocked above the knee,
> she asked, sweet as a lime,
> what country was I from.

The bitterness of the poem, which was distinctly a product of its period in history, was unyieldingly hostile to white Mississippi, a population for which I—who had come south as an advocate of black rights, to teach in a black college—was not about to feel sympathy. What an extraordinary sense of double displacement for a northern white woman—I was a girl, really—to belong neither to the dominant population nor, of course, to belong (I couldn't kid myself) to the world of my black friends.

"After the first exile there is no other," says one of my characters in *The Autobiography of My Mother*, a novel that followed a few years later. Some people, I was learning, are at home only in continuous displacement. In that novel I make alienation an overt theme. The mother in the book is a civil liberties lawyer named Gerda Stein who was forcibly removed from her native Alsace at an early age, bearing nothing intact except her convoluted Germanic syntax. Although the book takes place in New York, Gerda does something uncharacteristically passionate, even heroic, during a brief sojourn to Mississippi to argue for school integration. But she dismisses the act as not particularly courageous:

It was the act of an outsider with whom the consequences would never catch up. Having been cut free of my past the one, the first time, I was cast into a lifetime of freedom. One accepts such freedom of movement like a doom, a taste of certain death, do you understand that? I was not easily to be hurt or frightened. Perhaps that is all that is necessary for mere humans, not saints, not martyrs, to act. . . . (I) had come from nowhere, in whose accents I persistently spoke, and would soon return to nowhere. Mine was a privileged freedom which compensated—at such times—for my rootlessness. So you see, even the Lone Ranger could afford momentary lapses into heroism. They did not truly cost him so much, surely not so much as children believe, for he habitually vanished, did he not, into some canyon, some purple sunrise, leaving only his silver bullet behind. Should he not merely have been called The Exile?

In another place she says impatiently of her law partner,

I can better comprehend the life of a hoarse-throated, one-legged, blind, garlic-scented, God-fearing Malaysian who has lived in any twelve cities of the world than, say, that of my partner, Jack Tenney, who was born in Washington Heights and has merely rolled downhill a few miles to the nearest viable neighborhood, barring Harlem, to live in a building which must be nearly identical to the first; and so, except for a short lifeless sojourn to the barracks of Fort Dix twenty years ago, he has moved gently through his life yet to be truly surprised, I would wager, or truly inconvenienced. Snug Jack.

This is, I suppose, my own very personal sense of the paradox of mobility: Gerda's perpetually angry acknowledgement of her dislocation, with its concomitant freedom from hometown constraints, is the best and the worst one can expect. For certain purposes, we displaced persons have special powers; for others, no power at all.

Finally, I want to talk about my recent novel that is set altogether and most pointedly in Mississippi, some of it at the inflamed height of civil rights activity, most of it fifteen years later—1979—in a Jackson much changed, its racial mores (inconsistently) assimilated and less lethal, blander, its general profile less "southern," more American, all of that for better and for worse. I'm talking about my book because I think it's worth speaking of what I like to call the *Gulliver perspective* from which it's written: the stranger can comment on what he (in this case she) sees without bias. (Since there is no neutrality, of course, I should amend that: with the biases of the observer who has grown up on other sights.) Henry James in Europe had such a vantage point, or Paul Scott in India. Southerners do not often resort to it unless they, like Elizabeth Spencer, go to Italy.

My novel concerns a white husband and wife, Teddy and Jessie Carll, who are staying on in Jackson many years after the high season of their civil rights heroism. By now, so long after the exhilaration of that time, Jessie, who is one of those New Yorkers who came south for what she called the second civil war, is looking with a somewhat jaundiced eye at the world of her Mississippi-born husband. Teddy, a renegade in his family, has fought hard for his moral autonomy; has

67

alienated himself wholly from his childhood. When Jessie considers Teddy, she does so as a newcomer to his world, both attracted and repelled by so much that comes to her too late to be taken into her imaginative sympathy. I'd like her sense of the place to be illuminating to northerner and southerner alike: to show another New Yorker, say, what she might have seen and felt had she been in Jessie's place (for Jessie is a stand-in for any other alien's experience), and I'd like the southern reader to apprehend what it all must look and feel like to someone who's dropped in, Gulliver-like, from across the sea, or in this case, the Mason-Dixon line.

Because one's obsessions will surface wholly unbidden, I doubled the alienation factor. Without exactly realizing what I was doing as I chose the plot to pull the load of social observation, I forced the Carlls, by the accidental death of Teddy's sister and brother-in-law, to take into their house in an integrated neighborhood in Jackson their niece and nephew, who have grown up in affluent Birmingham in an emphatically segregationist household. These children are, not to mince words, little bigots, rich ones to boot, come to live in a commitedly ascetic (and, to them, a morally bizarre) household. Their world and the world of their aunt and uncle and cousins are 180 degrees—360 degrees—different, because ideology and its local manifestation, habit, can make rackingly different worlds out of the same point in space. No one in *Civil Wars* is living with the same sense of place as anyone else, even when they stand with shoulders touching. I give young Helen, who is 13 and one of the orphans-come-to-town, her own diary through which to show us what it feels like to be turned out of every comfort of home; her way of dealing with this tragic disorientation, finally, is to take refuge in her own unchanging solace, a good Southern solution, I think:

> No home there,
> No home here,
> No home anywhere
> But Jesus.

When I think of the writers whose rootedness I most envy, and they are too numerous even to try to name, I have to remember that there are a great many ways to feel sufficiently alienated from a situation or a place to be impelled to become an observer, not a passive or complacent participant. So many reasons to say, as I did in my first book, "Can't remember what I meant by home." For time and chance altereth all things. In my novel *Tender Mercies*, a woman who becomes crippled feels now the foreignness of the terrain of her own body. In Rebecca Hill's *Blue Rise*, by a writer with an extraordinarily deep grasp of local expectations, the narrator has left her small Mississippi town and come back half a stranger, to whom all is inescapably familiar and all is still impossibly threatening and insupportable. For Ellen Douglas in *The Rock Cried Out*, technology intrudes; in Joan Williams's *Country Woman*, time and the turmoil of the 1960s have twisted open the sense of possibilities for a woman still at home in the place where she grew up and married. Ernest Gaines's characters are black and powerless in Louisiana cane country; Barry Hannah's are rarely sober enough to remember *where* they are. Bobbie Ann Mason's characters are lost, like strayed deer, between the farm and the mobile home park. Though most of the time Eudora Welty feels like the one comfortable and unalienated writer among the ranks of the disaffected, her *Optimist's Daughter* comes back, comes home, finds some things changeless, but the behavior and the choices of her aging father new, bizarre, inappropriate. Yet the future he elects for himself turns out to be symbolic of great changes everywhere, and irremediable. And she, Laurel, has made her distancing choice even before he made his—she, after all, abandoned home and went north; she has made herself a visitor with no vote. In many ways this is the saddest of Eudora Welty's books.

Finally, of course, we come to the progenitor of so much southern writing: Faulkner was at home but never at ease on his postage stamp of earth, where time and all that is new, deadening, and uncivilized is creeping up on that good bear-hunting ground. ("The woods' old caves are flattened,/ dampness gone back under earth," I wrote in the title poem of *Some Deaths in the Delta*. "A sky away,/ pine survivors huddle together,/ roots in their hands,/ ready for the next step back.") Just so, Faulkner had to go nowhere to feel exile come to claim him in his native kingdom, though *he* had no intention of moving a single step.

So every writer comes upon the distancing element. I believe that no writer has ever in fact been fully at home anywhere, or he, she would sell insurance or decorate cakes for a living, or sit and rock and chew. Because home lulls and pacifies and stuffs the mouth with very simple song. Nostalgia complicates the song, or the angry conviction that all people do not appear to live equal in the sight of others, whatever one was taught in Sunday Bible class. Family politics and village politics and racial and religious and sexual politics wrench the harmonies of the song, and finally the suspicion, glimpsed early, that even the most peaceful home will one day perish, and the people in it—*that* modulates and darkens the most self-satisfied melody.

I want to close the way Flannery O'Connor closed her essay on the regional writer: "The writer operates at a peculiar crossroads where time and place and eternity somehow meet. His problem is to find that location." By such standards, even the stranger passing through can say, both proudly and humbly, "I think I'll sit awhile and listen hard, get warm, and maybe pay for my dinner by telling what I saw."

Postscript a few years later.

How our preoccupations haunt us. Each poem, each story or novel feels different as it presents itself: *Eureka! Something new here.* And each turns out to be rooted to the original stock, however obscurely. Biography, if it has some psychological reach, ferrets out these sites of connection. Meanwhile, this side of the psychiatrist's couch, we're left to discern them for ourselves. Years after I delivered this paper to the Southern Literary Festival in Chattanooga I visited the Soviet Union to meet with *refuseniks* in Moscow and Leningrad, and among the dozen or so bitter poems that came of those brief encounters, there had to be one about the unhoused spirit, the expatriated soul of the "successful" petitioner for emigration, both relieved and bereft in its new country. Thus:

Emigré (Houston)

Here you get yourself a car.
It takes you to town, it takes you home
at your own good time
and no one else's.
You have a house standing separate,
and a garage like a belly on the house.
Here's what you do at the end of the day: you ride up
fast to the house, put the wheels
between two little margins of short-haired grass.
(You have to keep it short.)
You point your finger at your house
and slow as a drawbridge the wide door yawns
up, up, showing your cans of paint,

your dog-eared valises to the world.
You inch into the dark, gently.
For a while you get to sit, then,
peaceful, like the cut-off motor cooling down.
Your hedge-clipper dangles on the wall, open-mouthed,
your exercise bike sits at the back
like a patient horse in its clean stall.

In Leningrad this is the hour
when they hang suspended in the Metro,
shoulder to shoulder to elbow to groin.
Nobody's feet at five o'clock
ever touch ground. When the full train lurches,
no one has room among so many friends and strangers,
not even an inch, to fall down.

An Insider/Outsider in Mississippi

J O H N   F O W L E S saw the French Lieutenant's Woman standing in black at the edge of a quay. Joan Didion watched a young woman in obvious distress stride across the lobby of a Beverly Hills hotel and make an anxious phone call. The image, real or imagined, begets the book.

In our case, the indelible impression, a man-begetting image, not a literary one, is of a gnome—round, bald, smiling, talking to us, although we were strangers, without let-up—eating a chop decorated, for himself alone, with a shiny canned peach. His table is covered with the kind of old-fashioned red checkered oil cloth that people and restaurants search out these days for its naive "charm." This table, only incidentally charming, is in the rickety, fluorescent-lit basement of a seedy wooden building near the center of a college campus in Mississippi. It is June of the summer of 1964.

There have, by now, been a great many anatomies of "the troubles," as a friend calls them with an appropriately broguish lilt. They have featured black folks, whose movement it was, and white folks, who were there as midwives but who also felt the ultimate freedom of their souls at stake. Bob Moses, Fannie Lou Hamer, John Lewis, Stokely, all of them have been written about, and many of the ancillary forces as well, private and public. But there are dozens, many dozens of other players who had their roles in this time of exceptional flux, this floodtide. Their influence was a subtle force, whose results are hard to measure. They need voices to *testify* (as they say in the little churches). Ernst Borinski, the man at ease in his own lively, peculiar and self-designed domain, wielded a very distinct kind of influence that has rarely been celebrated because it was *sui generis* and modest and in many ways seemed to run counter to the times. But it was genuinely important as one piece of the whole.

"The-three-civil-rights-workers"—that terrible phrase that came all in one word—had been missing for a week or two when my husband Marv Hoffman and I went to interview for our first jobs, at Tougaloo College, just outside of Jackson. As students we had stood on the safe sidelines of the civil rights struggle long enough, we thought; too cowardly to volunteer for front-line action, we answered the call of the Woodrow Wilson Foundation which was looking for former grad-school fellows to work in "developing"—i.e., poor, mostly southern, mostly black—colleges. Alternately brave and craven, we asked for a "safe" posting, maybe something in a border state, at the edge of the fray where we could do our little bit, which we saw as intellectually, not overtly, combative: one of us would teach English, the other psychology. They suggested Tougaloo, nicknamed "Cancer College" around Jackson for its place at the raging center. Tougaloo was a private college which had always been integrated—private funding made it independent of the kind of financial sanctions by the state that persistently threatened to sever the lifeline of schools such as Jackson State. At Tougaloo you lived on the campus, because off your safety was too difficult to assure. Even inside its gates, houses on the periphery of the campus occasionally took rifle shots through their windows; the sheriff chased you as far as the arch of the front gate. Intrigued, we went to have a look; compelled—the alternate placement in the border state suddenly rendered pale and tame by comparison—we took the jobs.

The June meeting with Ernst Borinski was by way of interview. (Six months later when we reported to work, the civil rights workers were assuredly dead, and a few more besides.) There he sat over his solitary dinner in the back room of what was called the Social Science Lab, although a conventional lab it was not. He had furnished the long, low-ceilinged basement room with a random, catch-as-catch-can assortment of unmatched and scuffed tables and chairs, and an equally motley collection of books—anthropology, sociology, psychology, history. I remember a particularly unused-looking copy of *Bleak House*, possibly, given his relative indifference to literature-as-such, shelved with urban studies.

The room in which we confronted Dr. Borinski at his chop—we couldn't bring ourselves to call him "Ernst" until many years later when we were bona-fide adults out of his employ—was partitioned off from the rest for a privacy that was only relative. It was never off-limits to anyone and student assistants roiled through it casually in search of assignments, conversation, life-direction. It was a combination mess-hall, office, and boudoir, a space so lived-in and so much a piece with its inhabitant that if there was no bed back there it felt as if there ought to have been. We were surprised when we learned that he actually had an apartment elsewhere on the campus—what else could the man own, or even care about, that he might put into it?

Ernst had an extraordinary accent and allowed himself a flamboyant indulgence of Germanic syntax, all inversion and circumlocution, which we soon understood he was not eager to lose. In Mississippi, where even the inflections of Chicago or Boston sounded foreign, his language made a kind of magical space around him, kept him enigmatic, and forever innocent (no matter how sly), moored, apparently forever, in foreignness. Every time he picked up the conversational ball he raised his eyebrows and said, in a rising tone of anticipation, "Zo-zo?" His speech sounded approximately like Sid Caesar doing Freud.

But Ernst played his myths for all they were worth. Once he told us that, spawned by his outrageous speech, rumors had circulated locally that he could understand every extant language. People began to bring him letters in Hungarian, Italian, and Russian to translate; apparently even in the most all-American of neighborhoods exotic needs will surface. Rather than dispel so convenient a reputation—who could guess what power and authority it might engender for later use?—he would put the supplicants off while he shipped their mail to the appropriate consulates with a request for translation.

Still, if he was not quite as extraordinary as he seemed, he was extraordinary enough. By the time he had left Germany, somewhere in Silesia near the Polish border, in 1938, Ernst had already had what would suffice many for an entire career: he was a lawyer and a judge. He must have travelled in prominent circles: Kathe Kollwitz was a friend. The advance of Nazi power was apparently more evident to him than to the rest of his family, who would not budge. Alone, he went to request a visa, was asked if he was planning to return and, where many of his confreres lied and said Yes, assuredly Yes, they only wanted a vacation, and were denied exit, he was straight-forward—"I'm never coming back"—and received one. He didn't use the visa for a long time, though, while he worked at persuading his family to flee with him. Lawyer or not, he could not convince them to leave. They stayed behind; every one of them perished. On the train, leaving finally, he told us, once again he trusted authority where many another would have found it impossible, with a Blakean innocence that had passed through experience, beyond hopelessness and beyond cunning. He gave all his money to the conductor, told him he was going to take a sleeping pill and did not wish to be awak-ened until they were across the border, did so, and was delivered. So went his story anyway. He landed first in Cuba as did so many refu-gees; came to the United States just in time to serve in the Army and, long before the English language imposed itself on his consciousness, became a citizen, along with a wildly assorted crowd of recruits in North Africa. (In anticipation of the arrival of the Germans, the U.S. government wanted to protect its German soldiers by annexing them as formally as possible.)

Finally he was able to get down to the business of reconstruct-ing a life: he worked in Rochester for Bausch and Lomb because in Germany they had had an adult education program he had been in-volved with, and somewhere along the way, probably later, he took a Ph.D. in sociology at the University of Chicago. Somehow he heard about Tougaloo and it too resembled the adult education work he had done in Germany. Suffice it to say that, although he probably did not have a multitude of choices, his arrival was no accident. (When I graduated from high school in 1956, one of my most culturally-attuned and serious friends chose to go to college in North Carolina because she said—and I was far too benighted even to have an opin-ion about the probabilities—that the next "action" was going to take place in the South and she wanted to be there to take part in it. There are those, apparently, who know at least one of two things, if not both: where there is need, and where there is movement, however potential, however seismic, coming to an underground boil.)

It was the late 1940s when Ernst surfaced on the campus of the small black college, founded in the late nineteenth century by white Methodists. There has always been white faculty at such colleges. The old photographs in the library showed us very sober young black faces—men and women buttoned to the neck, their collars sternly

75

starched—arranged in ranks or else in the random I'll-look-this-way, you-look-that-way fashion of group pictures of a century ago. Behind them, or in the corners, were their white mentors, modestly tucked out of prominence: they were there in the spirit of Christian helpfulness, and one imagines their ministrations—this was not terribly long after the Civil War—were gentle and more than tinged with noblesse oblige. They played a very necessary role in readying these young people—whoever they were, from whatever kind of tenuous, determined pre-middle class—for the worlds of teaching, of the church, and, once in a while, of the professions.

When we arrived in the mid-1960s, there were still white professors cut from the same cloth, with theological backgrounds and a cheerful air of service about them. Most were dedicated in the way of missionaries, or at least of ministers, with a slightly strained but rarely shattered patience in the face of intellectual shortfalls, and a set of standards just a little too forgiving to be wholly useful in the "outside" world. (For "outside," of course, read "white.") There were black professors too (Negroes then) whose tolerance, similarly, was often dangerously excessive: much of the work they accepted was barely of high school quality. But they were dealing with the shambles a poor and segregated Mississippi education (separate but nothing like equal) made of most minds, good, bad, indifferent, too often irreversibly, and at least their shared color and common experience gave them a different kind of edge. They could be sharp-tongued, even harsh, and it sounded parental. The old-guard white faculty tended to tiptoe because, stepping down hard they did not sound parental, they sounded *white*, and this was the deep South, and it was all too easy to stimulate connotations, associations, terrors, and watch ears and eyes close up and minds close down. They were sensitive to that, but generally helpless. A good bit of black higher education was felt to be in the hands, however benign, of the enemy.

Ernst, though—what to make of Ernst? He was, by careful design, not so much enemy as stranger. His origins remained in dispute; he was unclassifiable. (One morning in a sociology class, the question arose: How many Jews are there in America? Estimates ranged from 40 to 70 million. "Any here on campus?" "Oh no." "Borinski?" "Nah." "Feldstein? Hoffman?" Certainly not, our students said indignantly: they *liked* us all. Wherever the dangerous horde preyed, it had not yet penetrated the front gate here.) Ernst had a "complete

new concept" for where he dwelled in the imagination of Mississippi-
ans of all colors. It was more than mildly sociological, as were all his
ideas: he called it "inside-outside." "Some vays," he would say, rub-
bing his pudgy hands together like a man diabolically plotting, "some
vays zis vorks to everyone's advantage," implying, I think, that, like
drinkers who can excuse their behavior by blaming the bottle, those
who might be discovered yielding up their racist behavior or their
laziness in the face of difficult headwork—those caught living up to
his alien expectations whatever they might be—were merely victims
of his beguiling exceptionality, his empowered marginality. So he
went about building his empire of elevating aspirations, his labora-
tory of worldly enrichment.

The first thing he did when he arrived at Tougaloo set the tone of
daring pseudo-naiveté. Many of his students were recently returned
veterans, hungry for an education, more comfortable in the world-
at-large than their provincial brothers. He gave them an assignment
that must have sounded like the first command of a fairy godfather
to a prince in search of a kingdom: "Go," he ordered them, "und
bring back for me desks, typewriters, tables, bookshelves. Und do
not tell me vere you got them, zis I do not vant to know." Sweet are
the uses of ignorance. So they constructed the charmed domain of
the Social Science Lab in a boarded-up space beneath the building
that housed faculty offices. (Next door the administration ruled in a
pillared antebellum mansion that felt like the domesticated palace of
a conquered nation.)

The second use Ernst made of this willful blindness to "appro-
priateness" was a wholly unique series of weekly lectures he'd been
staging for years, to which all manner of speakers came, and all
colors of listeners. He invited to speak anyone who would oblige—
journalists, scholars, psychiatrists, activists—the whole assortment
of intellectually qualified passersby who, especially in the inflamed
60s, were flooding the state. From Ernst's point of view, which could
be irritatingly dispassionate, anyone with a firm perspective, any-
one who represented passion and brought along facts, was welcome;
his enemies were ignorance and stagnation, an inaccessibility to out-
side voices and multiple worldviews that is hard to reconstruct two
decades later. Somehow he trusted that along the way his listeners
would form their own judgments regarding morality, decency, neces-
sity. He'd have invited the Klan if they'd have come. (On our first

visit to the campus during that long hot dangerous summer, a black man from the village of Tougaloo nearly scared us into the bushes screeching up beside us in his tattered car. "Is this where the rabbi from Arabia speakin' tonight?" he asked us eagerly. And indeed it was: an Arab diplomat from some infinitesimal new oil country, passing through on business, was on the agenda that night, and the man from town was there in his workclothes to hear him. So came Indians, Japanese, Harvard professors, congressional aides.)

But that would not have been enough to justify Ernst's efforts. Very carefully he planned prelecture dinners to include, among students he thought could benefit, the small contingent of daring whites who would drive out from Jackson and not mind letting it be known that they were coming to this place of public contamination. The wife of the head of the Chamber of Commerce was a prize catch; even her husband was sometimes on the guest list. Two brave and significant civil rights figures who, in the 1950s, had been students at Millsaps, the white college in town, told us that Ernst's forums, to which they snuck out rashly under cover of darkness, were influential in their "alternative" education. A city like Jackson is unrecognizable today in its openness; no one much cares where you spend your time. You won't lose your job or your house or your life for "fraternizing." But in order to understand how unique were Ernst's efforts at rapprochement—his understanding that "casual" social contact could precede and encourage tolerance—one must reimagine the truly Gothic atmosphere, the sense of heart-stopping danger, in which his small but always growing cadre of white friends lived, and all they had to overcome to show up in the dazzling light of the Lab on Forum nights.

Working with Ernst was another story, although his scheme fit together better than we could appreciate at the time. We were very young (as was most of the hot-shot faculty—many programs were "plugging in talent" in those years)—and rather more aggressive and impatient about change than our experience warranted. And we were short-termers; Ernst, in for the long haul, had the larger picture and the lighter touch. He did not particularly encourage (though he didn't oppose) the kind of sit-in activism the Tougaloo students favored. He was rarely eager to confront the administration over its frequent and distressing lapses in commitment to the "movement." (The book has yet to be written about the ambivalence of black college leadership toward radical change and toward community, toward attitudes that include respect for the "unwashed" classes just outside the gate that so embarrass it, unless that book is the old standard *The Black Bourgeoisie.*)

In general, the old man (for so we thought him even in the face of our respect for his sharp analytical powers) favored conciliation. It was well for certain populations to petition and demonstrate, for others to raise hell with the powers that ran the college (while they, its leaders, dug in and prepared to wait us out, a mere rainshower of clamorous voices). But his role, he patiently explained while we listened with undisguised impatience, was to hold down the middle: he was the buffer we could shoot across if we chose to. To understand social dynamics we needed to learn to focus—"focoos" was the word—on the balance of forces. Dispassion was not indifference; disinterest was not betrayal. He regarded us more coolly than we regarded him: we were like impatient lovers, and the many crimes he saw us commit, he knew, were crimes of passion. Where would we be without his avuncular temperateness? We viewed his various conciliations with bewilderment. Given his background it was difficult to accuse him of fear so we accused him of optimism. We found him guilty of trusting his enemies and smiling when he should have been shouting.

Did he expect things simply to change without antagonists? Shouldn't he "of all people" decry silence in the face of injustice internal to the college or external? Didn't he sometimes put too much emphasis on delivering his students out of this narrow and embattled place—he cultivated every conceivable contact to get them off to distant graduate and professional schools—without considering the impoverished community right down the road? "Ve send avay children," Ernst insisted, "und zey vill come back to be leaders. Zo-zo, zis is vere ve fit in: ve uncover ze road for zem. Ve cannot take it for zem." (And many of them, degrees in hand, did follow it back to serve at home: lawyers, a young man I taught as a semiliterate freshman who brought his Princeton Ph.D. back and became chairman of the Tougaloo history department.)

We nattered on, and not always without justification, but in many cases we were the wrong ones to do the nattering, wholly sincere kids with good "eastern" educations, contemptuous of institutions— the black fraternity was one—far stronger than we, with histories we could hardly comprehend. Fashioned by other histories, we were relevant and irrelevant at the same time, resentful at having to give instruction in black pride and the righteousness of anger but patronizing in other ways we couldn't begin to imagine. We were role models chiefly for the sensitive kids who already felt alienated from local ideals, who could respond to our confident egalitarian chumminess. In a place where every hard-won higher degree placed an honorific beside one's name like an immovable stone, we—this was the mid-60s, after all—were the kinds of professors who asked to be called by our first names and had no patience when the homegrown faculty thought we were slumming. (In retrospect, we should have recognized a very familiar insecurity in needing to maintain all those letters: my husband's mother wanted to have his graduate degrees laminated and framed for her living room—he had done something no one else in the family had done.) Ernst understood far better than we where it was worth pitching battle: he was always Dr. Borinski and he in turn addressed every faculty and administration member by title, however absurd he may have looked doing so.

We left Mississippi in 1968 when we wearied of the mischief "black power" was making for white activists (by then—predictably?—having left the all-too-quiescent Tougaloo to work for the new and urgent poverty program). Ernst had no reason to move on. He had defined himself as a power outside the force-field of daily politics—"Today zis comes, tomorrow it goes. Zo-zo." He sounded like Billy Pilgrim. He was no Marxist, though his style was endlessly dialectical; he was not even a standard-issue determinist, but he would never be out of work—the conciliator's position would always be right there between the poles. Eventually, in the late 1970s, he cut back to half-time teaching (full time for most mortals), and he began to visit us every fall where we were living in rural New Hampshire, between trips—he was nearly eighty by now—to Israel, Lebanon, China, the Soviet Union.

He came to us in the fall in a cap with earflaps, wearing the clean white sneakers he had used to walk the Great Wall. ("Zey would not let me in the University Club in zese. Zey vere afraid I would start a new fashion!") Cast in a new role he was a remarkable house guest, having calculated carefully: a man with no family needs his friends. (He was our daughter's self-appointed godfather, and many others' besides.) Thus he called yearly on a regular rotation "in Vanderbilt University, in Chicago, in Columbia, here in ze deep country vere you play at Marie Antoinette and le petite Trianon." He insisted on cooking for us ("I must earn my keep, yah?") a series of unrepeatable dishes in the "Polish-Cherman-Chinese" style, heavy on soy sauce, mustard, and cabbage; he amiably accompanied everyone to work, sitting with fifth grade rural/blue collar children, a one-man lesson in geographical multiplicity; with preschoolers, letting them play with his accent as if it were a toy; with graduate students in administration, about whose work he had abundant multipurpose sociological theories.

Every Sunday afternoon, as regularly as a dutiful son calling his parents back home, Ernst would phone the president of Tougaloo, ostensibly reporting in and getting the news, in actuality demonstrating a courtly respect, honoring an absolute structure of command we had always observed with difficulty. Children of our time, we demanded "substance," "earned respect"; we easily dispensed with hierarchy which smacked of elitism, class division, "phoniness." But we Holden Caulfields had, since the last time around, grown up some. Now we could appreciate the care and nurturing Ernst gave out of his finely nuanced sociological grasp of the uses of seemliness. Where we had thought him a rank conservative and a sentimentalist, now we saw him for what he was: on the one hand a politician, on the other a good and decent man whom it cost little to bend the knee to ceremony.

The fluidity and playfulness of his mind, the ego that could withstand endless, because temporary, redefinition, all of it was disciplined by his belief that society is made up of groups who will avidly pursue their interests; and in the middle, a stiff-armed referee pushing the forces back a little on both sides, stands the virtuous and disinterested man. How could someone who had seen his family, just about all of it, fall to a madman in pursuit of *his* interests, stay quite so detached? How could an orphan of history restrain a passion for vengeance or for reparations? To what can one attribute the natural buoyancy that keeps some souls afloat in bloody churning waters— keeps them not only afloat but smiling? (We have known a few "boat people" in the last few years who came through such waters literally, not figuratively, and they suggest the same question.)

It would make good but not adequate sense to say that the fury of their reproach to circumstance could be so uncontrollable, so terrifying were it loosed that they have inhibited it, as people inhibit anger in their lives and present themselves safely encapsulated, repressed, undemonstrative in love and work. But Ernst doesn't fit the paradigm, somehow—perhaps his dispassion does and his apparent refusal (inability? unwillingness?) to create his own family. But, true to his own sense of the complexity of all things, he will not lie down and be analyzed. "Zo-zo," he might ask. "Und vut vill you learn if you answer zese qvestions?"

Years after we had left Mississippi, I had the only near-mystical experience of my writing career. I heard a voice—not a hallucination of a voice because I am too constrained by sanity for that, but a sort of echo of a familiar tonality, an accent I knew intimately. I heard this contorted Germanic language as a woman's speech that wouldn't leave me until I wrote inside it. I gave this woman a childhood shattered by anti-Semitism, pre-Holocaust, and I wished on her a daughter without much sense of history, to torment her when "outside" circumstance had finished wreaking its havoc. She became Gerda Stein, a not-very-lovable, and certainly not very buoyant character—I hesitate to say heroine—at the center of my first novel, *The Autobiography of My Mother*. Far from delineating my own mother in even the slightest detail, Gerda, I realized somewhere along the way, represented for me, transformed, the essential "secret," if I dare make his life into a conundrum, of Ernst's unmotivated serenity. Having been hounded into exile by historical catastrophe, both of them, real and imagined, had abandoned certain psychic comforts, such as the concept of home and biological family, and had taken refuge in that persistent "optimism" we had so deplored when we worked with him, that refusal to take a belligerent or rash or even hortatory stand on urgent issues. This was a paradoxical trust born of a pessimism whose roots were buried too deep, I suspect, for tears; an almost absurdist refusal to worry, let alone mourn. It placed an outrageously, demonstrably unjustifiable faith in the institutions of law, self-regulation, constitutional guarantees. Yeats's old men's eyes are gay in "Lapis Lazuli," having stared at "the tragic scene" long enough to have witnessed everything, and so were Ernst's, the darkest possibilities already having overtaken them. "Ya, zo-zo, some vays it vill all vork out," he would say, who had escaped by a shirttail the ultimate working out of the Final Solution. I don't think there was anyone in whom he had confided intimacies—intellectual formulations and analytic sangfroid stood in their place—and I wonder if anyone, since his arrival here, had seen him personally fearful, or even vulnerable. That he chose to be useful and to stay energetic and undepressed was a gift of temperament, but it was a gift wrung forever from its opposite, a hopelessness, a cynicism about outcomes, too dire to be borne. Thus were "the troubles" of one era connected by a slender thread to "the troubles" of another.

Ernst has been buried since 1984 in the little cemetery on the Tougaloo campus, a quintessentially southern graveyard inside a low gate under trees hung with Spanish moss. It is the kind of place that seems made for drowsy summer days, too antique to be threatening, too charming to depress a visitor. He is not the only white buried there, if memory serves, but surely he is the only one who was destined for the anonymous ash-heap of Europe; whose stubborn survival, even if he was never quite at ease, ultimately empowered him to be vividly present everywhere. It was a better use of exile than most people make of the safety of home.

The Jewish Writer as Endangered Species

A W H I L E B A C K, Woody Allen wrote an article for the op-ed page of the *New York Times* in which he expressed shock and disappointment at recent Israeli policies condoning violence in the occupied territories. The following week there was a spasm of outrage expressed in the Letters-to-the Editor column, a surprising amount of which centered on Allen's right to speak about Israel—or, rather, lack of right—as evidenced by his silence in his past work on issues of Jewish policy.

"Mr. Allen," says one writer, "is doing this (censuring Israel) because he loves Israel so much, and because those grand Jewish ideals get him all choked up. But it sounds a tad specious coming from an artist who, in his films and writings, exploits a now-extinct Jewish culture while scrupulously avoiding any reference to Israel, the Holocaust or any other relevant Jewish issue." Another letter ends by saying ". . . if Mr. Allen feels inclined to punish Israel by not allowing his films to play there, I don't think it will be a great loss to Israel. Certainly no more a loss than the money he says he stole as a youth from the blue-and-white Jewish National Fund cans." (Succumbing to that temptation is a bit he fesses up to in his film *Radio Days* and admits to again in his article.)

What is fascinating to me about both these letters is their presumption of what the duty of an artist is, and what constitutes such a gross abnegation of responsibility that, failing in it, he is seen to effectively sever his bond to his people and deny himself the right to care, to feel pain on their behalf, to have opinions about the fate of the Jews. Woody Allen has not referred in his comedies to the Holocaust or "any other relevant Jewish issue." When he does what he ought to be doing as a comic writer—in this case calling up a petty memory that he must share with a whole generation of first and second-generation Jewish children, filching pennies from his blue-and-white *pushke*—he is roundly condemned for early evidence of gross immorality.

Here is an example, and it's one among many, of a terribly dour, humorless, deadening approach to the presentation of Jewish life as it appears in art. It is first cousin to the other common misconception of the purpose of art, this one ecumenical—the fallacy that fiction is meant to be direct moral instruction, a sort of user's guide to ethics and self-improvement; the corollary is that, since Jewish life has been full of tragedy and loss, so must our every representation of it mirror that sorrow. Had the one letter-writer worked for some nineteenth-century humane society she might have shaken her finger at Melville for cruelty to white whales. What a burden to lay on literature! And what an insult to the revered ghosts of Sholem Aleichem, Mendele, Peretz, and all the other self-mocking and self-critical figures in the homey pantheon of Jewish writers.

The first letter-writer, a Ms. Berkowitz of Teaneck, New Jersey, accuses Allen of exploiting a "now extinct" Jewish culture, implying by innuendo that he's guilty of kicking it while it's down-and-out. Might we not just as easily say that he is celebrating and honoring it by keeping its memory alive? What exactly constitutes the skillful evocation of a particular time and place that is the work of any writer or film director? What, on the other hand, makes it an unscrupulous appropriation of something not rightfully his, a kind of thievery or worse—we might call it grave-robbery since Ms. Berkowitz knows a dead culture when she sees one? I myself would rather say that this culture is by necessity, and for a few good reasons, something like extinct, although I'd prefer a word like transformed. It is the late twentieth, not the late nineteenth, century and Jews are for better and worse at home in America, in spite of our continuing uncertainties and perils. Ms. Berkowitz, unless she is a Chasid trying to live in the eighteenth century, would probably really not prefer it to be otherwise. But precisely because we honor our parents and grandparents we surely should not take a vow never to talk about them, laugh about them, recreate them for others.

This is not to deny the profound quandary of the contemporary Jewish-American writer—or anyone, for that matter, who lives a hyphenated existence which implies the necessity of reconciling discrepant identities. Many of us are confused about what we should take as our best and most urgent material; who constitutes our audience; what should be our relation to our history, our present, our future as Jews and as middle-class, well-educated, rationalist, and therefore often skeptical and secular Americans. But it needs to be said that the confusions of the hyphenated writers are only those of American Jews in general in this next-to-the-last decade of the century; we are what the majority of Jewish readers deserve. We are, not surprisingly, their mirrors, neither better nor worse.

This confusion, of course, is no recent invention. As soon as the Jews stepped onto the wider world's stage (whether you want to begin with the French revolution or the Haskalah in the nineteenth century, the so-called Jewish Enlightenment, wherever we want to begin looking)—as soon as the walls of the ghetto were breached and ideals surfaced other than commitment to God and Torah—as soon as society condoned, not to say rewarded, *choice*—the Jews became a people in ferment. There is a wonderful paragraph in the writing of Peretz Smolenskin, editor of the exciting Hebrew monthly *Ha-Shahar* in midnineteenth-century Russia, that sounds so contemporary we might take it for something every contemporary rabbi has said in many a sermon. A father brought his daughter to Vienna to hear Smolenskin's advice, but she had nonetheless fled to Switzerland with her populist friends. The father complained bitterly that Smolenskin, who taught everyone else wisdom, could not prevent his daughter's flight. Smolenskin replied very coolly, "How did you bring up your daughter? You had governesses and tutors teaching her foreign languages. You sent her to high school, where she learned about other peoples. Did you teach her about her own people? Did you teach her our own language? Did you interest her in our own history, our own national aspirations? To whom, then, should you bring your complaints, if not to yourself?" This was written, remember, in 1868, not 1968 or 1988.

And thereafter, every so-called advance into a free society has brought the Jew, and concomitantly the Jewish writer, farther from a world and a language uniquely our own. Fiction, in any event, except in the Bible which we are not supposed to think of as fiction, has rarely been a useful form in which to teach theology. Among pious Jews, of course, the novel or story is an irrelevant, not to say heretical, form: if it is not Torah, Mishnah, Gemarrah—if the story does not exist to drive home the nature and supremacy of the Law— it is not to be entertained. Midrash gives plenty of reign to the imagination but there is, in fact, a strict harness on it: it is a beguiling kind of embroidery around an unyielding and particular purpose. Pure fiction, story-telling for its own sake, is a fairly young genre as kinds of writing go, and it has always been most comfortable as a carrier of information about the way people live, as a form of social documentation. Its means and ends, therefore, are profoundly secular.

And so the first of the writers who came to the United States devoted themselves, as one would expect, to documenting that experience. Abraham Cahan, one of the best of the early immigrant writers, who arrived in the 1880s and later edited the *Forverts*, was the author of the only kind of books a Jew becoming an American could have written then—not books about God, but books about Jews as greenhorns in the *goldineh medineh*, the golden land. There was nothing quaint about *The Rise of David Levinsky* or *Yekl*, which contained the poignant and amusing story that became the movie "Hester Street." Neither was there anything spiritual. Anzia Yezierska, one of the only women to become very popular in a world of male writers, wrote about immigrants saving their pennies to bring over their families and, only a little later, changing their names, denying their mothers, expunging their humiliatingly un-American pasts.

Saul Bellow's *Adventures of Augie March* probably marks the exact center of this century's fiction by Jews about Jews: the center because it linked together the immigrant experience with the American reality that engulfs us now: "I am an American, Chicago-born," Augie says in the voice of Walt Whitman out of Mark Twain, a most unspiritual tradition. It has been a fairly short step from that not-really-barbaric yawp to the assimilated—let's say barely even sociologically Jewish—short story writers such as David Leavitt, Tama Janowitz, Deborah Eisenberg—popular writers smiled upon by the *New Yorker*, who are identifiable as "ours" only because their names are clearly Jewish. There is a whole new generation of them, whose characters are suburban yuppies, grandchildren and great-grandchildren of the pioneering generation whose Mississippi was the Atlantic, and who sighted land and Castle Garden or Ellis Island in the same first glance. The cover of the paperback of David

Leavitt's book *Family Dancing* is a painting of wet footsteps around a backyard pool, which pretty well suggests the setting for the stories, figuratively if not literally.

But lest we see any betrayal in Leavitt and his assimilated generation, whose work is nearly interchangeable with that of any WASP writer who went to Yale or Amherst, here is the complicated question for us: What would Leavitt's grandparents have said, living cramped on Delancey Street, say, with a scummy bathroom down the hall and sweated work at disgraceful wages, had they been shown a picture of little David at poolside? Did they know they were making a deal, coming here to better their lives? Had they known what their side of the bargain was going to be with the Faustian America, would they not have made it anyway, most of them? This was not a generation that could ennoble starvation or persecution in the old country. And even there, in Minsk or Pinsk or Odessa, not to mention Berlin, were they not already beginning to give up their unquestioning piety? They would recognize their grandchildren; they would probably even applaud them.

There are, though they tend to be a little less popular because they're not very trendy, writers who are trying hard to connect with their vanished ancestors and to ask themselves what it means to write from a Jewish consciousness today. What does that consciousness consist of when Jewish experience is so thin or so unfamiliar to most readers, Jews among them? Why is it so hard to make artful narratives of Jewish lives? Does the problem—if you care to see it as one—lie in the art or in the life?

I want to draw on a very interesting, if often discouraging, experience which clarified and inflected that problem for me though, alas, it did little to suggest a solution. A few years ago my husband, Marv Hoffman, and I were invited by *Tikkun* magazine to become the fiction editors for this liberal, engaged journal that calls itself a "Jewish critique of politics, culture, and society." Our editorship meant that dozens of manuscripts passed across our desk. We read unsolicited manuscripts, we wrote to our friends, to writers whose work we'd seen in other magazines and liked—we took all comers— and yet, in spite of the rather astonishing number of stories we saw, we found very little that passed muster. The difficulty of finding good fiction is always hugely increased by limiting or in any way delineating subject matter or approach. I edited an issue of the literary magazine *Ploughshares* once, in search of stories written by men from a woman's point of view and vice versa—an exercise in writing as another, an other—and if ordinarily 1 percent of submissions might have interested me, I think I was reduced to liking about one-hundredth of 1 percent by the imposition of my thematic scheme. But for *Tikkun*, I think, we were looking for a much broader range of work, far broader than most people tended to understand. Well, what did we say we were looking for?

We started by positing that something needed to separate a *Tikkun* story from a *New Yorker* or an *Esquire* story—not that they might not want to publish some of what we printed, in fact we shared a number of writers—but rather that we would not find most of their work particularly relevant to our needs. What does this mean? Virginia Woolf, you may remember, asks at the beginning of *A Room of One's Own* what we mean by women's fiction. Fiction written by women? About themselves as women? About anything? Or fiction written by anyone about women? The Jewish Book Fair that sells 10,000 books every fall in Houston, where I live, is assaulted, I think, by the same slippery question as it relates to Jewish writing, and they solve it, or at least approach it, by casting as wide and perhaps as undiscriminating a net as possible. Thus books with absolutely no discernibly Jewish content are featured because their author's name is identifiably Jewish; I should add that plenty of people get passed over by such a crude measure. My first novel, *The Autobiography of My Mother*, which raises a great many questions for Jewish readers and features a heroine—perhaps an antiheroine—whose psyche is, I think, profoundly affected by her conception of Jewish history, was never marketed as a "Jewish" book, and since my name is Brown, it was invisible to the people who were out scouting for authors named Klein and Schwartz. Some, on the other hand, think they can swim into that wide net by making rather casual adjustments, like the writer who sent a story to *Tikkun* in which he'd crossed out the name of his protagonist, which I think was Neilson, and quite visibly made him Bernstein—circumcised, right before our eyes, by a flick of the pen. We were not so easily deluded.

Because, I think, they reflect the popular understanding of what constitutes "Jewish" subject matter, I want to give you a short list of the most common species of story we received—or maybe the species is Jewish fiction and each of these is a genus. It is a close-up view of what Irving Howe has called "a crisis in subject matter," abetted, as I see it, by a crisis of form as well.

By far the most frequent subject, we found, is the aging parent or old person, often an immigrant; if not, then someone still in touch with old wisdom impossible to duplicate today. If a younger consciousness is represented in the story, he or she (clearly a surrogate for the author) is fairly abject with helplessness and grief at the declining state of the Old One, or with eagerness for moral or religious instruction, presumably before it's too late. These stories are not often deeply engaging; they tend to be dutiful and guilt-struck and they let the character—and perhaps the author—off the hook rather easily, as if to say, well, that's the end of that, and go about the business of their secular lives without finding a live and vital source for their Judaism. This is a kind of death rattle Judaism, spasmodic, a short phase. (I have to admit I've perpetrated a few myself: my father-in-law has had plenty of time in my stories, but I've tried to avoid the worst pitfalls of the genre by focusing in fact on a foreground character whose life has its own dramatic trajectory.)

The next most frequent subject attempts to deal with the Holocaust. It's not so much that these earnest stories trivialize the horrors they approach; and in a certain sense it's admirable that our generation, and a still younger one, wants to try to feel some fragment of that pain. It's just that their sheer inadequacy is either deadening or unintentionally *chutzpadich*. The Holocaust is a black star; our little words implode and leave a gaping hole where feeling needs to be. And no surprise. They would do better to leave it alone.

Next most popular, I'd say, is the memory-of-Brooklyn story, which sometimes takes place in the Bronx: Bar Mitzvah lessons at the hands of a barbaric, or sweet-and-impotent, or grievously-misunderstood-and-underpaid-but-profound old rabbi who usually smells of garlic and whose pants are shiny with wear. Or beatings-in-the-park-at-the-hands-of-goyish-thugs stories, vaguely derivative of Isaac Babel. And so on.

What you can probably see emerging here is a pattern—namely that the majority of these stories document old news. The word for that is "nostalgia"; the operant adjective is "sentimental." What is identifiably Jewish in the lives of the writers lies almost entirely in memory now, a pool not newly replenished because their current lives are not notably heavy in what you might call Jewish content, nor do they understand that for the purposes of fiction-making they could with less strain subject their own moral lives to a kind of questioning and accountability that some of us would recognize as specifically, if not exclusively, Jewish. They are reflecting, distantly, and with a certain poignant sense of loss, the disappearing Jewish lives of others, which for them are the only ones in sight. If I want to think Jewishly, these writers seem to be saying, either I remember Bubbe and Zaide, Auschwitz, Reb Mordechai, or the time the O'Brien twins nearly slaughtered me and left me for dead in Crotona Park.

The two obsessions with current life (to which I am quite sympathetic but which are rarely worked out with sufficient complexity) are the I-am-a-woman-and-I-will-assert-myself-somehow-in-the-patriarchal-tradition story, and the American-in-Israel story, usually—in fact, in my experience, always—fragmentary and inconclusive, the main character torn apart by contradictions and inconsistencies but appreciative nonetheless of the vitality and beauty of the sabras, not to mention disgusted by their—whatever: arrogance, belligerence, sexism, cruelty to Arabs. Aside from the larger issues of identity, it is impossible for an American Jewish writer in Israel not to respond to the sheer human texture of the place, the vitality, the color, the rasp and crackle of so much street life, even if he could leave aside the hard questions. But perhaps as an act of humility born of limited experience in Israel, our response seems always to be fragmented, provisional, a gathering of random impressions.

Now you might say, mediocre stories are mediocre stories no matter their subject matter. Here I want to raise some writerly questions: being "p.c.," politically correct, or "c.c.," culturally correct, does not guarantee that you can make art of your concerns. So. The stories I was speaking of tend to suffer from a confusion about what the writer's gaze actually takes in or pauses over. Over-earnestness about searching out relevance and significance tends to make them sociological rather than artful, heavy-handed where they need to be light-footed.

John Hollander speaks most wonderfully about this problem in a recent essay on American Jewish poetry, published, in fact, in *Tikkun*. He quotes Dante; using an apt phrase from *The New Life*, he speaks of "a screen for the truth." Dante is referring, Hollander says, to an unnamed lady past whom he was looking, in a church full of people, at his secret muse, Beatrice d'Este. This lady sat in his line of sight, and everyone believed he was looking at her, but of course he had made of the lady "a screen" for his true preoccupation, at whom he could look his fill, but obliquely. For poets, Hollander says, and I add fiction writers with little hesitation, "the result will always be that the subjects of poems are no more what they are 'about' than their verse-forms are." Substitute stories and forms of stories in the sentence. But many Jewish writers are uncomfortable in the presence of so-called Jewish subject matter: they don't live it much, or think consciously in its terms, and so you can see them taking a deep breath before they plunge in and swim hard to get to the other side of the unfamiliar and perhaps dangerous waters. The poet Paul Celan called his Judaism less thematic than spiritual; one might have said the same about Kafka's—it is a useful distinction for our day. The majority of the work we see, on the other hand, is thematically hard-breathing and anxious. And where its spirit is I have no idea: lost somewhere in a confusion of soft wishing and hard reality.

Part of the problem of finding good but subtle stories that would make provocative reading for our *Tikkun* audience lay, parenthetically, in the difference between novels and stories. A novel can use the Jewishness of its characters as a background color (by which I don't mean incidental, but rather encompassing), can utilize and exemplify the assumptions that exist in our universe as Jews—historical, circumstantial—without necessarily making them the sole focus or subject. When Jay Neugeboren, for example, writes about Jewish gangsters in *Before My Life Began*, we aren't asked to spend much time saying "What a phenomenon, a Jewish gangster!" Their Jewishness is a given; it is their universe. What do they do within it—that's what interests the author. What are these gangster lives like? The sheer length and complexity of a novel militates against simplification. Novels have the amplitude to paint characters into a rich landscape but landscape, except in man-against-nature books, is background; stories, on the other hand, tend to search for a single symbol which will contain meaning. Because the story is so compressed, so aimed—too aimed, most of the time—it ends up being, as Hollander said about poems, only what it is about; it is, all in a rush, no more than its subject. In addition, many of these stories keep referring to an offstage life we are presumed to understand because we have shared it: they use Jewish culture as solely private reference, its challenges and absurdities agreed-on, like an in-joke, a poke in the ribs between familiars. They are, in that sense, intensely parochial and exclusive and haven't much independent life. It seems to me that a good story is amphibian: it can live in its native waters but can also exist comfortably on the shore amidst readers who are not part of the *meshpachah*—family.

Anything a Jew thinks can make a Jewish story. Anything anyone else thinks on subjects a Jew gives thought to can make a story of interest to Jews, though not perhaps a Jewish story. How one chooses, well or badly, a road to walk; how one knows the Law in its day-to-day manifestation, whether it is called the Law or not. Sometimes these stories will ask their questions in traditional Jewish terms, whether visionary or pragmatic, or restore some historical scene for our imagining, fleshed out like Midrash around a laconic text. The person asking "How shall I live? Am I my brother's keeper? And who is mine?" does not need to be named Shapiro and he need not ask the urgent question before the Western Wall or the open ark or over his open siddur; he needn't ask it in steerage or on 7th Avenue or Maxwell Street. He, or she, will ask the question of history and of himself or herself. And if he or she believes in God, he or she will be heard by God. We are coming to the end of Yiddish accents and the Evil Eye but we are still a people who share ancestors and geography and a tradition of bold and sometimes—often—heretical questioning. The new grandparents live in Florida and tool around artificial lakes in pedal boats. In another half-generation there will be no more pinochle. But theirs are not the same ancestors who came on the Mayflower, or settled in Minnesota straight from a farm in Norway, or died in slavery, or swam across the Rio Grande. And so I presume we ask our questions in a slightly different tonality. I do believe in what Amos Oz calls, quite simply, "a shared set of sensibilities."

Here is a case in point. My own most recent novel, *Civil Wars*, concerns a couple, old civil rights heroes; it is set in Mississippi fifteen years after that momentous time in American history, and it poses a number of questions that we've often heard spoken: how one is obligated to act toward the stranger in one's midst; the terrible costs of unyielding—self-righteous—commitment even to a good cause; these and many more. The wife in my book is Jewish—a red diaper baby, whose father was an old Communist who went underground during her childhood in pursuit, perhaps excessive, of his ideals. Her husband is not Jewish; but she is for the first time conscious of her Jewishness when her niece and nephew, who come, like a doom, to live with them, turn out not only to be little bigots bred in a segregationist household but also Christian fundamentalists. It happens that the civil rights movement was rife with Jews and with the sons and daughters of ministers who took their father's sermons seriously. And so, making my character Jewish was historically plausible, even probable. Making her self-conscious about *halakhah*—the Law—or observant, or even preoccupied with her nominal religion, would have falsified my experience of the 60s. And yet I see *Civil Wars* as a "Jewish novel" because—simply—it tries to place a Jew in history. It tries to describe a moment when the progressive, left-wing, more or less secular background so common to American Jews intersected with a formative moment in twentieth century American life.

Another book comes to mind, *The Organ Builder*, by Robert Cohen, which concerns itself with a young man named Heshie Friedman whose father, a physicist, was part of the Los Alamos project, again a not uncommon situation for a Jew in his time. Does it matter that Heshie is Jewish, even though he gives no specific thought to his religion? Of course it does: his father became the man he was—a scientist who finally abandoned his work on the atomic bomb for reasons of conscience—within a moral and historical context in which his background played a decisive part. He was a Jew in American History; he was not anonymous.

Of course I wish American Jews knew more about their religion, their history, knew Hebrew and Yiddish—knew more about what I would call their Judaism as opposed to their Jewishness, which is cultural (sometimes only culinary) and often delicately balanced on the edge of obliteration. But I wish those for a lot of reasons; I am not really sure how much knowing those things would change our fiction today. I agree that one's writing comes out of the whole of oneself, and the more one concentrates on some things the less one concentrates on others. The reason those nostalgic stories or the dreary recreations of anti-Semitism and Holocaust memory constitute the major preoccupation of would-be Jewish writers is that their lives as uneducated Jews are impoverished, defined by what dregs of the spirit might be left twenty years after the obligatory Bar Mitzvah, by defensiveness and unpleasant relations with the relatives or the world at large.

But even with a more profound and willing Jewish education, contemporary writing will never literally—only obliquely at best—concern itself with *halakah*. Even Cynthia Ozick, who has in the past been known to condemn just about every Jewish writer for not concentrating on Halakhic Judaism, has broadened her definition. She mentions, in a recent interview, some formative ontological questions, questions of knowing, she assumes a serious Jewish writer would consider: Why are we here? What is the meaning of consciousness? Our lives as Jews and Americans, as men and women, are very complex, and we are pulled at one moment in one direction and at another in a different one. The fact that I keep a kosher kitchen does not always or even often affect my choice of subject matter, let alone my technical choices. Nor, frankly do I want it to. Just as, a woman writer, I feel blessedly free these days to write about any subject, any character I can imagine, so, as a Jewish writer, I do not want to issue myself a kind of edict that will make me apologetic if I find my material, sometimes, outside my life as a Jew. I need to pray for a long enough life in which to do both. (The most recent novel by Hugh Nissenson, who has written frequently about Jewish subjects, is the diary of the ur-*goysiche* character, a man named Thomas Keene who travelled to Ohio in the year 1812. Max Apple's is about Howard Johnson and Walt Disney. My own, predictably or not, is this time concerned with a piece of Jewish history, the Am Olam movement that brought men and women from Russia near the end of the nineteenth century; they knew nothing about farming and did very badly at it.) Even Israeli writers, who are rapt so much of the time in stories of the divisions within their tormented country, must often want to write about their cats, or about sexual rapture, or the way a soccer ball reverberates against their foot. Writers are not people you want to instruct to stay "on task" like assembly-line workers.

Meanwhile, to return to *Tikkun* as it tries to define contemporary Jewish writing. In the end the best definition of our hope was that we could find stories whose territory was lit with the light and heat of moral engagement, and an openness to whatever new and as-yet-unpredictable forms Jewish life will take as time goes on. Nor, we always said, like the old Levy's rye bread ad, did contributors even have to be Jewish. If, say, Melville were out there today and had chosen to send a chapter of *Moby Dick* to us, would we have printed it? We might have, no matter what Mr. Melville's provenance, on the grounds that as Jews we have a pretty well-seasoned interest in judgment, vengeance, powerful faceless forces, and passionate commitments to rid the world of evil, especially when they're couched in Biblical cadences. If the good story is, as I've suggested, amphibian, then perhaps the whale comes close enough. Certainly we would have urged Mr. Melville to try his work on us, stamped, self-addressed envelope included.

A recent issue of the *Reconstructionist* magazine contained a disturbing article by a professor of English named Herbert J. Levine. He describes a project of the Kaplan Institute of the Reconstructionist Rabbinical College that called together six Jewish poets in 1985 to spend three days with notable Jewish teachers studying texts that ranged from the Bible and Talmud to Yiddish poetry. Professor Levine was disappointed that the poets, whom he saw as representatives of the decayed cultural situation of secularized American Jewry, did not at the end choose to respond by announcing that they had discovered an instant sense of community. Instead they read their old poems, written in the isolation of those who do not give much detailed thought to living within the covenant, side by side with others who do the same. These poets, he implied, a little too stern and literal for my taste, use Jewish references and metaphor as a sort of interior decoration, accidental, undeserved—Woody Allens of poetry, to go back to where I began—exploiters not sufficiently devoted to the teachings of the fathers. I agree, in the case of Allen Ginsberg, that I have often wished the man were as interested in finding in his own religion of origin the meditative experience he needs, the merging of his consciousness with a traditional Jewish universe rather than his Eastern one. Like so many, he does not know what he has overlooked in his own all too familiarly weedy backyard.

But let that be. Here is a very moving poem by one of the poets Professor Levine condemns for the inadequacy of her specifically Jewish content. If we expect to take many writers into the fold of *chaverim* and *chaverot*—friends and compatriots—a poem such as this demonstrates how we can expand our definition of Jewishness to embrace moral engagement, a willingness (as Philip Roth does at the end of *The Counterlife*) to take one's place publicly and proudly at the set table, an eagerness to see oneself in a continuum in which one cares about others as oneself and is humble before the mysteries of life and death. If many of us are lonely nonetheless, and miss the camaraderie of ceremony; if our *kavanah*, intention, is inadequate to let us pray, that should not mean that we are cast out as Jews testifying to Jewish experience. Here is the poem in which Linda Pastan identifies herself with all Jews, past, present, and future, in a single line that comes in the middle, five lines before it and five after, the fulcrum of eternity on which the rest is balanced. What a pity the Professor, bound in the coils of his narrow definition of piety, could not appreciate it.

Poet

At his right hand
silence;
at his left hand
silence;
ahead of him
the yahrzeit glass;
behind him
silence;
and above his head
all the letters of the alphabet
to choose from.

POEMS

From *Some Deaths in the Delta*

I   THE DELTA

Some Deaths in the Delta

I

In Itta Bena there was a yearling hog
lived on statistics. A few percentages
made a meal.
It fattened better than anyone had hoped
on its diet of rare slops.
But the day the farmer slashed its throat
that barrel body split its staves
and a family of nine
drowned in the blood of its numbers.

II

The woods' old caves are flattened,
dampness gone back under earth.
A sky away,
pine survivors huddle together,
roots in their hands,
ready for the next step back.

III

The secret ceremony,
old, grave,
warms the darkest room
where the silver lives.
On the eighth day of his life,
swaddled, brown skin, in bridal satin,
the child is held before the man who smiles.
Bloodless, quick,
the whip-sharp knife snaps
and the baby's tongue is out;
ripped off,
gently,
the small simple leaf on its pink stem.
The satin is taken away, the child drifts back to sleep,
naked again.

IV

The fire caught.
A breath of laughter shook the houses
and their meek bones came loose.
Vanished the first day: Sunflower County
and most of Tallahatchie.
Bolivar caught slowly and was holding firm
till it exploded,
and a howl of blood splashed up
and dried like egg on the sky.
Sharkey and Issaquena gave at the center seam
and years of dust flew out,
or ashes.
In Yazoo, when the June fields buckled
everything green went under.

As logic demanded,
it was only the tinder-poor who died in the fire.
But for a week the air was flying bone
and sour tides of smoke.
There was no levee against it.
So the others—
even those who owned the air—
drowned breathing, heads under the wind,
a sack of kittens in the pond.

V

The children who live see clear through the dark.
They hear what silence hears,
and search at ease with their hands.
In the shortest season,
lavender flowers gape from porches,
singing out of the grave.

Night upon night
clouds swam down the sky
in a black current.
Now I know where the fish hid
live and helpless
going voiceless over the world's edge.

If (people were to say)
the fish had carried flowers
which were (I remember) profuse that year,
and therefore inexpensive;
or something edged with mother-of-pearl;
or perhaps, if nothing frivolous, then
a book; or a reed attesting to
skill at a wind instrument—

but they were themselves,
bare, every third or fourth
lit as if from within,
travelling beneath a streak,
cunning red or silver,
shaped and greased for speed.
Bearing (if anything) something jerry-built
and undeniably personal.

The clouds were fog off the Pacific,
washed up on the sky's far edge.
Painlessly they tore apart,
and they were never less (I remember)
than beautiful.

Now it seems there were fish
chased over the edge; they
had no hands to carry the ransom.
Their scales came down on the underside
of every rain.

When I splashed my feet,
I must have taken them home
in my shoes.

Absolute for Death

for E.K.
Mississippi 1961–1967

Everyone had that moment.
Certain connections burned out,
dangled like shorted wires.
Life at any cost was the last one gone.

Unrancorous, never alone,
they lay down on their hands,
absolute for death,
each behind his own uncrossable line.

Some escaped with half a face
since half was worse than none.
Under the knee caps, gun-butt blows
hacked bone away,
leaving a trick of perfect skin.
Fire ate wood, water ate men.
The old familiar way.
But everything fit then—
deaths echoed and hung in the air
like honest words nearly impossible to say.

The moment had to cool.
Now pain is pain again. Subtraction and division
are all that work.
Survivor's slow, bitter arithmetic.

A Wry Music

Seven are convicted at Meridian

Wind
a wry music
the piney woods give it off like their own
chill
spice

Pelahatchie
      Big Black
           Tishomingo
rivers thick with leaves come moping around the long curves
walking on faces
on long bones
on men's bound ankles narrower than flint

October
cotton-light
Summer lies in drifts
in dunes
high on red wagons
Unwincing light   the shadows of nothing human
pick at it

In a hundred years
one bee
may forgive the worst in us
may stop to drink honey
from a murderer's ear

To a Friend Who Is Leaving Home to Save Herself from the Sin of Despair

After the talk and anti-talk,
the balancing,
one jumpy foot on the point
where this time meets this place,
you find you've dashed knee-high
into the amber of your choices.

You will live with books and unglazed pottery
in a house the wind dare not touch,
conspicuous among admirers
for what you might have been
were it not for them.
Your children will not chop cotton.

But this island of black soil,
of fierce vines swallowing space,
of mutilating smiles,
good brown-beer wit,
these hundred rusty car-skulls
with poppies in their eyes—

will you dare forgive them
that rawheart morning drowned in snow
when they try to choose you back again?

A Book of Months

I

Against a forest of leavings.
My hand is closed on the dried cornstalk.
I stand at attention
holding my paper spear.

II

A Mississippi Cypress,
from the kitchen window.
All night it spatters nut-sounds
over the skimpy roof.
Down the road a mile
a hundred ram's horns call us
and call us again.
The heifers begin their howling as soon as the sun goes down.
They live in the dark, in pens,
and fear for their lives.

III

Across the reservoir named for Ross Barnett,
somebody shot at Mr. Winston's daughter's
eye last night,
and shot straight.
She was sitting on a porch like this one,
giving not one blessed thought
to her daddy's politics.

IV

The next-door hogs (in shadow)
churning and pitching
our new spring grass.
That's Sammy who isn't
all there by a longshot
come to take them home,
grunting the words they love him for.

V

M., kneeling
in a swarm of yellow gnats.
Or a thousand flowers.

VI

There's Pat against wild purple,
her back in wisteria.
Eddie dancing to the music,
taking care of business by himself.
Helen in better days,
wide as a full-open flower
about to draw back in.
Me again, already remembering,
already missing them.
The baby's beginning to come clear,
if you look hard,
under my folded arms.

VII

Six Hinds County police cars
blocking the road before it goes
clear out of their grasp.
They are waiting for a killer
or a madman who shook himself
good and loose from Whitfield State,
or a car-thief,
a dumb-ass nigger
who looked crosseyed at a deputy,
or the one Jew too many
for The State.

VIII

The sky is whipped thick. Clouds
group and regroup, coming down dark.
This was the night our first tornado
picked up the other side of town,

ran with it like a football
and fumbled it.
Poor-to-middling whites out there,
living around their first real supermarket.
You could hear the roar crosstown—
six hundred boxcars,
all downhill.
I didn't like a single soul
in all South Jackson . . .

IX

How I looked walking the public road,
an eight-month's child
going before me.
Friends warned, lectured,
the logic of the Mississippi male
does not take kindly to a White Girl, Pregnant,
out alone, flaunting,
in this Black town.
They roll their windows down
and speculate.
I walk along the edge of 51,
picking the reddest clover I've ever seen,
daring no one,
eyes down
but open.

X

Dead fall sucks the sky bare.
Slowly it spits back sharp rain.
Good dirt is turned to stone
in the hollow cowfield.
My neighbors' old dark overcoats
inch up the dim side of the road,
and the frozen flag
is snapping at the post-office pole.

XI

Full-face, house.
The evening news (local) lands on the porch.
(National) floats out through the screen
in Huntleybrinkley's salt-free voice.
They drop into a casual stew—
all together, one square meal
served up at seven, central standard time—
law-breakers, home-breakers, record-breakers,
custom-breakers, ball-breakers.
The faces we know are bloody,
more than likely.
The tall grass you see under the windows:
that soaks up the sound
and holds it down,
dust that it is.

XII

We are leaving.
My face has almost closed back over.
I thought I remembered all my secrets
but this smile that has no corners—
I have to guess—
it is about living out of sight.
Boxes are stacked on the porch
and the door behind me is cracked
on nothing but swept floor.
I am holding the baby,
my hat is slick and yellow
to take the rain.

In Rooms

I have been alone in rooms,
in houses, even—their doors barricaded
with snow, a month from the news.
Nothing is like it:
Talk and you wonder if that could be a voice.
And you lie lightly, skimming the cream
of sleep off the top of an endless night.

I have been alone in rooms
with cats dozing—their bodies like snakes
coiled around air.
Nothing is like it:
Talk and they hear you and don't hear you.
And you sleep tacitly guarded by their claws,
at the side of their breathing that flows and flows like a river.

I have been alone in rooms
seething with strangers—their presence demanding
my captured presence.
Nothing is like it:
Talk and they blink and answer and do not hear you.
And you see through a film like sleep how you are drifting
into a whirlpool, down, down to yourself.

Who It Is Who Could Not Wait

Off in that other room, sleep,
you hear the faintest jangle—
bottles pushed aside, wind-chimes—
then the bell rips through like light.

At night all phones are answered
in a leap, less than a breath.
Fear snatches half the first ring
and asks in a readied voice

who it is who could not wait,
what news from the unsleeping.
From far off, what surprise strange
as the dream it shook you from?

And it is no one. Hanging
like a curse in its hollow,
silence pulls you in, holds you.
You riffle years of pages,

the closed accounts of friendships,
for one hint of a joker,
and your neck crawls with the cold.
Something like your own guilt then

starts in the motiveless dark.
The click cuts you away, free.
Three o'clock in the dark night
of someone's soul, who had to hear,
shaken, your voice before he slept?

Neighborhood News

Notices to Homeowners

Plant trees.
For every tree build a fence.
For every fence get a dog.
Let the dog use the fence however he pleases;
you will sleep, free to dream,
your investment protected by trained teeth.
(Consider a second dog for your car.)
You have responsibilities now:
You have bought your island
for $24.99 and a handful of that
dried fish the natives like.
You do not like it,
remember.

Notices to Renters

Keep your milk off the windowsills.
Count your kids each night.
The number should be constant or decreasing.
Search their eyes for needle marks.
Stay in the house after dark—there is no
walking without a destination
in a Transitional Neighborhood.
(If you have a car, you may drive it.)
Make small fires, if you wish,
under the stairs, in the bedclothes,
fire being an approved agent of change.
Stay in and watch the pages of the dictionary
projected on your shades,
flowing like a river,
Spanish into English.

Notices to Store Owners

Rinse out the blindfolds that hang like banners
CERVEZA FRIA   OPEN SUNDAYS.
Feed the cat that gritty fish
beached on a rice sack,
feed the mouse that cheese souring on months.
Burn the candles for yourself,
the kindergarten reds   greens   blues
WELCOME HOME   SAFE CROSSING   DEPARTED BELOVED.
You have been notified
in case of emergency.
The A&P is coming with a black glove
on its closed hand.
There will be no clues.
You will be found shaken to death,
your deliberate fingers still on the register keys,
the drawer wide open,
none of your money gone.

The Famous Writers School Opens Its
Arms in the Next Best Thing to Welcome

for A.B.

Good writing, the book tells you,
begins at home.
If it's anything like charity.
Hope for the best, try to relax,
and ignore the spelling.

You are obedient. You write about your kitchen.
"Everything I hate.
It is the place where all the accidents happen."
You are standing at the stove
shaking the saucepan
the way you'd shake a child,
to hurry along the coffee-water.
Oh it is green in here,
the green that punishes public walls,
never the color of leaves or moss
spreading, soft, on the shady side.
The pennies in the linoleum cracks
you're leaving there for luck.
The walls, the floors, the chairs have their flesh scrubbed off,
flayed no-color. All of it shatter-lines,
but holding.

"I think I have something to say,"
you say, separating some of your children,
always tangled up like hair.
Once a year you can expect to disappear
so far down your own throat and belly
a doctor with a miner's lamp
comes looking, calling out names,
some of them yours.
He tells you
you mustn't want to be destroyed
ever again,
admires your youth, your height, your hair,

whatever catches his nearest eye.
But you are the place
where all the accidents happen.
You have a cache of reasons
he isn't going to see.

This morning, though,
with a branch of sunlight
moving against the kitchen window,
words are—cheap? free?
No. Possible.
In the air.
They blow around
in the wind of your dreams.
"I was dreaming about the word 'surprise'
with a 'z' in it.
Nothing else happened, there was only this word
coming out of my typewriter.
A tickertapeworm, surprizesurprize."
You laugh, slouch a little,
and wait for something surprising to begin.

To saddle the word "surprize"
and ride out the kitchen window forever
over the limp roofs of Brownsville,
across the stone badlands,
Red Hook, Gowanus,
right through the twin castles,
empty purple castles of the Brooklyn Bridge.
Or out to sea past the softening
Staten Island meadows,
dotted with old trees and genuine, pale lakes.

You pour the water
into the Maxwell House,
and turn to the paragraph you've made
with your own limber hands.

You are turning soil,
looking for the place to plant fresh syllables.
The only garden on your block.

Going on Thirty

They still let us in the swamped
doors of the Fillmore
if we have our straight's five.
I'm hunched toward the stage,
a strange tidal bending, and it is
the blackest sea this side
of the moon.
Red lights, buoys stranded,
burn across dead space.
Those are the eyes of undersea gear
that hauls up sound
naked off the ocean floor.

When the waves, blue to purple to good-blood red,
have battered all our ears back into
these sober undefended heads,
the dark comes on again. The lonesome
little eyes stare back. No recognition.
I stiffen for a hard shove,
myself against myself.
Oh I pity me! me! and trust no one,
I who love the stage dead,
nothing begun,
and the dark stalled up there, empty-handed.

My mother's mother
   began her worldly progress
slow as a great ship,
   ballasted with children.
The first to say Ekaterinislav
gave no farewell parades,
   still, she would add,
she studied it from the outskirts long and hard.
At his own intervals, Grandfather sent
money from Baltimore,
   which got them scant
herring and heels of bread.
   Moored in a single place
months at a time,
   Grandmother peddled lace
to ladies, bone buttons to gentlemen,
till, fresh with impatience and some coins,
   again
they'd forge the sea of the continent,
   island to island;
were fruitlessly robbed;
   left the baby buried
in a shroud of yard-end lace
   at a quiet roadside.

It took two years
   and one long lurch of a crossing
to land them here.
   Not strengthened—
pared, whittled to a point, drier than wood,
two sons marooned,
   my grandmother's hair half white.
She slept a full three days
   in her cousin's bed
in Baltimore,
   saying that she could wait
to see the land, whose promises would keep

if they were real. And she awakened
to see them all,
   like cups,
casually broken.

In Refusal

"When we say we are living 'in refusal,' they think we are speaking of their unwill-ingness to let us leave their country. What, after all, do they know of our refusals?"
Refusenik, Moscow, 1985

7 A.M., Leningrad

The empty street fills
from the edges in.
A man with a long straw broom
idles toward the center, poking
at nothing. One black car,
     a vertical slash,
          hunches toward the streetlight,
waits
     while nothing but ghosts
          cross over.

Behind this dusty curtain
I watch a mother in a kerchief
pulling her bundled child across
the stagnant junction. They are running.
They too have heard the rumor
that morning is coming toward us from the east,
unstoppable.

Bounty/Leningrad, September

We come to you with our hands empty.
We come to you with our hands full

of the pettiest parts for the mechanism
of your daily life, these screws, these replacement ratchets
to help it fumble along another day.

Here is a camera
    (Now you may record your friends' sweet faces
    before they disappear).
Here are black thick socks
    (In the endless ache of Leningrad winter,
    nylon sticks to the knees.
    There is so little purity in our lives: we have brought you wool).
And fine pens like the fingers of one hand
    (to write those letters that will promptly arrive nowhere).

Every day, obedient, you line up
to chip a bit of sustenance off the rock of the state.
Your fingers bleed into your pockets.
Your city gives you nothing but agèd beauty
to chew on, the Winter Palace,
the Mojka Canal, this stark and unconfectionary
Venice.
Beauty is truth,
perhaps, but you'll waste away
on such a diet. Here: a bottle
of vitamins in the shape of fish, pink and shiny
under the cotton.
Kids' stuff. One-a-day. The best we can do.

We sit amidst the strange detritus
we've dragged (economy class) across the world,
drinking tea, eating crackers heaped with sweet
white cheese, rounded and rich as cloud cover.
Vodka, clear as water but heavy, heavy,
and tea again, the essence

and then the boiling water,
ritual endless as breathing.

We empty our insufficient hands into your hands.
We leave with our hands still full.

News Update

Light years late the news arrives:
They have beaten him in the street
and left him unstrung, unconscious.
They have made off with a bag of "evidence"
that might be anything: love letters,
poems,
dictionaries
in the enemy language.

I am walking along my own home street
looking into the faces of my neighbors, innocent
on their way to getting and spending.
On the other side of the world the sun comes up
every day on the evidence.
But there are only words, nothing but piles of letters
in the dictionaries,
not a single sentence. There is no path
they can follow, page upon criminal page.
There are only the broken stones, unstrung,
of language.

Communal Apartment,
Archipanovna Street

for L.K.

In the one room
a man and a woman,
two girls, the suckling baby.
The stuck smell of someone else's cooking.
Thicker than dust,
the books, the photographs, the paintings, the poems.
The candlesticks. Under the beds
the empty boxes
going somewhere. The crammed boxes
staying here.
The crayon alphabet, *aleph* to *tet* to the moon and over.
The flushing toilet, all night the sluice of water.
Silence nowhere. Suicide in the mirror,
like a grackle,
sullenly watching.

The reel-to-reel music of never-was,
never-will-be. The ice
of remembering, always at melt
across the floor, children beware.
A cold pipe
and the clever business of fire
held in the match. Spite
under the cushions. Murder. The vodka
tinted with cranberries, color of blood,
for keeping wounds clean.

The New Man, the Last Leader

(1985)

What will he be
like, they ask, the new man?
All they can see to measure by
is people begin to line up for
vodka, for salvation, hours before
the little shops open: a line like duty
down the block. You can miss out,
God forbid, and have to spend the weekend
sober. They shake their heads.
"It's no way to endear yourself."
They argue right
versus realpolitik; nation of drunkards/
nation of whatever's the opposite
of drunkards. They raise an eyebrow,
say We'll see, say
Show us. You be
the one we say goodbye to.
We will praise you with our backs,
honor you with goodbyes. Be our last leader
and we'll name our children for you.
In Tel Aviv, in Sheepshead Bay
a thousand little Mikhails, peeling their Russian off
like a heavy coat, dropping it
as they run.

Emigré

Here you get yourself a car.
It takes you to town, it takes you home
at your own good time
and no one else's.
You have a house standing separate,
and a garage like a belly on the house.
Here's what you do at the end of the day: you ride up
fast to the house, put the wheels
between two little margins of short-haired grass.
(You have to keep it short.)
You point your finger at your house
and slow as a drawbridge the wide door yawns
up, up, showing your cans of paint,
your dog-eared valises to the world.
You inch into the dark, gently.
For a while you get to sit, then,
peaceful, like the cut-off motor cooling down.
Your hedge-clipper dangles on the wall, open-mouthed,
your exercise bike sits at the back
like a patient horse in its clean stall.

In Leningrad this is the hour
when they hang suspended in the Metro,
shoulder to shoulder to elbow to groin.
Nobody's feet at five o'clock
ever touch ground. When the full train lurches,
no one has room among so many friends and strangers,
not even an inch, to fall down.

Vow

I vowed I would come to the station
to wait for the black mammoth engine
and not see Anna, like an omen, start
from the shadows, dark hair
pulled back austerely,
a few perfect strands escaping.

I stood where there should have been steam
and should have been snow
and would not think of Anna
rising off the platform, for all the weight
she carried within her, rising,
beginning to fly
upward just a few inches in a hopeful arc
before she began to come down.

Wedding Day

It is a custom for newlyweds to visit Lenin's Tomb directly after their wedding, or to drive into the Lenin Hills where they break a wine glass and look down over Moscow.

Double ring on its roof, the little
car rolls merrily forward. This long haired bride
is young, her bridegroom younger. Eyes
wide, they are off to the Wedding Palace,
twelfth couple of the morning,
to consort with the Law,

and then to Lenin's Tomb where
they may jump the line
this single time. (Their finery pleads
their case, her bridal white
brings tears to the eyes
of strangers with bad lives
and good memories.)

Inside, in a holy light, their ultimate father
propped in his single bed, waxy
and more complete than in his dangerous life,
is murmuring words only they
are meant to hear, only
today.

Soldiers goose-step around them in the slowest
motion, Nazi t'ai chi,
in a tightening ring.
What is he asking of them?
Anyone can see the faithfulness of their bodies
is all for each other, they sway and almost
touch (but the soldiers will not allow it

and Lenin's eyes are closed.)
They are humbled by his bright
indifferent face as we, on a road in summer
under the stars more infinite than faces,

know ourselves tiny, know ourselves
mortal, swell and diminish
until we are nothing at all.

STORIES

One of Two

M O N I C A had always wanted to have an enemy. A life of rancor and vendetta was not what she had in mind exactly, but it did seem obvious that if no one disliked or disagreed with her vigorously, she must not stand for anything. (*Stand for?* she would challenge herself, scrupulous. What does that mean, *stand for?* People are not ideas or political platforms, and her life was no debate.) Well, then: if everybody approved of you, you must not cast a shadow, that was all. Invisibility was what she worried about; "mousiness," she and her friends had called it when they were twelve and heartlessly critical of other people's friends. She even discussed this with her husband, Rudy, and they decided that it would be fine with them if they were not so universally considered decent and admirable. Not that they were planning to go out and start fights—they had to trust that in a life properly lived, enemies, like wrinkles or laugh lines, would naturally occur.

Rudy acquired one first, though it never came to much, this nemesis. He had, years ago as a new graduate student, done some work for a professor, in the way of those unequal relationships in which the student does the work and the professor takes the credit. They had been studying the relationship of physical activity to dreams and spent a great deal of time submerged in the watery darkness of the sleep lab, monitoring rapid eye movements, recording narratives of escapes down narrow corridors, falls from heights, the dead returned and the living dispatched to hell.

(This was what Rudy had been doing when he and Monica got married, and it made for a strange backdrop to the beginning of their time together. Because he spent so much of the day in unnatural dark and silence, tiptoeing around his experimental subjects who slept with wires clamped to their heads, Rudy had trouble sleeping at night; unrested, he went around tired and irritable all the time. This underwater stage lasted nearly a year. Monica, who was a cellist and lived in bright stage light, thought that if their marriage hadn't survived the strain she'd have sued the professor for damages.)

When, years later, Rudy submitted his thesis, which was called "Dream and Daily Life: A Correlation," his exprofessor wrote him an offensive note on the stationery of a minor Canadian university accusing him of thievery of ideas and insufficient gratitude to his mentor, whose name had been mentioned only five times and whose "intellectual parentage" was insufficiently acknowledged. It was a paternity suit, Rudy liked to say, filed on university letterhead.

Rudy had, in fact, sighed for the stinginess of the complainer and the desperation of the complaint, for the visibly reduced circumstances of his old professor who must be chafing with jealousy out there in that prairie province while Rudy was setting himself up in his first job, a good one, at a northern California school of solid stature. He had the amplitude of spirit to see through his professor's threats (of a lawsuit, of informal blackballing "in the profession"—scurrilous stories, in other words, but who would hear him from so far away?) to the dreadful anxiety and weariness beneath. "That's no way to treat your first enemy," Monica complained, "by understanding and forgiving him. You're not going to be good at this at all." But Rudy had shrugged: the man was still doing papers called "Dreams and Jogging," "Speed of Arousal Response in Athletes," "Exhaustion and the EEG"—the same song in the same key. He had lost interest in all that a long time ago.

When Monica opened her mail one day and confronted her first enemy in earnest, she understood the difference between a sloppy pot-shot and a lethal blow. It seemed to be the mail that brought them the news of their offenses; certain kinds of people clearly preferred to fight unseen, and from a safe remove. Nonetheless this letter felt as dangerous and real to her as the one genuine fight she had ever been witness to, on a winter afternoon in the Automat in New York, when two men had begun to throw chairs and actual stunning, breath-stopping blows—noisy popping sounds—to each other's chests and shoulders. Solid hits they were, and the receiving body kicked each time at the open-handed slap like a rifle after a shot. What was terrifying about the fight, and so unlike even the most vivid movie bar scene, was the way it threatened to engulf all onlookers; how the metal and leather chairs flew from the cleared center of the circle, out of control; the way the two men, red-faced with rage, kept turning to any spectator who dared say a word of disparagement, even of encouragement, and offered to deal with him next. She had edged away, terrified, to the back of the crowd, and even there she would not have been surprised to have received a ketchup bottle or one of those familiar Automat chairs right in her face, which felt, suddenly, irresponsibly bare.

The letter felt like that fight to her, even if it was only words— real anger wildly spinning towards her, dangerously out of control.

You bitch, it said, where *Hi!* or *Darling Monica* ought to have been. *Now I can tell you this. All the time you thought we were friends I was hoping I would never have to see you again. You must have known whenever we were together for all those endless sessions I felt I was being cut up a hundred times with razor blades. You never supported me or wanted me to succeed, you only wanted me to feel terrible about myself. Maybe you were jealous of me and my talent, how should I know? Just realize that you never took me in as a dear friend, your behavior is cruel and if the world does not know it now they eventually will know how underhanded you are. If you will change and reform, we should be able to go on being friends. Otherwise I hope I never have to see you again. It is your move.*

The letter, which Monica read in a single intake of breath, was typed; it was signed *Glenna* in the generous blocky girls' prep school handwriting she had been reading, it seemed forever, on post cards and notes written from country cabins and distant cities, on birthday cards and the little tags that had hung from Christmas presents. The last time she'd confronted it, at the end of a thank-you note sat the straight-forward *G*. Glenna had been out to see them on a transcontinental trip only a few months ago, and when she got home to Boston she'd sent a bread-and-butter note and three color snapshots of all of them in Golden Gate Park, plus one of herself squinting into the sun at Seal Rocks.

Rudy had said nothing as she'd picked up the envelope. The letter was open but back in the pile, under the *New Yorker* and the dunning note from the Alma Mater fund. They had the kind of marriage which allowed, even encouraged, them to read each other's mail on the supposition that they'd discuss every letter anyway, as they would every encounter. Why, Monica always said, be coy? Now Rudy watched her make her way swiftly through Glenna's outcry. He stayed thoughtfully on the far side of the room so as not to crowd her as she took the painful blows, her long freckled face reddening, one hand flat and open at her throat as though to protect her jugular.

When she had finished the letter, Monica looked around her angrily as if the room might suddenly have filled with people who were staring at her. Rudy came to her side, quickly and silently, startling her. He put one arm around her shoulder. "Honey, I hope you won't—"

"What *is* this?" Monica demanded, and shook out the page. She was staring straight ahead.

Rudy was relieved. "I was afraid you were going to take it to heart, you always blame yourself for everything—"

Monica finally turned to him with a look of fresh fear in her eyes, the way she might look if someone were at her heels then and there. "But I *do* take it to heart. I take it very much to heart. Only that doesn't mean I blame myself." She made a pained noise—his mother, dying under the slackening kindness of morphine, had made such vague aching noises whenever there was anyone to hear. "Oh God," Monica said, "Rudy. I don't even—" Her voice dwindled and she read the letter again, for the third time, moving her lips as she arrived at the outrageous words, the unjust accusations, like a child whose reading is still insecure. "I need a drink, would you get me a beer or something?"

Rudy ran to get her what she needed. Monica, seeing him hurry to oblige her as though she had met with an accident and needed ice, and bandages, thought, I have, I've been attacked from behind. Glenna was one of her oldest friends and she had tried to kill her, there was no other way to see it. A spiritual mugger. She thought of those bewildering murders where there are no broken-down doors, no jimmied windows: "The victim appeared to know her attacker." She said all that to Rudy, trying to laugh, as he handed her a sweating can of beer. She would never be the same again, she thought. It can happen that fast! Even when she had straightened up and stopped hunching over her new wound, she would be diminished by suspicion—of herself, of others.

That night before she fell asleep she thought about the time, long before "no fault," when she had argued angrily with an adjuster at the insurance agency after her car had been hit from behind on Memorial Drive. (It had in fact, been hit by another car that was in turn hit from the rear—classic blameless chain reaction.) "It doesn't matter to us whether you were at fault or not," he had said. "Statistically, you were involved. You were there to be hit, not somebody else. We have to take a long hard look at who gets hit." But, she had argued, when you've taken that look, what do you see? She had not understood, let alone agreed. The guiltless guilty?

But tonight she was ready to accede, if only she could put it differently: They were right, such guilt didn't have to do with fault or no-fault, or even with such imponderables as chance and defensive skill. It had to do with the future, with who you became. She would be marked forever now, bleeding internally. After an accident, she understood, one is never innocent again.

They were musicians, she the cellist, Glenna the pianist and—it had once been hard to think of the two of them without the third—Dot, their violinist. In college they had called themselves the Bizarre Trio, with a laugh and a nod at the Beaux Arts. Everything about their time together had been auspicious, even—as the school newspaper loved to report because the reviewer didn't know enough about music to comment on their performances—the way they represented three styles of beauty. Well, it wasn't beauty exactly, but they were a quaint combination that looked almost too carefully cast: Glenna with her peasant's buxomness and floating blond curls, Dot the dark one, long straight hair a sluice between her shoulders, and she, Monica, pale-skinned, red-haired, at her worst all freckles and invisible eyelashes, at her best vibrant and odd, a bold light springing from somewhere under that copper helmet of hair like the color of certain trees in autumn that seem to shine from the inside out. They received mash-notes from their audiences, sometimes communal, sometimes divided according to the taste of their admirers.

They went to Tanglewood together the summer after their senior year and sat, each of them, at the rear of her section, similarly reduced in status but very busy, very happy, wearing matching painters hats that said BIZARRE!, gifts of the Music Department at graduation.

When Dot left Boston to go to Curtis, Monica and Glenna shelved their trio scores and invested in duets. There were some accommodations to be made. Two was not one fewer than three; the repertoire seemed to decree that Monica suddenly be the soloist and Glenna the "able accompanist." But they worked hard at their collaboration, listening to the way Rostropovich and Richter worked out the balance in the Beethoven sonatas, and Du Pré and Barenboim the Prokofiev. Glenna was not naturally assertive, though neither, really, was Monica. Dot had been the grandstander among them, the one who wanted to be a soloist, who dipped her head deepest when they bowed. She thrived on adrenalin while the other two held each other's hands and yawned with nerves, took trips from the green room to the bathroom, suffered mouths as dry as cotton balls. They took refuge in their numbers, finally, each responsible but not entirely exposed. But Glenna seemed to be shrinking, now that Dot had gone. "I am never going to upstage you, my dear," Monica assured Glenna when there were just the two of them. "These pieces will feature the two of us or no one. Only you have to play as if you mean it."

Glenna had bitten her lip. The solution, Monica had suggested as gently as she could, might be extra-musical. Perhaps it had to do with Glenna's overbearing father (a Congressman and a flirt) who had tormented her childhood by saying to her whenever they were in public, "Speak up, damn it, speak up!" but who never wanted to hear a word from her at home. Or she might look to her super-efficient mother, a professor of nutrition at the school of public health, a consultant and a columnist for the daily newspaper whose name everybody knew. (She couldn't cook so much as a breakfast omelet but she wrote *Your Menu For Health*, instructing greater Boston in how to make tofu doughnuts and low-calorie pies with cauliflower crusts.) She wore a lab coat wherever she went: it made her daunting even at the dinner table. Perhaps Glenna had once been the shy dreaming girl who played the piano to be alone; she had also, Monica insisted, played to be heard, and now there were people who genuinely did want to hear her. She was a good pianist who was cheating herself.

Glenna heard Monica out, agreed that her problems were standing in the way of the music, and found herself a psychiatrist to see why she could assert herself when she was one of three but not one of two. Monica probed to make sure she hadn't hurt her feelings suggesting such a thing but Glenna said no, quite the contrary. She was grateful for a friend who cared about her—not only for the music's sake. Friends had the right, after all or—her eyes had clouded over with tears—what were friends for? Anyway (briskly) at the very least she had an obligation to Schubert or Mozart or whomever to hold up her end: pianists were not meant to be invisible, inaudible, insubstantial. Everything about Glenna, her cheeks, her bosom, broadened as if her gratitude were a yeast. Being cared about made her soft and cozy-looking.

But first she had a problem, not a very original but nonetheless a real one. There was no way to pay her psychiatrist without somehow involving her parents' money.

"Well, your trust fund isn't *their* money," Monica argued. "That's for you, isn't it, to do with however you like. I mean, if you want to go skiing in St. Moritz with it, isn't that your business?"

"Still," Glenna answered, and when she shrugged her round shoulders she really did make herself look like a small child about to do something she knew was wrong. "The money has their fingerprints all over it, somehow."

"Oh look, everything any of us does has our fingerprints on it, our interest in music, our talent, it all comes from somewhere, doesn't it? My mother and her silver flute, that beautiful old—"

"My parents despise music. It doesn't accomplish anything, you know, it just *is*, and they're not about to forgive it that. The way it just sort of wafts around on the airwaves, it doesn't get bills passed or establish the dietary requirements of school lunch programs."

"But Glenna, look, there's the first thing you have to talk about with your therapist—how you staked your first rebellion on loving what you love."

"Hating what I hate, you mean." Glenna smiled bleakly and ran her fingers through her pale curls as if to wake them up.

"God knows it's true, any psychiatrist would tell you that you get a lot more mileage out of saying 'no' than 'yes.'"

"What do you mean 'mileage'? Where have I ever been going?"

"Out of their sight, I guess. Someplace your parents can't follow. Or won't."

Glenna shrugged again; it was the dismissive movement she made more than most. "I'm not sure they ever noticed."

"How could they not notice you've got your back to them, you live your whole life in a place they're not comfortable in. It's a declaration. I mean, can't you see your piano says this very loud 'no' to what they are? They're not deaf." (Or maybe not loud enough, she thought but did not say; it was a little too neat, as if the day Glenna acknowledged it, she would bring her volume up.)

"Pretty close to deaf, I've always thought," Glenna was saying bitterly. "You're a lot cheaper than a shrink, you know. What if I buy you a couch and we start—"

"Really, Glenna. These are things you've got to understand. I'm not kidding."

"What does it have to do with Haydn?" Glenna looked away. Her lips had narrowed like those of a spiteful girl.

Monica shook her head. "And what does Haydn have to do with food stamps or the ERA?"

At first Monica feared the cure was going to be superficial. Glenna began to accent her white blouse-long black skirt recital uniform with bits of brightness, like a bird bringing home random twigs and strings to her nest. People's vision was drawn, by design, to her striped Equadorian belt or the vivid fuchsia bow that sat in her pale curls like a maraschino cherry in a cocktail. Well, all right, Monica thought. She, Monica, had to sit forever in the middle of the audience's vision whether she wanted to or not, poking up like a Maypole, her red hair vibrating under the lights. Maybe that was something pianists resented. Let her draw all eyes, share that attention. Anyway as their teachers used to remind them, music is no competition. Whoever won forfeited the game.

But Glenna's playing improved. She did gain volume, she advanced her own ideas, sometimes she even refused Monica's interpretations and put forth her own. "Good!" Monica would think. If a piece went spectacularly well, she'd say it out loud. "Oh, Glenna, much much better!" They were wonderful, she thought—in perfect balance, each assertive, each reticent by turns. At their best, Monica thought of them as swooping on the most flexible wings, bobbing and skidding around invisible corners of wind. Such ecstasies, shared, made them triumphant and vulnerable, somehow. Sex might be one way to unclothe and exercise the soul; surely work, this mutual holy sweat of the Brahms second sonata was the other. They held each other's hand taking their bows and hurried offstage joined like children swinging up the street together.

Monica found a job teaching cello at a small Catholic girls' college in Rhode Island where her students were genteel and accommodated music in the tradition of the nineteenth century when one played as one embroidered, as one perfected an epistolary style. Glenna freelanced as harpsichordist with a few chamber orchestras and accompanied dancers at two studios. On the side they hired themselves out to schools, to college lyceums, cocktail parties, graduations, and weddings, often in the company of a violinist or two but more frequently by themselves when they could sell the unique idea of "the intimate duo"—"Sunrise, Sunset" in that throbbing baritone voice of the cello. It was cheaper than a quartet and, they tried to imply, classier. The work didn't demand enough to keep their standards up but considering that Glenna was still at the conservatory and Monica was studying hard privately, it was satisfying. They were employed musicians, young, hard-working, in business. They had printed cards, an answering machine in case people called about jobs while they were out; they even hired an accountant as income tax time drew near. The subtleties, Bartok and Elliott Carter, they attended to in their offhours.

Then Monica met Rudy. Glenna had already married a law student named Cy, but that did very little to alter her schedule or her relations with Monica. Cy was easy-going and perpetually busy. He was one of those gentle fair-haired midwestern men who look comfortable and unconstrained in tightly buttoned shirts and three-piece suits and who, accustomed to obeying their fathers, yearly pour into the good law firms to do whatever is asked of them without complaint; he was impossible to dislike.

Rudy, on the other hand, disrupted everything. He too was unexceptional. Glenna approved of him from the dark top of his head to the sneakers on his feet. He and Cy played squash together, the two couples ate in all the restaurants in *The Underground Gourmet*. But he had his doctorate, he had served two years of a postdoctoral fellowship and now he had a job. The job was in San Francisco.

Given the other choices—Arizona and Arkansas—Monica was ecstatic about the move. Could anyone have dreamed of a better city to be sent to? (One tended to think of first jobs with all the pessimism of military assignments.) They would finally have a wide-awake honeymoon surrounded by hills and bright Mediterranean-blue water.

Only the parting from Glenna was difficult, and the knowledge, inevitable from the start, that not only would she need a new teacher but she would have to begin again with another partner, learn a thousand intricacies of temperament and timing and, even at that, hope for the best. As the two women clung to each other on the eve of Monica's and Rudy's departure—their little car looked like an Okie truck, Monica's cello shrouded in its case, carefully buckled in a rear seat belt, a rack full of Rudy's experiment printouts on the roof, and a U-Haul the size of a small room full of irreplaceable junk and wedding presents bobbing behind—Monica said to herself, but not to Glenna who was still and always would be fragile, that chamber music was not a friendship as she had always called it, but a marriage. Perhaps it thrived without sex and generation, but it was a compound of thousands, millions of moments of intimacy incommunicable to another soul, and the end of it, the cessation of everything from hard work to exaltation, was like a divorce or a widowing. A partner was irreplaceable.

But, as with divorce or widowing, after a good many months of nostalgia in which she envied her old self, the way things used to be, the pain of her defection slackened and the need to replace her pianist began to seem natural again. It was hard to find someone she really enjoyed working with, but given sufficient time to play the field, she found a partner. This was a woman considerably older than Monica, unlikely-looking, suburban in her dress and habits but positively European in the fierceness of her devotion to her music. Her name was Sandi—complete to the "i"—and she had played for years with a very fine chamber orchestra. As Sandi beat time in her flat-heeled Capezios, her leg ticking in its plaid polyester pants, Monica worked at eradicating one more stereotype from her repertoire—taste in music and taste in clothing, or even that hideous makeshift that covered all the rest, "lifestyle," were not correlated and just as well. (Neither, she had learned a long time ago, was "intelligence," if by that she intended to say articulateness, or maturity, or even literacy.) If the best moments of the best composers were unpredictable, why should their performers all be cut from the same cookie mold? As long as Sandi didn't wear those slacks to concerts. . . .

She and Glenna wrote to each other faithfully if not frequently, and indulged in an occasional long phone call. One December a few years after the move, Glenna herself materialized for a visit, en route to see an aunt in Spokane who was footing the bill. She was rosy and pregnant; her pale hair, no longer so curly, had grown and she was wearing it up in a sophisticated sweep that made her look older. "More finished," Rudy said, beaming at her in surprise. It was true. It looked as if the swan in Glenna had finally emerged from her chubby duckling's down.

There had been no awkwardness in their reunion. From the first moment they were comfortable, their conversation quick with gossip about the music world and with ordinary talk about nothing Monica could remember long enough to tell Rudy how they had spent the day. Glenna brought the news that Dot had signed a record contract; she was going to solo with the New York Philharmonic next winter. They shook their heads in wonder. Dot's was an ambitiousness they had always recognized but had only irregularly dared imagine for themselves. They were journeymen ensemble players who loved their work, not soloists manquées. "She can have it," Glenna had said with one hand, mocking, on her heart as if the whole idea of such a life might make her swoon.

Monica showed her friend every lovely street, parking with her wheels carefully turned in toward the curb to keep her car from becoming what San Franciscans so quaintly called a "runaway." They drove to Sausalito for Sunday brunch on the water and went to the best and ugliest restaurant in Chinatown. Glenna now played regularly, piano and harpsichord, with a chamber group that met in a downtown Boston church; they had a full schedule of reviewed concerts and their notices had been quite good. It was easier than duets for sure, she said. "More satisfying? Less?" Monica asked. "Less strain," Glenna answered, smiling in acknowledgement of all they had pushed through together. "I'm probably backsliding—I'm one of eighteen!"

This was the last free time she would have till spring. The baby? Well, she was lucky to play piano, wasn't she. (She had taken to saying she played piano, as though she worked nights at some South Boston bar.) She had sporadic hours and no heavy work as long as she didn't have to move the damn piano herself.

This time, putting her on the plane for the duty leg of her trip, Monica laughed instead of crying. The ties of work broken and both their futures settled, she was free to enjoy Glenna as an old dear friend who had been something far more and was thus assured her own permanent niche in memory. "Goodbye, goodbye," she murmured into the top-knot that seemed like someone else's, that measure of Glenna's growing-up. "Next visit is mine. And when the baby comes—"

"You get the first call."

"After your parents—"

Glenna had smiled and shrugged as if to say, "What do you think," and disappeared down the accordion-pleated runway to her plane.

Months later—how far along had Glenna been in her pregnancy? —well, however far, enough months later Monica realized that she had never heard a word about the baby. April had been the month, she was sure she remembered that, something about producing the baby in time for the church's great Easter concert. (They had laughed and sung, spontaneously, together, "Unto us a son is given . . .") Was she afraid to call? What if there had been a problem? How could you check on someone a continent away only to be told that something dire had happened? But such a good friend, Rudy had insisted. Surely it would be no secret. By then, though, Monica herself was pregnant, and it would be cruel, wouldn't it, to stir up any news Glenna had not wanted to send her? Because of that, when Marcie was born Monica did not send a birth announcement to Glenna— she couldn't bear to hurt her, if that was what joyous news might do.

And now the letter. Monica folded it very slowly, following the direction of the sharp fold-lines as if it were a road map, and put it into its envelope, which she placed neatly by itself in the middle of the dining room table. Sitting there alone it looked as if it had repelled all the life around it.

"Is the baby sleeping?"

Rudy nodded. He had picked up Marcie at the sitter's on the way home from school. "Mrs. Ames said she didn't get much of a nap, so I put her down again."

"Okay. Good." She walked around the room as soundlessly as if she were circling herself. Every part of her was raw. Of course Rudy was right, she was blaming herself, how could she not be? Even if she had never intended to hurt Glenna, what had she done? Why had Glenna come to see her if she was so "happy" when they'd moved away? It was a hideous joke, cruel and impenetrable. She saw poor, shy Glenna bent over the piano, her back in a low flat arch as if she wanted to put her chin on the keys, saw her hold a long note, rocking her whole hand around the extended finger exactly as she, Monica, did on the fretboard of her cello looking for a motion to contain the energy, to fill motionless time, quarter, half, whole note tied and tied into the next measure and the next, her eyes closed, counting.

Post-partum depression, she thought quite suddenly. Nothing else could account for it. One of these days they would hear from Cy, who would be apologetic, grieving, as confused as they, that Glenna had gone insane and this had only been one of her outbursts. If that didn't turn out to be the case, Monica would never trust anyone again, not Sandi, not even Rudy, no one she knew. If a friend could harbor such hate that she became an assassin out of the blue. . . . As if to assure herself that her pain was only beginning, she hit the table top so hard with the palm of her hand that it smarted; anger enough to inflame the flesh, then. This was a new experience for Monica, who could usually talk herself around impediments and through depressions, comparing all disappointments to final losses, thereby rendering them petty, even laughable. She felt sick with this—it *was* a finality—and enlivened at the same time; adrenalin washed through her in waves, preparing her for fight or flight but instructing her for neither. She stared at her throbbing hand as if it didn't belong to her.

Sincerely, but without conviction, Monica began to catechize her friends. "Am I such a bitch that I don't even know it?" "Do I hurt you accidentally when we're together? Don't laugh, think about it." But her friends would not cooperate by telling her she was oblivious, insensitive, competitive. They shrugged and shook their heads, which she was to take for comfort.

"Wouldn't I tell you, Monica?" Rudy would ask her. "Wouldn't *I* see the worst, if all that was a fit description?" Loyal Rudy. She seemed to look at him from a great distance filled with experiences they had not shared.

"I know husbands who defend insane wives," she told him as if she were defending herself. "Remember Jim Papilardi, who tried to get his nutcase wife rehired when they put her out of the lab? I don't think he ever believed what they said about her." Rudy didn't think the comparison held. Joan Papilardi had been found out of her clothes, flank on flank with a Harvard senior who had been asleep with electrodes attached to his scalp; he was not the first experimental subject she had awakened, he was only the first who had protested. True, the woman's poor husband had fought for her job, but that was not the same, and anyway, the man might be expected to maintain his pride.

I'm trying, sweetheart, Rudy seemed to be saying to her, I'm trying harder than you are to understand and to help you resist. But he could feel in Monica's grateful embrace that she was comforting him, somehow, was humoring him in his diligent efforts at her acquittal. It was all, he would murmur, a tragic mistake, undeserved, as if Monica had boarded the wrong plane and it had gone down in flames. No, she was even less implicated—as if she had been standing on the ground minding her own business when the plane fell burning out of the sky. But Monica refused his generosity—this was not a mechanical failure. People are bound together, even if we don't know how. Miscommunication, maybe, but not engine breakdown.

Over the next few years whenever Monica thought of Glenna she winced with pain. She no longer felt more than a passing shadow of shame when she remembered her. She had finally decided in her own favor: Glenna was mistaken. But she was also lost to Monica as surely as if she had died, and what was the use of that? Who was being punished? Nor could she ever modify the judgment, that was the other part that felt so final. Once, when a friend who knew the story mentioned her "enemy," Monica stared for a moment in disbelief. Having an enemy ought to become a two-way proposition, she thought, even if it didn't begin that way; and she, who loved Glenna, hated no one.

Dot brought the news that Glenna, not long after her visit to San Francisco, had tried to kill herself. She had been put in a clinic in the Berkshires for a few months, had emerged dulled and silent, undoubtedly drugged, ignored her new baby—there *was* a son, a beautiful boy born on the first day of spring that year. Dot saw her whenever she passed through Boston, although it was, she swore, not a lot of laughs.

"Does she mention me?" Monica asked sadly. She had turned so pale she thought she must look guilty of something.

"Once she said she hadn't seen you for a long time. But frankly she doesn't seem to have much energy or emotion to spare for anything." Dot, beautiful and unchanged, cocked her head. "Whatever in the world did happen between you two back then? Nobody's ever accounted for it any way that made sense."

Monica couldn't say. "I must somehow be to blame," she concluded experimentally, wondering if Dot might possess some new evidence. "Otherwise it's nothing but a shaggy dog story."

"It's too noble to assume you're to blame, lovey," Dot told her in her efficient, emphatic voice that plunged through its subjects like her bow across taut strings. "People can be their own worst enemies, you know, without any help from anyone else. We all know what kind of problems she had." She thought for a while. "She sounds jealous."

"Jealous?" That was absurd. "If she was going to be jealous it would be of you, not me. I'll tell you what I think. I should never have tried to help her. I was being critical when I ought to have let her—".

"Absurd." Monica's own word. "For whose sake? You were her friend. That doesn't mean you're sworn to silence, I hope." Dot had a rich dark face, ripe as a plum. If she had doubts, she throttled them out of sight. "If I see her, do you have a message you want me to give her? I'm going to be in Boston again in a little while." Things were still breaking well for Dot, the concerts multiplying, her name becoming known. The calm with which she accepted all of it, Monica thought, proved that she deserved anything she had— it was a natural movement and her energy stayed free for the music. "You hope she'll change her mind, or you miss her or anything? Or are you too mad?" Dot looked at the nails she kept filed for the sake of her work. Her fingertips looked tough. Musicians' fingers always had hard pads at the ends, a special brand of beauty. "I know I'd be too mad if somebody savaged me like that."

Tell her she has scarred me forever, Monica thought, looking away, her eyes filled with tears. Hadn't she told Glenna herself that "no" speaks louder than "yes"? And if she is my enemy I will have to hate her whether I want to or not. And then—for she knew, suddenly, what this felt like, she remembered her old idle desire, hers and Rudy's, to be despised for cause—then if I hate her hard enough (that would not be easy, oh Glenna, she thought, seeing the futile drop of red ribbon beading up on the transparency of that fine hair) she will come out of her invisibility into the world and be seen.

The light on the coffee pot had come on. Dot was waiting for a message; even if the joke had no punchline somebody had to have the last word.

"Just tell her you saw me and I looked wounded." Monica spoke firmly, as if she were giving her words of absolution. "Tell her I told you I would never forgive her."

"Okay." Dot nodded, satisfied. "I'll tell her you're sworn enemies. To the end of time." She shrugged, her thin shoulders rising like wing bones, and took her cup of coffee out of Monica's hands.

Good Housekeeping

S H E   P U T the lens of the camera up so close to the baby's rear that she suddenly thought, what if he craps on the damn thing? But she got the shot, diapered him again, lowered the shade, and closed the door. Turned the coffeepot so a wan light barely struck off the half shine under the accumulated sludge on its side. Held it over the toilet bowl, tilted so the camera wouldn't reflect in the ring of water. In the laundry mountain looking out. Carrots, parsnips, onions— then she stopped, put the camera down, shaved them all, and flung them into the long pile of their own curled skins. That was beautiful, the fingers of vegetable, the fat translucent globes of the onions like polished stones, absolute geometric definition picked out of the random garbage heap, focus on the foreground.

She was working very fast, the way the idea had come to her, before the tide of possibility receded. She laid the camera in the rumpled bedclothes so that the sheets formed great warm humps and valleys, the plaid of the blanket coasting off out of sight on one side. There was a faint impression where one of them had lain—it was more or less on his side—like grass that hasn't risen after someone's nap in the sun. Like photographing a ghost. She pulled her underpants off, sat on the bed, put her legs up the way she did in the doctor's stirrups, laid the camera on the bed—well, she couldn't see into the damn viewfinder but it seemed to be aimed—ah, it was the shutter that came, that sound of passionless satisfaction, its cool little click sucking in the core of her, reaming out the dark with its damp sweat like the seeds of some melon. So long it had been her face, she might as well have its puckered features in good light, for posterity. Some faces gape more meanly, anyway. This was so very objective, it would transcend lewdness, anger, the memory of passion. The lens like a doctor saw only fact. She found an unused box of condoms lying half covered by socks. She opened the box, arranged a few randomly, only their rolled edges peeking out, surely recognizable. Then, like a teenager nosing in her parents' drawers, she put them neatly back again and buried the box where she had found it.

And the dirty window, its shadowy design as regular as a litho. The soil in the pots waiting for the seedlings to show, that made a lovely stipple where they had been watered, light on a grainy dark, pearly vermiculite on peat. There was something so neat and purposeful about the shelf of pots. Magnified the soil reminded her of little girls she'd known who wore white blouses with Peter Pan collars and sat with a certain obedient stillness no matter what raged around them; for years and years sat that way. Her pepper seedlings, her tomatoes, under there, primly incubating in the still, protected dark.

The food didn't work, neither the lined-up cans nor the omelet she made just for the occasion, heaping it up into ridges—too much like *Good Housekeeping*. Oh, yes, the drawer in the kitchen table that held a little of everything—keys, bills, warrantees on all things electric, seed catalogues, a display so wanton she smiled. Cigarette papers—the grass to go with them was in her spice bottles marked FENUGREEK (though it looked more like basil or tarragon, finely ground. Wait till some visitor in her kitchen tried to cook with it. . . .). Straight into the bore of the pencil sharpener, a terrifying snout at 10X. Wallpaper they couldn't hide: symmetrical and graceless, cabbage roses with stars between. The welcome mat, its disordered grass lying all tamped down, caked perfectly with half-moons of mud, as though a horse had wiped his feet.

There was a little pile of feathers she had found in the bathroom—the cat had killed another bird and, proud, left this gift of fine, unmutilated evidence. They were mottled on one side, a combed gray on the other, their barbs unevenly separated as though by movement. No, that wouldn't be understood; some objects implied their function, or at the least, how they got where they were, but the feathers needed the cat and even then . . . are murdered birds a part of every household?

She was thinking of the way the show would be hung. Utterly random, on flat matte. No implicit order, no heavy ironies. In spite of the fact that the chemicals in her darkroom had probably spoiled by now from disuse multiplied by time, no bitterness. In fact there was such beauty in these banalities up close that she felt humbled. Like a lecture from her husband the evidence piled up, orderly, inside the shutter, that she was wrong again. That she was right and wrong. She walked on the balls of her feet, spying into all her likely and unlikely corners, elated.

When the baby woke, screaming and swallowing down huge hunks of air and screaming again, she took the camera coolly into the little hall room, seeing herself from a great distance, doing an assignment on herself doing an assignment. She pulled the shade all the way to the top and then knelt in front of the crib bars. So much light you could see the baby's uvula quivering like an icicle about to drop. . . . When the baby saw the camera he closed his mouth and reached out, eyes wide. Eyes like cameras. His mother looked back at herself in them, a black box in her lap with a queer star of light in its middle.

"No!" She stood up, stamping. "No, goddammit. What are you *doing*?"

The baby smiled hopefully and reached through the slats.

She put her head in her hands. Then she reached in and, focusing as well as she could with one hand, the baby slapping at her through the bars, wheezing with laughter, she found one cool bare thigh, the rosy tightness of it, and pinched it with three fingers, kept pinching hard, till she got that angry uvula again, and a good bit of very wet tongue. Through the magnifier it was spiny as some plant, some sponge, maybe, under the sea.

What Does the Falcon Owe?

F., 27, 5'5", 122 lb., hair medium brown worn long (sometimes in gold clip), eyes brown, glasses for reading (tortoise frames). Morning 12/13 had approx. $40 (known), car keys (car left parked outside MP's apt. house). Took few clothes, overnight bag (blue plaid), portable typewriter, small b/w etching ("Clown" by Daumier), 2 small eskimo masks, removed from bedroom wall.

REMARKS:

MP and H(usband) had been writing book (study of Kwamiack Indians of Saskatchewan); typed chapters were stacked neatly in basket on desk where husband says they usually were kept. On top of file was found Enclosure (C), with Enc. (A) in typewriter. Enc. (B) was taped on bathroom mirror. Enc. (D), a stapled set of yellowed newspaper clippings, was found by H on MP's pillow, which was neatly covered by bedspread. H claims apt. had been cleaned while he was out that morning. One coffee cup drying in drainer. Approx. 24 hrs. after MP disappeared, H received telegram (night letter, sent from phone booth, this city), Enc. (E) which H identifies as Navajo prayer which he taught MP before marriage. No further communic. from MP; none of couple's friends rec'd communic. H received two bills for dept. store charge account purchases, one for a sweater, the other for a number of novelty items identified as (1) Ventrillo Wonder voice-thrower (2) Fur-head, a bar of soap shaped like a face, which grows a beard overnight when placed in water (3) a set of trick mirrors (4) plaster-of-Paris mold outfit called "Living Death Mask Set." Purchases totaled $14.53, which H paid.

End file. See attached Encls. A–E.

ENCL. A:

Words = Artifacts
Sentences = Ritual

First prayer of UNBINDING.

† Hohman's Powwows on Arts and Remedies (Eagleton, Penna., 1837) claims following:

a good remedy for hysterics
a remedy to be used when anyone is falling away
a remedy for calumniation or slander
to attach a dog to a person
a sure way of catching fish
to mend broken glass
to prevent the Hessian fly from injuring the wheat
to prevent cherries from maturing before Martinmas
to prevent the worst kind of paper from blotting
to remove a wen during the crescent moon
to make a wick which is never consumed
to compel a thief to return stolen goods
against every evil influence
to charm enemies, robbers, and murderers
a charm against shooting, cutting, or thrusting
to prevent being cheated, charmed, or bewitched
a charm to gain advantage of a man of superior strength

ENCL. B:

Dream of a hunter wearing his hooded falcon
Blind on his wrist. Then watch the bird escape.
Forgetting hunger, remembering he has wings,
He feels his way on the under edge of the sky,
Threads through the clouds,
Comes down in the safety of distance,
And wonders: The falconer is gentle,
Has fed him well, has taught him all he knows,
And keeps his sight.
Can you say what the falcon owes?

ENCL. C:

Once in a land that perhaps exists, there lived a king and his little daughter, the princess. They lived in a regulation castle and were all

155

the things they had to be; in fact (in spite of their perfection) they were even believed to be happy.

One day in spring the king put on the lightest cloak and crown in his closet and took the hand of his lovely little girl. "Let us go for a walk around the palace grounds," he said to her, and she threw down her golden doll and came to him with a smile of true delight. (She loved her great father perfectly and it was clear to the whole world that he reflected her love just as a still deep pool reflects a star, drinking in its light without a movement, without the hint of a ripple. He never scolded her or made her cry; he was a true king and a forgiving father.)

Hand in hand they strolled the walks in the garden, past the purple berry bushes and the roses strung up with silver twine, past the shore of the little pond with its pearl cup of a boat tied up on the grassy beach. When they had been once around the grounds and their feet said nothing, not a word of reproach, the king suggested they walk out past the village into the countryside. The little princess had never ventured beyond the gates of the palace and she was thrilled. And she could walk longer with her splendid father, her small hand in his large one!

She was so excited that she chattered, chipped at his ear like a woodpecker. She laughed at her father's dignified silence and twitted him for talking so little. "Well," she would say, "perhaps kings are not supposed to talk as much as princesses. I'm sure that's it, and my king"—she tugged at his sleeve to reassure him—"my king always does what a king ought to." Though she was a mischievous child, often a trying one (since he never restrained her), she had no standard by which to feel herself judged. He said nothing now but walked steadily beside her. Every now and then, try as she did with her short legs beneath their heavy skirts, she could not keep in step with the king. She would run a few steps, raising the dry dust under her slippers, and match her strides to his, then she would fall behind again. Finally, feeling the pull of her hand, her father slowed his pace to match hers, and they kept on, slowly.

After some time the king stopped. He dropped his daughter's hand and said, "Dear child, I am very weary." He sat himself on a large flat stone at the roadside. "Little queen, if you want to, you can walk on a bit. Why don't you go through those trees—" He pointed to a stand of pines that loomed abruptly like an island in the flat sea of meadow—"and on the other side you will find a lovely brook full of fish with rainbows on their backs."

The princess could hardly restrain her delight. She gave her father a kiss and ran off down the road and across the spongy earth that rose and sagged beneath the trees, mountains and valleys of pine needles. She could see light pricking through the solid darkness in sudden ragged flashes like sunlight glinting off a sword, and the child ran toward it, rolling the hoop of her eagerness before her.

A low growth of bushes stood barricading her way when she approached the light, and she had to skip through it, holding her breath as each thorn scraped through her skirts and through her skin. With an anxious little sigh, she brought her leg high over the last hurdle and down with a decisive thrust, and before she could see it, she had tumbled flat on her chest into a ditch. The ground near the stream was rocky and damp and she had dirtied and torn her velvet dress in a dozen places. Winded, she shook her skirts out with a fury that was all the more painful in her throat because she was not sure where it came from or where it wanted to go.

There at least was the stream, and it would be cool on her raw ankles. It had been dusk; now the light seemed to dim and go out, and the rainbow fish had gone home, or had turned their promised lights out. If there were rainbow fish. The water darted at her bruises with cold fangs, and she waded back to the bank stung with pain in many places. Something caught at her foot, bit through with a crab's mean grip. In terror she kicked and kicked till it flew off and, wide-eyed, as she saw it arc against the black water and tumble in, she could just make out the rainbow lights winking at her. She pulled her skirts up to her knees and ran, expecting to feel a hand or a claw at her shoulder, in her hair, at her feet, as she felt her way dumbly through the fence of thorns. The forest was blacker and quieter than sleep, and cold—she felt the sudden cold as if someone had slammed a door behind her. Only the unfamiliar sounds of the night harried her home.

When she had flown across the lawn of the castle and rattled the door open, she found her father sitting calmly with a book, wearing his heavy crown again. She could not speak.

"Child, you are home," he said to her simply, as if he were telling her something of value. "Did you see the rainbow fish?"

"Father!" The princess stood still as a thorn tree.

"I couldn't wait for you," he said.

"Father!"

"My precious one, understand. This has always been so. You talked so much. You walked so slowly. You took so long. You could hardly expect—"

She swayed in his words. "But why did you say nothing? You said nothing at all."

"What should I have told you, little one?" He was well returned to his patience.

"I could have done something! I would have been quiet! I would have run! I would never have left you. Or I would never have come."

Her father smiled faintly, quizzically. "Ah," he said and spread his large hands wide.

ENCL. D:

VIOLINIST SCORES WITH BACH, TARTINI, BEETHOVEN, BRAHMS

Jan. 23, 1924

The splendid warmth and style of Alexei Tartakoff were again in evidence last night in a recital which brought him back from his celebrated European tour to an audience that jammed Carnegie Hall. Mr. Tartakoff chose Bach's second partita for unaccompanied violin to open his program and in the Bach and the notoriously wicked Devil's Trill sonata which followed, he showed himself again the unrivaled technical master of the era. His fingers seem to have the strength, speed, and certainty of a mechanical instrument which is powered not by a motor but by a great and magnanimous heart. His tone is ripe and brilliant and he has a wealth of nuances in tone and tempo which he uses to ravishing effect. The limpidity he achieved in the slow movement of Beethoven's very familiar Spring Sonata was so lovely and cumulatively so moving that the audience applauded at the end of the movement. This crowd knew where protocol can leave off and passion begin. Mr. Tartakoff's accompanist was Frederick Hopper and his collaboration was exquisite. Mr. Tartakoff has always exercised fine judgment in picking his assistants, but there is apparently more to it: he can elicit great commitment from all who share the stage with him. His personality demands response and gets it. The audience gave it to him last night; there was a ten-minute ovation followed by four encores that left the crowd shouting for more.

August 6, 1948

The Music Shed at Tanglewood was the scene last night of a rather disheartening concert by the Boston Symphony Orchestra. The program, perhaps, was to blame. It was war-horse night, with a stable of old winners trotted out for the automatic approval of a loyal audience which, itself, is not quite as young as it used to be.

After the Leonore No. 3 and the Haydn Clock, about which there was nothing the least bit diverting or unique, Alexei Tartakoff was the soloist. Lexy, the old Russian who used to be billed as the Liszt of the violin, is still a drawing-card, whether for musical or extra-musical reasons one cannot tell if he doesn't feel the hypnotic pull himself. (This reviewer must admit that he doesn't, but perhaps his parents did.) This reluctance to be moved by the charming smile and courtier's bow, and the still ample crown of free-floating hair, leaves one's attention, unfortunately, free to listen to the music Tartakoff produces. It is flamboyant and undisciplined and yet somehow conventional, for all the unconventionalities his sloppiness of phrasing and intonation allow. He sounds temperamental à la Russe, but it is all so familiar, could his heart really be in it? This style would be so easy for a young violinist to learn to ape, with a bit of application, from old records; and one fears that a younger, more limber man could do it better. These days, at least, we must demand more from our orchestras and our soloists than they gave us last night.

SEASON CLOSES WITH VIOLIN DUO;
TARTAKOFF FINALE SEES PUPIL BOW

April 20, 1958

Last night was a most peculiar one for all who attended the much-publicized closing concert of this season's Philharmonic at Carnegie Hall. Judging by their response, the audience was as bewildered as it had every right to be. The evening was to mark the farewell appearance of the great Alexei Tartakoff, who has appeared in New York only once in the last ten years. Mr. Tartakoff, now a worn-looking 72, has continued to concertize across the country within the last few years; therefore, what was at first announced as a return from retirement for this special concert could perhaps more honestly, if less euphemistically, be called a return from obscurity. In any event, the occurrences of the evening make one wonder what the intention really might have been, and one is at a loss even to conjecture.

A good deal of newspaper attention had been given as well to Mr. Tartakoff's plan to present at this concert his only pupil and protégé, so that the occasion was to be one of more than sentimental interest. It was to be both a farewell and a debut, and the latter, judging by Mr. Tartakoff's reluctance to sanction any other student over the years, made one quite naturally curious and hopeful that a worthy heir would be proclaimed by the abdicating king.

How to say it? To be blunt, the concert was a fiasco, and an extraordinary one. Harlan Temple, who is 23, has the manner of a master—he swept onstage and bowed from the waist, a more athletic replica of his teacher, dispensed with even the customary gesture of interest in the tuning of his instrument, strode out into the deep waters of the Dvořák A Minor, and promptly drowned. One could not attribute such fundamentally faulty playing to nervousness, especially when not a hint of discomfort was in evidence. On the contrary, Mr. Temple was more self-possessed than most proven professionals, even suspiciously so. But his technique was wretched, his intonation slapdash, his tone ugly, his general level of sensitivity and musical feeling so low it was virtually absent. This pleasant enough concerto was suddenly ghastly and endless, and when he had done with it, the soloist bowed profusely to a paralyzed audience from which a ragged little sound of applause issued briefly. But Mr. Tartakoff was onstage, clapping proudly, and the orchestra, with Rouben Der Tartesian on the podium, joined with him enthusiastically. No one but the audience looked troubled. One shook oneself to see if it might have been an acoustical fluke or an after-dinner dream. But for confirmation, the master and his pupil were paired in the Bach G Minor double concerto, and the impression persisted. And next to Tartakoff, the untalented boy was an even greater outrage. What a lovely tone and what a cat-squawk juxtaposed! By comparison the aging violinist was the perfect musician again—soaring, agile, strong.

This reviewer, grieved, confused, even angry, cannot help but wonder what will happen to Harlan Temple when he is properly launched (horribile dictu!) and on his own. Considering that he already parades like a child moviestar, he has apparently been brainwashed into believing that he will have, or already has, a career ready-made for him. If so, Mr. Temple is in for a colossal disappointment.

ENCL. E:

	(H's translation):
Sike saadilil	My legs for me restore
Sitsat saadilil	My body for me restore
Sissis saaditlil	My mind for me restore
Sini saaditlil	My voice for me restore
Tadisdzin naalil sahadilil	This very day your spell for me you will take out
Naalil sahaneinla	Your spell for me is removed
Hozogo tsidisal	Happily I shall go forth
Hozogo nadedisdal	Happily I shall recover
Sana nislingo nassado	My feelings being lively may I walk

All This

S H E I S sickened at all she knows:

—about the many ways to make gray with watercolors, creeping up on it from yellow and blue and red with a lot of water or down from black or purple. And brown, brown can edge into gray too somehow.

—about corruption in the unions, every union she can think of, a history of hypocrisy among the representatives of the have-nots, the have-a-littles, and the haves. Jimmy Hoffa at the bottom of a river. Or compacted. Or incinerated.

—about the relative caffeine content of everything, tea 50 percent as potent as coffee, 42 percent more potent than chocolate. Cola drinks are worse, even the innocent-looking ones, orange pop, Mountain Dew. And the lurking carcinogens—hot dogs, hair dyes, early sex, stones; the very boulders of the earth storing up radiation. Sucaryl and the Grand Canyon. The whole earth is a death wish.

—about daisy wheels and azimuth projections, Stanford White, the Negro Baseball League, how to make loquat jelly. There are 24 ribs, 88 piano keys, 227 differentiable squashes.

—about what to do with her teeth during variations on the sex act which would upset her mother even to contemplate. She has an aunt, though, whom she suspects of compendious knowledge arrived at over decades of serious attention to the subject.

—about four causes of a disease called toxoplasmosis that destroys the nervous systems of unborn babies during the last three months of gestation. One cause, which involves cats, she would rather not consider.

—about how many million dollars every movie loses, how much it earns, how much it cost. She knows someone who worked on the catering crew for *Star Wars*. Tubs of roast lamb at crazy hours, time-and-a-half. $4.50, $5 at the door for lamb, mint jelly.

162

—about the need for the shoes she wears for aerobic exercise to be broader and blunter than running shoes.

—about the speed at which Cape Cod's beaches are eroding; and what about the danger of the warming of the polar ice cap?

—and the year of moveable type. Year of the Irish potato famine (and how in a different blight, ergot invaded potatoes and made the extremities of potato-eaters turn black with rot). The year of the first two-tone car and the Buick with portholes. Year of the pill. Joplin and Hendrix's death years. Jim Morrison's she can never remember because she doesn't care.

—about the trim levers in an airplane and where to find the horizon indicator, and what is called the fishplate on a traintrack and what a clerestory window is; subways used to have them. Once she lived in a windmill for a week: she knows fantails and helmaths; also all the parts from tassel to blowpipe on a bagpipe. (At her father's funeral, a lone bagpiper wearing the clan tartan had walked from the canopy over the grave to the cement path and up the path until he was gone.) She could name ten basketball players who average 15 points a game. She knows that the joker in the deck is called mistigris and that the card Charlemagne is the Suicide King. Forte, presser plate, feed dog. Bellows, many kinds for many purposes. Narthex, nave, and apsidal. Ironwood burns hottest, applewood sweetest. She can replace a zipper, classify columns, anatomize an arch. She knows that Laurette Taylor was the best Amanda Wingfield, that Cincinnati has a good zoo though she's never been there, that some commuter airlines are better than others, and a few to keep away from. She sits toward the tail section because in case of trouble she would have a .06 better chance of survival. She knows a pome when she sees one, and a carapace.

In addition to an unending list of certainties, she has a set of speculations she would call bankable, if it comes to that. And she has all sorts of lore that attaches to her work—she is a specialist in education programs for a foundation and she carries an unholy amount of comparative, not to mention absolute, data in her head: successful and unsuccessful examples of solutions to the merit pay problem; competency test scores; factors mitigating, factors exacerbating; last year's buzzwords, next year's; a short list of people she trusts at work, a long list of those she suspects of sleeping on the job, or with each other. Where each of them slept on the job before they took this one.

She has the specifics of her family's history filed in two places— over there: Lithuania, Morocco, and Edinburgh; there are interesting stories to her grandparents' meetings—and over here: a generation-and-a-half of desperate poverty, then the ascent into the middle class with college, though not a very good college, graduate school. (Despite her rages against it, this is a freer country than many); and after graduation (at which six people she can still name were given degrees *honoris causa*) the shelves of cookbooks, a comprehension of the peculiarities of the Volkswagen carburetor, retirement accounts, good ski slopes in cold and warm climates, growing conditions of ficus and areca palms, variations on the sulfa cure for urinary discomforts, stereo components on any prudent person's hit list, B-vitamins and their best sources, B-1 through B-12 plus niacin and thiamine and what's this about selenium preventing cancer? Scenes from the intimate lives of John Lennon (that album cover with weird Yoko where his penis looks like an aged vegetable) and of Sting who wrote "Every Breath You Take" for his wife who left him and of Mick and Bianca Jagger separately, who really did meet at the London School of Economics, credible or not, together or not today.

Then she has her own history, happy or unhappy depending on how, like the nap on corduroy, one looks at it. Joan, Harriet, and Anny, Christin, Jeremy, Nat, Russ, and Walter and another Walter later. Friends, enemies, loyalty, cattiness, deflowering, long-ripening love, loss of love, souring, shrinking, shopping for a therapist, a corner turned, two-day ceaseless conversation, new bloom on the plant, new set of keys: for every friend, every lover, a thousand details— likes coffee without cream, three teaspoons of sugar, no sugar, does not like ears kissed, will shop only in boutiques, never a (God forbid) chain store, no sex after grass, can't spell, sends semiliterate letters—but look at the *substance*—borrows shamelessly, clothes, food, money but also gives and gives, insensitive to boundaries, called from New Zealand once and would not get off the phone while the meter ticked, will always break a date for rescheduling of analyst appointment, embarrassed by prominent collar bones, sullen in the morning, sullen after midnight, a fiscal conservative, a fiscal radical, eats compulsively—butter, spoonfuls of mayonnaise from the jar— loves teal blue, has a secret crush on Jesus.

There is also building politics, office politics, bedroom politics. There is the location of voting precinct, which lane on the FDR Drive for which exit, when the E train stops, or does not stop, at 23rd Street. Lebanon and El Salvador. José Marti was which country's greatest poet? Not Grenada. Which Mozart she likes, which betrays the fact that he was ten when he wrote it. Which Indian lamb dishes are best, which Chinese dishes contain the intolerable taste of cilantro. Which Faulkner has a girl walking down the side of the road barefoot, newly pregnant. The beech tree is the one that looks like a chestnut (horse or American?). The chestnut is almost extinct. Snakes too—of course she knows what shaped head the poisonous one will show her before he strikes, and what kind of gun is least visible in someone's pocket. Some few bars are friendly, like pubs, others exist for those who are asking for it. She actually knows of two people whose maids were murdered, one Ola, one Odette. Certain brands of clothing tend to fit, Prime Cut pants and Maverick, sometimes Orbit. Never Gloria Vanderbilt. Which stores take plastic, which demand cash. How to tell if jade is genuine. Which branches are the suckers on a tomato plant. Where does the "h" go in Lhasa Apsu. Apso. Acid soil for gardenias, what for oxallis? Which tall ship had the highest rigging the year they spilled, beautiful, into the harbor. How to remove the front wheel of a bike to keep it safe in a hallway. The time someone disappeared with the seat.

It is too late to become a primitive in the outback, or in New Guinea, where, according to the *Times*, it is even too late for the New Guineans. If only she knew 27 names for snow or sand and not the names of the supers in the last three buildings she has lived in, not to mention the supers' wives and children. Could she run away to live a new life where she would know nothing she needs to and be in actual danger? Where? Cuban Miami. The docks in Cardiff or Piraeus or Baku. At the women's military academy. Cambodia. (Are they still starving in Cambodia? Whatever became of Pol Pot? There are things she does not know.) She could be one of those guileless Americans who wanders across the border from Israel into Jordan, smiling, saying later, "I didn't know, I didn't know I was so close." Very backwoods Mississippi, is there anywhere TV doesn't reach, or New Orleans, where her accent would be an irritant. No; New Orleans is all T-shirts and tourists. Where would it be an irritant, make people say "Why are you here, what do you want of us?" She knows why her friend Nessa went to Nepal, walked along a mountain trail in thinnest air. All she knew how to do was put one hiking boot before the next, no supers, no names at all in her head anymore, no best cheese for onion soup, no vinegar for sweat stains, nothing but how not to make a sudden move over the sheer drop. She brought back saddle blankets and hepatitis. The insides of her ears and nostrils were vibrant, yellow as carrot juice. What if she went to Bessemer, Alabama and worked in a steel mill—do women work in steel mills yet?—or to Josslyn, Nebraska to work in the village bank which has opened a second branch. Learning every face, studying gossip, whose grandmother loved whose grandfather and no one ever forgot it after sixty years. Could she find a job she wouldn't know too well after three weeks?

Ronnie, who owns $13,000 worth of photographic equipment but can't afford to insure it, who becomes disagreeable when women cry, who has a tiny white scar beside his left nostril called a keloid from an accident on a motorbike, who makes beautiful oboe reeds and tolerable bathtub saké when he can get a good deal on rice, suggests she either become a doctor because only the mysteries of the body are endless—why not an astronomer? she asks—or give up all her money, all of it, and go on welfare so that she can relearn the city in a new, an "instrumental" way, or else shut up and stop sounding ungrateful.

He's right, Nessa says. Think of brain damage, senile dementia. Alzheimer's disease. Syndrome, Ronnie says. Syndrome. Okay. It's everywhere these days.

Just plain dying. A smart girl like you, you think you'll know all this forever? Where did you get this brie?

The International Language

I M I S S E D the first step: it was like being doped, asleep, for the birth of a child. They arrived at the airport without me, I did not watch them touch down, did not see their faces bloom into light as they came through the entranceway to Customs, the children thinking—no, feeling—*The earth has stopped moving, we are on solid ground*, the parents thinking—not yet feeling—*Safe! Safe! No one is armed, no one is starving*. Weapons and hunger are too subtle to be seen at first glance in Boston.

They drove out of the city in the dark. Was it different from Saigon, I wondered. Saigon has no interstates, no electronics plants, no U-Hauls (where everybody hauls), no skyscrapers, no malls. They slept in the back seat, flung together like a family of cats, as light, as silent, as unknowable. In my mind I watched them coming north to me.

I stayed home from their arrival because my daughter had driven her bike into a tree—arm broken in two places—and was not ready, a day later, to be abandoned. An obsessive, I sat at the window near midnight looking out to the deserted Vermont road, thinking, Some children are lucky enough to break their bones at play, to be abandoned by their mothers for only a few hours, to sit on a gigantic patchwork pillow and watch color television for a cure, eating Rocky Road with a spoon in their bad hand. I thought Mandy a spoiled, rich, protected, uninteresting child. This was not fair but I thought it anyway.

The young minister is in charge of settling our immigrants. He has convinced me to join his group of samaritans: I have the room, the time, the temperament, he says, of a teacher. I have no way to defend myself against the facts or the flattery.

Around one o'clock his car draws into the false dawn of the porch light; he leaps from it as if it were burning. The Phongs are the eighth family he has retrieved from the International Arrivals gate, why is he afraid of them? (Most have moved away to places like Houston and Tucson in search of steamy weather. Vermont is not the tropics.) He loads my empty hands with reassurances of their health, their charm, their gratitude. "Everything will be okay," he says, smiling the strange smile he has that runs nearly perpendicular to his nose: is it irony, a tiny premature stroke? I know his father; actually it runs in the family.

Inside the car there are many dark heads. It looks like a circus car when they unfold and come shyly forward. Quan comes first, man of the family, hitching up his loose pants with his elbows. Later when I remember his arrival, I'll imagine his pants held up by a piece of rope. It turns out to be true, it is his belt of choice. I don't know why. His face is indistinct to me—dark, smiling upwards into the lamplight, a wide mouth showing all its slightly convex teeth, yet somehow deeply turned away, as if he were here against his deepest will. Unlike the rope belt, this will turn out to be untrue.

His wife, Anh, follows, bent shepherding the children, who straggle along groggy from car-sleep. She is very young-looking, at least from here, and exceedingly pregnant, though the blue dress she wears makes no accommodations for her state. She looks uncomfortable. I am surprised the plane would have her. Her stomach is perfectly round, like a melon with a smooth blue skin. There is a lot of chatter between them, where the voice goes lightly up and down to hit its "tones" and change the meaning—what sounds like the voice out of control is actually profoundly under control, at home in a language of shades and levels. Right now in the half-dark, it seems to me she's yodeling.

At the door we make a lot of eager noises at each other. I gesture them in. Then—I am making it sound more portentous than it should have been but I do nothing lightly—we are a little knot of strangers standing in a brightly lit tweed living room (long thin paintings on the wall busy with the brushstrokes of another, more famous, Oriental civilization) with nothing easy enough to say without language. The little girl begins to circle her mother's skirts and cry, I try to pick her up, she doesn't want to come but a word from her mother cautions her, I would guess, not to kick me. So I am for the first time holding Truc, who will later come to know me as the lady who brings chocolate (which her mother doesn't believe in, with an almost superstitious mistrust, and which therefore appears to be twice as sweet to Truc; adolescent and four-year-old rebellion have a lot in common).

They are going to stay with us about a week. There is a lot I wish I could explain to them: that my children are asleep, that my husband, who builds houses, hospitals, schools, all kinds of buildings both useful and useless, is at the moment away on a sailboat whose crew includes a woman or two but never his wife. Oh, oh, Quan would say, if he could, or maybe Anh, you should have gone, we hope you did not wait for us. No, no, I would assure them: I get seasick, I get hot and cold and queasy, I stay at home to straighten up the closets, repaint the kitchen, my husband thrives on the company of other men's women, likes to be trapped with them in a tiny space where every time they pass, nearly touching, the golden hairs on their arms stand up helplessly.

The irony does not escape me, in fact I indulge it, roll it around in my mouth as if it were warm and liquid, that the Phongs were boat people, whose tiny hairs, if indeed they had any on their smooth dark arms, would never have risen in passionate anticipation at the passing of a fellow boat-person of the opposite sex. They were looking only for water, for food, for space to sleep in, they were trying to keep their children from falling over the side. Their boats were laden with the dead; every day, even, sadly, the last, someone surrendered to the lack of some vital element and was tipped over the edge into the bottomless dark. My husband at this moment is eating a good double Gloucester on low-cal crackers, and drinking a fruity white wine. (Oh no, he isn't, I had to admit; he was probably asleep.) One way or the other, this is a juxtaposition so obvious it should shame me, but it is real, not forced, and it makes me sick. I have not found subtlety particularly useful in the last few years.

Anh and I go to the kitchen because I have convincingly pantomimed "Something to drink?" I comment, with my eyes alone, on her neat globular stomach, she taps it like the melon it resembles, giggles, asks by raising eyebrows and gesturing around her into the empty air if I have children. I hold up three fingers. Sleeping. I lay my head on my hands and close my eyes. Ah, she says, and it could

169

be English. She approves; we can be friends. "Three," I say. "Fee," she echoes, and bends her head toward her stomach as if to repeat it to her baby. "Fee."

I have made up beds for them in the two guest rooms, parents in one, children in the other, thinking they might like a bit of privacy after months of the forced emergency-shelter life of the resettlement camp. Chattering away with impunity—having a secret language is a little like staring at a blind man, you cannot offend him—they let me settle them in. They are docile, exhausted, perhaps grateful, perhaps not. There is no way I can tell them they are going to their own apartment in a few days, when they feel ready, when they've adjusted a bit, learned a few necessary things. I hope someone down the line who speaks Vietnamese has discussed this; frankly I doubt it. I put my own head down on my pillow trying to imagine myself wholly passive, my life, my family's life entirely in the hands of, say, Quan and Anh in Saigon. I try to imagine Walt delivering himself up without force, without language. His broad shoulders, long back, small brainy head full of particulars—dimensions, symmetries, materials, vectors of force on load-bearing walls—all useless, taking up unnecessary space: he is about to become a night watchman, a broom pusher in a large factory in a country across more than one ocean. Would he hold his shoulders the same way, like a doctor about to begin an operation, or a general about to launch an attack? What would he do about not knowing how to look humble? Opinions and survival are not related: one is a luxury sport that would be left behind with the egg cups, the recliner in the den, the sailboat, and the cooler—abandoned, cut loose. We too would be very light, unballasted, without our taste, our petty choices. We would float away until we could be safely tethered by new possessions, given us by charitable strangers: a wok? a cleaver? a pallet for the floor?

In the morning all the Phongs are in one bed, heaped in the middle like kids struck quiet in the middle of their horse play. They sleep, unmoving, till close to noon, then rise and gently decline breakfast because it is not rice. I make a pot of white rice for them, the first of many. Somehow it fails to be quite satisfactory. I point to Anh and say, "You, you do it next time." She laughs. I turn on the water, shake the box at her, offer it, repeating, "You. Anh. You."

"You," she says, and takes the box tentatively, looking it over as if it might announce itself in a recognizable tongue. On the back there are pictures of pots and measuring cups that she finds immensely funny. "Fi shaw?" she inquires, still laughing. "Fi shaw? Li?" She shakes her very small hand over the unsatisfactory rice. It turns out (it takes me days to discover) that it is fish sauce she is looking for, for the rice, for everything: fish sauce must be Vietnam's major product. This is only the first of the failures of America. Later I will hear, as their vocabulary thickens, still missing its final consonants, a litany of our material inadequacies. At this moment, sitting over a rejected plate of toast, piled between the jam jars and the assorted cheeses, I am closer to tears than they are (though the six-year-old, Thanh, is sniffling perilously, hungry and uncomfortable in the tight new jeans issued him when he left the resettlement camp). I want to go away where no one needs me, where I have to love no one, where there is neither failure nor success at anything.

In the next room Miranda, my oldest daughter, the one with her arm in plaster already strewn with inked daisies and signatures, has stopped trying to keep order. Judy, also mine, is ungraciously pulling at a toy that Truc has dared to pick up. Truc, her bangs as cute as every Oriental girl's, her eyes like dark nuts, has a serious, even a ferocious, grip. When I come back from separating them from their toy, which I discover you can do without much moralizing speech, Anh is quietly weeping over a plateful of cold gummy rice. She raises her head and smiles at me. Her teeth are perfect, one at the side is slightly crooked but in general they are like the teeth of certain horsy WASP girls, stony, large, glowing blue-white with interior health in the face of every reverse. She smiles and weeps, weeps and smiles: sun on a rainy day. The smile is polite, meant to acquit me of blame. I envy her her legitimate cause—that her tears originate in the actions of governments, dictators, liberators, national destinies. Mine are personal, and craven. I shrug and heave the rice down the disposal. Where do we go from here?

Where we go, unexpectedly, is that I fall in love with her husband. I understand this entirely as a phenomenon: let us separate the fact that my marriage, my long association with Walter Baxt, my abject disappointment at his habits and his attitude toward me, have annihilated my self-esteem, etc., etc., from my respect for my intelligence, which I know to be sufficient for most purposes. I am smart enough to understand, for example, that an angry, emotionally neglected woman will—may—attach herself to any male who happens to fall within her line of vision, even like the Beast whom Beauty's father promises the first creature his eye might happen on. But Quan was unlikely, even so. I ought, by rights, to have wanted the minister who brought him to me, it would have been simpler. But, aside from the fact that he was ten years younger than I, and blonde and heavy in a way I could never have liked, I think the minister does not much fancy women. This is unfounded speculation, intuitive. The fact is I like to think of everyone suffering a secret it would ruin him to make public. This makes every encounter interesting.

Approve or not, it was Quan. The day I settled them in their apartment, led them wide-eyed from living room to bedroom to bath, I saw him for the first time as something other than a toy, appealing and amusing as a child in his incompetence. There was always a lot of tsk-tsking and condescending laughter, not meant to be cruel, among those of us who sponsored these international orphans. It reminded me of the mocking, genially tolerant way my friends who worked in hospitals and mental institutions dealt with the absurdities of their patients' demands and refusals. ("You'll never guess what Maisie did today.") When Anh threw out a loaf of white bread because it had gotten soft, or when Quan put fish sauce on his strawberries, we shook our heads and pushed back our amusement. These little people were littler than we really wanted them to be. They needed some context of their own in which to regain their size, like some dehydrated substance, shrunk for shipping, that plumps up again in water.

But this morning I touched Quan on the arm accidentally when I was showing him the bedroom, and recoiled like a twelve-year-old in the presence of a crush. Pinky Tice and John Logan, two good church-going souls, one underweight, one over, had laboriously moved a slightly ragged donated queen-sized mattress into the center of the floor and left it covered with a sprigged sheet. I figured, having seen the Phongs in a single bed at my house, that they wouldn't want the children out of their sight, that they'd end up together in that bed again. But I watched Quan stop to look at it a long time—the first time I saw him drift away from his family, their needs, their high-pitched nattering noise. What was he thinking? What did he see? I knew what my husband would imagine if he stopped to study a bed before climbing into it. (He wasn't entitled to his midlife crisis yet, it was ten years premature, but he was already a fool for young beauty as if it were all nostalgia and the beginnings of loss.)

But what would Quan dream of? Anh seemed very shy to me, the kind of girl/woman who undresses behind a screen, or not at all. Perhaps that would make a woman endlessly, virginally appealing? Maybe as he stood there he was simply remembering her before there arrived a roomful of children. Or he was thinking that it was better than a cot: now he might get a good night's sleep. He was a slight man, his pelvis tipped slightly back, his elbows pointed behind him, hands reversed on his hips as he stared out at the empty room. His face had two modes: a heavy impassivity, everything withdrawn, the eyes distant, perhaps cruel, perhaps merely waiting; and a wonderful sparking animation in which his eyes narrowed and his cheeks took on an autumn color. He had a sudden laugh, its own syllable, as quickly silenced as a bark. Somewhere in the large range between the two, which were really moods, Quan's natural temperament seemed to lie waiting for a natural life to present him with occasion.

Shamelessly now I stood beside him thinking how gentle such a man's hands would be, how he would delight in modesty, how he would never betray his wife in all her gaiety and confusion. (It had been while I walked around heavy with Judy, and not particularly receptive, that Walt found his first alternative to a wife. She was the nurse who helped me deliver Judy, in fact, a very nice woman who prodded and eased and then wiped me up. This is a small town. I thought that was obscene to the point of kinkiness, though he never understood.) After all these years with my husband, who was a star linebacker in college, and dean's list, too, the fact that Quan had a smooth sunken chest and narrow shoulders, an absence of hips—the frailness of an adolescent—was, in its way, seductive, a mystery. He posed questions I would have loved to hear answered: how could his potency have lain coiled so invisibly? If I narrowed my eyes to see it, there was force in his wiriness, intensity in the sudden crack of his laugh. There in his boy-sized clothes, he was no child.

That I would allow myself to think of Quan romantically was not so much absurd as it was somehow demeaning to him, but I'm not sure why. Was it that his suffering—the death of so many of his family, the brutality he had seen, the horrors of his escape, his crossing—disqualified him from being a sexual object? How unfair, then, how doubly wounding! I was prepared to be outraged on his behalf. Or maybe it was exactly the opposite—I had no preference. I suspected that his history was, in fact, what made him attractive: that he was a survivor, one of those exotics, a black swan. The odds on his escape were like a number on his arm. Then how gruesome, I told myself, and how purifying after all my years with Walter's wine collection, his thin-soled Italian shoes, his aesthetic imperatives—travertine marble for the lobby is old-hat, we need a long thin window in this wall for better ventilation, let's have a semicircular fanlight over the door in the Georgian style. I was appalled at myself, but I understood. I think that's what I wanted, censure and self-disgust. But I forgave it.

I'd have been in their house daily even if I weren't drawn there by Quan. For one thing they needed English lessons. I used to teach but it's been years since I've set foot in a classroom; I abdicated, gladly, I recall, for my own little brood, and Walter gets very unaccommodating whenever I murmur about going back. But this I would be good at— I went with a set of kindergarten-style cards and helped them get their loose-voweled mouths around "kitchen," "stove," "over" and "under," "store," and "hungry." Anh hung back, giggling, not trusting herself; Quan leaped into language and sank and got angry at himself, at his wife, even at me. Bad speech came easy, approximate globs of syllables they flung at their subjects, and missed by a mile. (Both of them reduced my name, Lucy, to a soup in which the consonants had been thoroughly pureed, though the vowels were enormously complicated, inflected lovingly, as I had never dreamed them. "Oo-ee" is more or less what I became, as if I were always to be summoned by an exclamation of wonder.)

One morning while I was still in bed I picked up the phone on one ring and heard an urgent babble I had to fight through like a dream. I thought it was a mental defective, one of the retarded kids who live in the shelter downtown. It was Quan, asking me when he could take the driver's test, when he could buy a car. He had just the day before begun his job sweeping at the clothespin factory, at minimum wage. I told him to wait, to be a little patient, I tried to make clear that if he'd like I would teach him English from the driver's manual (though I remember thinking, English? That poison? Motor Vehiclese is a distantly related *patois*). Walter was already up and out.

I hung up and closed my eyes and saw Quan looking down at me, my plump American breasts splaying out under his hands, saw my hands tight on his dark narrow shoulders, the bottomless eyes above his high flat cheekbones trying to find a word, nasty and sweet and pronounceable, for what we would be doing. Who, I wondered, is the missionary in this position?

There were others to help out with this project, of course, meetings at which we discussed their progress, and that of the huge family of Cambodians, the Tetashrivathlongs, who had come to live in the next town over the mountain. (The Phongs had barely begun their family compared to the "Tets.") Somebody suggested we add birth control to our teaching; somebody else thought it might be offensive to their beliefs. Some of us were relativists, some absolutists when it came to mores. All of us were fairly ignorant of who and what we were dealing with, and no two cultures were alike in any case. No one had time to research in depth the places our charges had come from. We had some guidelines, too vague to be useful, we had dictionaries for when the going got rough, and a phone number for emergencies. But we were playing by ear, with our own raucous domestic melodies in our ears.

Just before Labor Day, the church gathered the Phongs and the Tets and a few other Asian families from not-so-distant towns to the social hall one Sunday for a dinner. We wanted them to meet each other, we wanted, I suppose, to celebrate our own charity. They were all dressed up for the occasion. Anh wore a pair of pink and blue cotton pajamas that had been in a batch of contributions that came in a big plastic bag. Probably she thought the bodiless fabric a bit bizarre, but surely the Americans had finally found the appropriate style for her. The children were adorable, Thanh in jeans, Truc, who was very tiny, in a lavender baby jacket over a long white nylon dress that must have been someone's confirmation outfit; her age seemed to quiver like a barometric needle somewhere between one year and eight.

As for Quan, oh Quan, I had to look at him a long time before I comprehended what he had done, confidently, as usual, without submitting to the quenching effects of advice. Hardy's, the downtown department store, had donated winter jackets for all the Phongs, smart blue-and-green ski parkas to offset their first Vermont winter. Quan, I surmised, had been cold already—even high summer in New England is cold when you come from Saigon, that sauna—so he had cut the sleeves out of the parka, leaving a sort of jagged-edged vest, with batting peeking out like marshmallow fluff, that he wore zipped to the chin indoors.

I took Walter to meet him and watched them join and unjoin their so dissimilar hands. After a mumbled greeting, Walter had nothing to say. I tried to pretend he had picked up suspicious vibrations, that he was jealous and would not talk to Quan, but in fact he very simply had nothing to say. Though he never quite admitted it, I know he thought intercultural rescue efforts were ladies' work and their recipients wimps, the runts in some divinely ranked moral litter. So he had no desire to be here, where we (male and female) ladies of the town were beginning to strip plastic wrap off potato salad and oohing gratefully over the chicken wings some generous soul had sent as an alternative to The Starches. "Where's the fish sauce?" somebody asked, laughing, but it was no joke: poor Anh, poor all of them, confronting yet again the massive loneliness that must have sprung up out of the steaming casseroles, the trays of just-sliced homemade alien bread, the pickles. Maybe there are Vietnamese pickles, I understand they eat a lot of salads, but I am fairly confident there is no Vietnamese egg salad.

Walter smiled a lot, looking strained, shook the proferred hands of all the darker adults in the room, grimly, as if they were on the receiving line at a funeral, and escaped. He had a lot of wood to split; winter was coming. The children whooped around like any children anywhere, my Tony and Judy and Miranda in her grimy arm cast among them, and squabbled over hot wheels and corn poppers, while their parents who had nothing in common except the generally Eastern provenance of their origins, stood shoulder to shoulder and smiled as if they were under the gun. Seroi Tetashrivathlong had been a scholar of some kind—not languages, surely, but of something revered in his homeland and lost over the ocean. He did not appear to be particularly interested in speaking to one of the Cambodians from Montpelier who, as far as we could follow, had farmed in the mountains. Similarly, one of the Vietnamese families had two male mechanics in it, good at fixing motors of any kind—cars, blenders. The younger one, who looked thoroughly American in dress and demeanor, had enough English to tell me he could deal with "all small devices."

Quan had been a sign painter ("no goo' "), a collector of scrap metals on the side, and, most important, a musician, a singer of native music of some small renown. He performed; he was appreciated; I don't know if he was famous, that was too fine a distinction to survive our blighted communication. The other Vietnamese family was from Quo Nongh province and Anh and Quan were big-city, not medium-sized city, people: Freud speaks somewhere of "the narcissism of small differences." They would find nothing to say to each other. The young minister, who could, out of Christian devotion, find something in common with an Eskimo, was staggered by what he kept calling, obtusely, "ingratitude." But gratitude, I thought, was a terrible hunch in which to have to stand for more than a few minutes. Survival was their right. We hadn't brought them here to be grateful to anyone for anything.

Someone asked Quan to sing. He pantomimed a long, rather intricate action which I think explained how he had left his instrument behind. Imagine it, whatever it was, wood, I suppose, some bulbous carefully shaped, delicate viol, like an extra child to be protected in flight, in a boat at sea, in his foot-locker at the resettlement camp— it had been abandoned, he was sorry, he was apologizing. He spread his hands to indicate the inadequacy of what was left.

But he sang anyway. His voice took on a wholly different quality from the sound he was grappling with for English. Full of glottal and more improbably situated stops, it seemed to emerge from a part of the body that was all sunken pits and sharp rises and declivities, all in a mournful scale that lived unheard between the notes of ours. He was, of course, a far larger man when he sang, not exactly a glamorous character but no pathetic waif either. I had discerned something real in him, I was relieved to see, besides vulnerability. There was no way for me even to approach the abyss beyond which he sang in a purposely quavering voice: whether he sang well or not would have been, for me, like telling you if a bird flew well, some bird I'd never seen before. But he had a calm authority I could appreciate, and a painfully faraway look in his eyes. Once in a while he closed them and vanished from our presence. I was humiliated to be using him as a fantasy, surely that was an exploitation he didn't deserve. But we

are all exploited, I decided, looking around the room at the couples
about some of whom I knew more than I should, each animal gulping
down the next smallest in the chain. Who, I had to wonder, watch-
ing Quan bowing deferentially to his applause, smiling abashed and
proud, was having Walter on a plate, whom Walter was not in turn
having himself? I didn't know who but I surely hoped someone was
doing it, sharp teeth, sharp claws, and no apology.

I wasn't sure how I could get my message to Quan. His music was
so alien, perhaps flirtation proceded by different rules as well.

He was hellbent on being American now. I sensed a split between
husband and wife on the subject of loyalty to their origins. Quan
had developed every taste he could see was indigenous: for hot dogs,
"Dallas," jeans; he had begun to dream, aloud, of a motorcycle. He
borrowed the minister's guitar—it said GOD LOVES MUSIC in decals
on the front, a recommendation considered useful for Youth Fellow-
ship—and, lowering his head, tried to hear the sort of chords that
wanted to come out of it. Anh, on the other hand, had gathered
around her every Vietnamese cooking ingredient we could find for
her in Boston; she stared at them all, and sang to herself that mysteri-
ous music, her hands around her stomach as if they were circling the
globe, feeling for the South China Sea. I remembered watching her
walking with her children along the river road one morning, pick-
ing devil's paintbrushes and daisies, moving very slowly, smoothly,
like the women I had seen in photographs threshing the rice paddies,
their broad hats caught between their shoulders, nearly motionless.

The speed of Quan's defection, I'll admit, was a little disappoint-
ing. Had he no past, no inner life to protect? Perhaps it was encap-
sulated, safe, and he had accepted one reality unsentimentally and
gone on to another one. One day I knocked on their door and when
no one answered, hearing noisy music, I rattled the knob and went in.
Quan, in his saggy donated underwear, was dancing, elbows sharp,
pelvis twitching in perfect teenage American style, to the television
set. He had a long purple scar across his lower back. "Oh, we do
this Sai-gon!" he called out merrily. "No new this. I knowing this
far—far back, time!" Of course he had. Saigon was not so pure as
I pretended, these were no Montagnards. Anh had not spun flax all
those years, she had sold watches, cameras, God knows what illegally
gotten goods, to God knows whom, under I couldn't dare imagine

what circumstances. Her innocence was only conjectural, a reverse prejudice on my part. Still, she was sitting huddled in a big maroon University-of-Louisville sweatshirt in which she looked like her own child, staring at Quan angrily as if he were trying to humiliate her.

I think she couldn't wait for that baby to come free so that she could occupy herself with an enterprise entirely her own, unsullied, intimate. We had taken her to see the hospital, the delivery room, the whole foreign set-up, so that it wouldn't frighten her when the time came. She had nodded, smiled, yielded nothing. I had no idea if she'd ever seen a hospital, let alone been in one. About Truc and Thanh she had given inconclusive testimony: hospital yes, hospital no. Maybe it was one of each kind of birth. She looked indifferent to the question. She had a long scar down one cheek, far more delicate than Quan's, that must have been stitched; it was like a pencil mark all the way along her slender neck. She would say nothing, politely. She gave us her sign for "How very nice," a sort of tsk-tsk with the teeth, and thanked us. I'll bet she went home and talked to her stomach; I'll bet she begged the baby's forgiveness.

Here's what I did about Quan. A very sweet retired man had been giving him driving lessons; they were going well. One day the man couldn't take him for his hour, so, my kids off to school and play group, I took him myself. He drove along the highway too fast, smiling broadly, then swung abruptly, at my suggestion, down one of the shady one-and-a-half lanes on which, I pleaded with him, one had to reduce one's speed. We hurried along under the trees, through which the sun smacked us like a strobe light, the radio blaring away, Quan humming vaguely his newly discovered cadences. "Slow down," I implored, "Quan, please take it easy." And finally I said, "Why don't you stop over there?" and pointed to a little turn-out into the woods where the hunters must park their cars to go into the bush. "I want to talk to you."

I had no idea how he might react if I made an inviting move, I had never in my life done what I was doing now; even my husband does all the inviting in our own bed. I put my hand on his arm and looked at him as insinuatingly, as shamelessly as I could without feeling too stupid. How did Walter do this without simpering? (I suppose women expect it of men and that gives the come-on something like dignity.) Quan cocked his head to one side quizzically.

"In America," I began. He smiled, that automatic polite smile that covers every social hesitation, still bewildered, so I leaned forward until my face was right there, ready to be kissed.

"In America?" he asked, rather gaily I thought, and obligingly kissed me, lightly, without flavor, without lust. "All right you here?" he asked me unintelligibly, and put his hand on my breast. I felt how white and assertive it was under his palm, another pushy American presence to be accommodated in his life, a wonder like baseball and Carvel and "Hollywood Squares." He didn't move his hand, which felt hollow, like *papier maché*. He was trying to read my expression for a go-ahead, I suppose, for permission that said "This is your next lesson in Being Here."

"Next time," I told him then, having learned what I needed to about his adaptability. Now I'd have to go home and discuss the rest of the course with myself to see if I meant it. "Tomorrow maybe," I said, and nodded praise.

He shrugged, started the car, smiling slightly, but before he took it out of neutral he seized my hand and put it for just a few seconds in his lap. "Goo' teacher," he whispered and pressed it there so I could see that I had achieved—he had achieved—the required response. "I study—hard." His first English pun. He laughed, I laughed, and he had the car at sixty in an instant.

I decided to stop just this side of humiliation. And I hated to give Walter the satisfaction by default—even if he didn't know about it—of having driven me to this.

For another thing, Anh had her baby. She went into labor a few days after my reconnaissance mission and, terrified by everything in the hospital as though we had never taken her there to reconnoitre, she lay bathed in tears the entire length of her stay. She said something about missing her mother; I didn't blame her. She had produced a perfect tiny girl, to be called Sue-Mei, which Quan promised would soon be simply Sue, the first American in the family, and whom Anh called Mei and, spraying her with tears, could not hold enough. The nurses took her from her mother only when Anh surrendered to exhaustion and slept.

Quan called me aside in the hospital corridor on the second day. "I surprise Anh," he said, more or less. "I my driving license, I come for her, for Sue me alone. We go car." So in his much-used, ugly, bashed-up new car I took him for his license, which he got from an officer so stupefied by his incapacity to understand Quan that I think he'd have passed him if he'd driven up a tree. Quan moved his finger across every word of every answer of the written test, letting the words crawl up his fingers like ants until he felt them bite.

He came out holding the license more proudly than he had held his baby. "You me cerebrate," he announced, and I fought back the old condescension to the clown that displacement could make out of the most dignified of men. (Was Quan dignified? I will never know.) He sped us off in the direction of the woods, singing "I Heard It On the Grapevine" and patting me chummily on the knee. I had been the agency of his admission to America in so many ways, I could feel his pride and gratitude roiling under his skin.

"No, Quan, we can't do this," I began. "I'm sorry."

But he had the license and the wheel. This time, unbidden, he pulled the car deep into the woods, under a roof of leaves. He had worked this out in his head, alone at home—or surrounded by his children but free of Anh: that he could celebrate this arrival with me, the first long step out of his past, all that loss, that old rending pain. The motor still racing, he kissed me without preliminaries, a very long kiss in the international language, a real, not a dutiful kiss, in which I tried not to acquiesce. He was following the lesson plan of the last time, moving to my breasts, which he uncovered and almost violently bent to look at, blinking, as if he had to learn the differences between the familiar ones at home and the kind they have over here.

All right, one look. I turned off the motor but I stopped him there. I was so full of apology he finally apologized for me, graciously. But then just as I thought we were past it, that he had understood, he reached out to my breasts again, first one, then the other, equal time, trying but failing to say "Beautiful!" When he held them high and kissed them I thought of nursing—I always do, once you have done that you have returned your breasts to their real reason for being, and the sadness of that lost time swells like a heavy wave. (Could Walter know that? Could that be our problem?) So I was distracted. Then I remembered Anh alone in her hospital bed clutching her baby tight every time a nurse walked by. She kept nursing and nursing, they told me, even without milk, so that they wouldn't try to take the baby from her. Again, I tried to wrestle myself away. I tried to apologize for being a tease. It was hard without the words, which are abstract.

"You no show me?" Quan asked simply, holding out his empty hands. "I learn American. After, I go show Anh."

I laughed a little bitterly. I asked him, probably sarcastically, though he couldn't have known that, if he really thought he needed lessons. I kept my hand on his bony arm so he wouldn't think I was angry.

Oh, they had met and married so young, he told me. She was a child, hardly finished growing, and sex embarrassed her. She believed in darkness, stillness, silence. He watched the servicemen, watched how the prostitutes acted with them, though he would never have gone to one. He assumed it was different here, every part of it different: light, movement, noise. Somehow he managed to say these things. Maybe he didn't. I thought he said them.

"It isn't better here," I told him. Somebody had to defend Saigon. "It doesn't mean so much. It stops mattering." We could all use a little forbidding, Walter first, and now me. Good.

"And chi-ren," he added, "always Truc, Thanh, same room with us, they bad see." He stared at my treasonous breasts like a virgin. His eyes were pained, he gave a little moan that seemed to me to come precisely from the center of his music, frail, in an unfamiliar minor key, and lowered his head to them again with the greatest dignity, unguarded, grateful. "Please you do," he murmured into them.

Walter, I thought when I felt the grip of his mouth, firm as a baby's, on my nipple. That nurse ought to have stopped you if you couldn't stop yourself. It's an old story, the loneliness of men whose wives are involved in giving birth: they can't be ignored for a minute. Jealousy it was, not only hunger. They're jealous of her other love, her new love, they don't want to be alone. Walter will learn to be alone, I thought dizzily, barely able to call up his face. I'll give him lessons.

But I breathed in hard enough to hurt. I couldn't do it. Betraying Walter would have been a cinch, and God knows I was hollow to the core with simple longing. But Anh, it was not sentimental to remember her, Anh was the one I could not betray or subtract from, even if she never felt the loss. The problem with morality, I can say now that the fog of lust has dissipated, is that so many of the calculations

of loss and gain are secret: you're alone with the choices, the renun-
ciations, all of it, like fidelity to God that nobody really sees. You
keep the accounts with yourself. "It isn't fair to Anh," I whispered.

"You show me, I show her, no tell. Three mother—three baby—
time now." Time to be immodest? Wicked? Time to share, as they
say in kindergarten? His eyes teared; he closed them. "What mean
it, 'fair'?"

I had taught him everything I could about kitchens, supermar-
kets, plural nouns; had tried to tell him about winter in Vermont,
which he refused to believe, about basketball, libraries, income tax,
innoculations. But when I remembered this scene was all my doing,
I saw I had been carried away by the versatility of the good teacher,
the undreamed-of dimensions of welcome.

"'Fair' means Anh is my friend," I said reluctantly, and coaxed
his head up so I could look into his face, which was bewildered, on
the edge of anger.

Again he promised not to tell. But I apologized for ever having
begun. "'Fair' means you and Anh—" and I held my fingers close
together emphatically, the way we say of friends or politicians,
"They're like *that*!"

Whereby I cleaned up one outstanding debt I had had to myself
since the time Judy was born: I proved to myself that some things
are within your control, others are not; let each of us keep count and
not shoulder more blame than we deserve.

"Anh friend you," my student Quan said petulantly, and tucked
his shirt into his roped-up waist, poking his fingers violently into his
pants. "You no friend me."

What I had done, he meant, leaving him foolish on this brink, was
a sin in any language. I wasn't going to argue. I apologized again
and patted the shirt pocket that held his license. It made a little rus-
tling sound under my knuckles. "Anh will be happy," I said. And
we drove toward town in silence, listening to the textures under the
tires: pebbles, blacktop, hard concrete.

Re: *Femme*

Senator Joseph L. Tender
2366 R St., N.W.
Washington, D.C.

Dear Senator:

I hope you will forgive me for this intrusion into both your time and your privacy. We at *Femme* magazine are attempting, in this first year of a new decade, to construct a new image for the young woman who reads our pages. We will continue, of course, to present the fashions she must have to put her best foot forward, and many of the features that will help her to create what we like to call her "special ambience" (makeup and hairdo hints, menu and entertaining ideas, furnishing tips, and so on). I enumerate only because a man who is familiar with the *Congressional Record* may not have had the occasion to flip through our pages recently! (Your hairdresser undoubtedly provides *Playboy?*)

In addition to these features and the outstanding fiction we have always showcased, we are expanding our articles department with a sharp eye on where today's woman has come from and where she is going. We will print the most penetrating analysis we can, from all corners, in our effort to paint *Femme*'s realistic full-length portrait of the American Woman of the Seventies. We are working now on a double issue for early next year, a very exciting one we think, to be called "Beyond Liberation." And this is where (we hope) you come in.

We are putting together a collection of short vignettes, by their husbands, of women we consider to be gracefully "liberated." With all the hostilities generated by the rhetoric and militancy of many of today's girls (yes, we do have quite a few right here in our ranks, and they call us counterrevolutionary, but we are trying to do something about that!) we would like to publish tributes from men whose wives are still charming, still loving partners in marriage, who are probably still, if you'll pardon the candor, wearing their bras, but who have either their own careers or an irreplaceable part in their husbands' careers. Women like your wife. We think our readers would be interested to learn from a famous man of politics how his wife feels about the limelight she lives in, the duties she fulfills as an official hostess, the things she does with her spare time, and how she stays as lovely as she is in her pictures.

We are trying for pieces of about 2,000 to 2,500 words, to be paid for at our standard rate (see enclosed). Deadline, say, September 15. (Perhaps a member of your staff could prepare the copy from your notes. We certainly wouldn't object!)

Thank you, Senator, for your time. I do hope you will agree to join the distinguished contributors to the new *Femme*.

Sincerely,
(Mrs.) Harriette Moritze
Editor-in-Chief

Mrs. Harriette Moritze, Editor
Femme
230 Madison Avenue
New York, N.Y.

Dear Mrs. Moritze:

Thank you for your letter of July 9. I am sending two articles to you, per your request, written, thank you, without the assistance of my staff, who have more pressing matters to attend to. Perhaps I should send the first of these to your office address and the other to your home, on the theory that just as we senators do have our private lives, ostensibly conducted at our homes, so do you editors have yours outside the halls of business. And to that life the second of the enclosed may speak; surely not to your corporate half-life?

In any event, even for the delectation of your staff, if the second response should fall into their Arpèged hands, I send both to your editorial offices to challenge your promise of candor. The American Woman Exposed? The true woman, e.g., my helpmeet? I suggest you publish my words as a foldout à la *Playboy*. Hair and nipples would demand less bravery: the whole woman has them and more. I hereby throw down my gauntlet. Please do (at your standard rate) pick it up.

Yours,
Joseph L. Tender
United States Senate

I. CLOSE-UP: A SENATE WIFE

The last time I had the occasion to thank my wife, Meg, publicly was on the victory stand two years ago where, in the flash of spotlights and popping bulbs I felt as if I were standing drenched in a hot shower, while she was as always cool, glowing, and absolutely calm. No one, anyway, listens to those routine-sounding acknowledgments. But now, presuming a willingly, charmingly captive audience, I can broadcast the secret that being a senator's wife is not as sweet or as simple as it might appear at those well-lit moments.

My Meg:

—waits dinner for me six nights out of seven. She eats with our sons (aged fourteen and seventeen) when they are home from school, but otherwise dines alone, doubtless cursing the caucuses and study groups and other official playground business that keeps me. We employ a cook only for formal dinners; otherwise Meg is alone with her *Joy of Cooking*. (She does enjoy it and the kitchen is a little United Nations. Her favorite dishes are Korean, German, Greek, and Mexican. Her chicken mole is the equal of anything I've had across the border.)

—reads at least three books a week, nonfiction generally. She tells me she has enjoyed *The Naked Ape* recently, *The Greening of America* (which our older son sent to her), and (this has me worried) *Sexual Politics*. Also the historical novels of Cecelia Holland.

—is the best backup secretary no one could ever hire for a price. If she is unsalaried, she knows she is indispensable (worth how much a week?) as witness the time she answered a call that turned out to be a threat on my life, cleverly pieced together a few vague clues, alerted police and FBI, and finally helped them to apprehend a man insanely angry because (though I had tried) I could not obtain clemency for his son on Death Row. There was no reward for his apprehension but . . .

—has opinions on every major piece of legislation that crosses my desk and has never been known to mince words. I would describe

186

her as an intuitive liberal, hard-headed but basically a chance taker and a truster of people. About welfare she says: "I have never met a man who didn't want to work—provided the work was human." About education: "Our children must be taught to think no matter the subject, and to recognize authority alongside freedom. By 1984 our problems will be unrecognizable. Will a child in kindergarten this year be equipped to answer questions that don't yet exist?" About women: "Freedom, yes. But I pity the girl who forgets the first lesson, that the word 'woman' contains the word 'man.' That tells me a lot about what our significance should *naturally* be."

—has changed very little since we married after college nineteen years ago. She is, remarkably, more slender than the girl I married, and if her hair color is helped along a little—well, she has that in common with many of the men on Pennsylvania Avenue. I like to think she keeps herself alluring out of respect for both of us and the hundreds of thousands who had faith in us, both of us really, to represent their state and themselves. When she began to tire near the home stretch in our last campaign, she laughed and said, "I'd better iron out these circles under my eyes. You never know when people will begin to wonder if you beat your wife!"

—spends a good deal of time being attentive to little things. She is frankly in charge of those sweet spots that I could never get to while I'm attending to my somewhat more salty life. She enjoys sending gifts, flowers, cards for birthdays, a note here, a phone call there, often to constituents who have made special requests or written about problems. She feels that we do our work as a team, each with our traditional duties.

—once warned me, when she disagreed vigorously with an opinion of mine on domestic policy, "You'd better be careful in '72 or you'll turn around and find *me* running against you." So I'm pretty careful. It would be quite a contest.

II. CLOSE-UP: A "SENATE WIFE"

What would you Ladies Incorporated, pulse feelers of America, say about a woman who:

—calls you "Senator" in bed? (Knocks you to the floor, all sharp elbows under satiny skin, and thinks, "Dear me, I've pushed The Senator out of bed.")

—touching you, gets newsprint on her fingertips?

—poses for cameramen in the broom closet and looks for voyeurs in the bedroom window? Hoping.

—Ladies, what would you say if I told you I am jealous of my own name?

Which was still Joey when I met her. A college junior who shaved twice a week, up from hardscrabble Southwest farmland. My woolen slacks itched something unbearable because my skin was denim-cured. I spoke about like an out-of-tune guitar, thwanging behind the beat. But I did speak, plenty.

I haven't recovered yet from what it took to get Mary Margaret to notice me. I lied so hard, promising that I was worth one glance of her simply blue eyes, that I wound myself into a steel coil; then I let go and I'm flying still. Truly. (For which, perhaps, I owe her some thanks of one sort or another.) One night in the middle of a laugh I told her I was going to be a congressman, a senator, maybe a president. That meant noise, bands, microphones, speeches over the little gate at the rear of a train like the kind I'd seen as a kid on the Santa Fe tracks, and easy lies that sounded like careful calculations. I knew I was good at those—the whole elaborate pitch was a dazzler in the tradition of the campaign promise. I'm not sure I know more now what it does mean than I thought that night, pulling it like a lightning bug out of the dark air.

But she listened. Her whole sorority liked the idea. "*National* politics?" "Well, why not? Far as he can *go*. I guess." Like a trip, all you do is buy a ticket and be there on time. What happens to you along the way no one can promise. It was better than being quarterback on the Aggies with no prospects, like her previous boy friend. Who was my last competition: a fist, naked (as she never saw him, since everybody's grappling in those days took place in furtive corners of the Alpha Mu house), he must have had padding sewed under his skin. His head was a mess of cuts and numbers, still (permanently) preliterate. What if I had lost out to him?

I took her along. She had a bag of Southern girl's stuff. (If we ever went to court on it, which of us could prove entrapment?) Fancy Samsonite luggage: words in it that broke their vowels in two, but with no violence. A strange language to use for a weapon, it had no points, more a kind of sucking action that pulled you into a windy hollow. Breasts in it, with nipples that bit back. Leg spread that could snap closed and take a fellow's hand off, never mind what-all else, if she didn't have a mind to. In the bag—dresses that needed replacing whenever the air so much as hit them. A shovel to dig up every word or act you thought well buried. Bleach, kerosene, cleaning fluid: each used (only once, and not used exactly—selected for display), poured with a shaking hand into one of the goblets her grandma left us. "You Joe, you're pouring this down my throat!" when all the time she's bloody well doing the pouring but tempting me, tempting me . . . Goddamn! A life of high comedy. I wish I could be abject enough to aspire to all that again. I try to remember what it was like and it all runs together: did I dare consider running for senior class treasurer, did I dare dream of Mary Margaret? Such pure joy, such pure terror.

I'll tell you when our first son was conceived. When the votes were in from the last decisive northeast county (and I was smashed; she was never smashed). Mary Margaret whispered in my ear so my campaign staff wouldn't hear, and led the new state attorney general to her scented bed to see if it was different with an elected official. (It hadn't, you see, been so good with an appointed one. Let me not begrudge her the truth, however; it did get better.) By the time I made it to a national office, yes indeed, the girl had worked up some good limber exercises to demonstrate her pleasure. Ambition for ambition. If ever I declare for the Presidency and am found dead in my bed in the morning, you can tell the coroner it was her gratitude that did it.

Which means what? Let other people tell you what you need to know about your husband? Good God, what if their opinion really hinged on politics? If issues of tax structure, farm subsidies, SEATO, determined my election, what could she take for her cues? My real nature speaks a foreign language and her own emotions speak none at all. Then again, she and the electorate cannot ever fail each other in this life: both love something beside the point, that lives in newspapers and spot ads in election years, in gossip columns and gala state occasions. I'm not there when they look at me and they elect each other.

So it's a sort of psychic gang-bang for my lady Mary Mag—like fucking every voter in the state. My beloved wife, whose chastity when she brought it to me had been guarded in a gargoyle crouch by a many-brothered family of crack shots, a phony churchman of a father, sorority sisters with scissors between their teeth, and her own melting-eyed, strawberry-tongued, utterly icy control of her destiny—was she feeling a sexual tremor every time Luke Thompson or

Willie Mae Johnson X'd their ballot or threw that red lever back to get out of the voter's booth? Her quaint, wordy husband was putting it, putting something, on the line, but decently. They were saying "Yes, yes" out there in the sticks, and she throbbed with affirmation as if their approval had been an invitation to a trip to the bushes. What an orgy an election can be, if you're so inclined.

So you see, she *is* a devoted Senate wife. If she remains unconvinced about how worthy that dreamy Joey was without the crazy sword and buckler he concocted for her, she shared with him the hard-assed unrelenting side that made him the renowned and noble man you see before you today. Our public life, bless it, is every bit what it appears. Her most genuine smiles are For the Press, her concerns are duties shouldered graciously, the funds and charities and luncheons of dyed bread, inspired aspics in the shape of crippled children or recycled garbage. I can't ask what sort of life we'd have had if I hadn't taken that blind running jump onto this lurchy bandwagon: by definition, if she married me I would make it. It is her empyrean, she furnished it herself, my eyrie in the Sam Rayburn office building. All it lacks is a beam of light emanating from some mysterious source to play gently on her picture, our sons' pictures, in full but somber color on my desk. It sounds like a Greek curse, an arrangement of the Fates, or maybe the Calvinist dream: not that I didn't have to work my ass off to get here, but she seems to have been waiting here all the time, expecting me.

Is that what is meant by standing behind a man? It is a fine old virtue, then, more ancient than those poison goblets of her grandma. You do know, sheltered ladies, what some mild men get from behind.

The irony, you understand, is my own response to my wife's to-do about who I am, or who she is. (You wives do seem to enjoy meeting her every bit as much as you do me, though you pretend to be thrilled by my teeth, my six-inch cuffs, my airblown hairset. Taking my measure by taking hers? Your screwing by conduction?) She demonstrates nothing but an indifferent breeding and all the perspective of a lifelong hysteric and secret camp follower, but it's enough to put me in my place. A senator? A king? A damn fool elevated by vain ceremony to an exquisite subtle shame. I see her posturing in my name and ask, so that's what we look like from a distance? All the public irrelevancies magnified in her makeup mirror, the glossies and blowups to improve on my face, and the shopping bags bearing my name into the supermarkets. What in the hell: then a senator is an expensive presence, a personage created, chiefly by mirrors, for scaring the crows of the other party.

From a flat corn-covered dusty yellow square of earth comes a boy with a wife and her luggage. He holds the reins of a scrawny talent and she holds his two little balls in her lotioned hands. (Can this article have pertinent technicolor illustrations?) We are still riding, just so—you see, it has been nineteen years—and you must understand from that why Mrs. Senator Tender hasn't had a free hand for doing much more through the years. Beyond liberation, my good editors. We are both that, in our ways. We are that.

You may print this.

Inter-office
To: H.M.
From: Cathy Klein

Harriette, where to begin??! You (We?) have got a choice to make. This letter is symptomatic of what *Femme* should be dealing with. I know you don't approve of some of the things I'm into, along with a growing number of others around here. (Though, disapproval or no, I notice we're running a feature on "braless fashion" next month. Why don't we have a new department called "Co-optation"?) In fact, I have to admit to myself in fairness that I don't know how you really feel about some of the implications of what the mag. does. There are people with real and serious cases of tunnel vision and then there are those who find that a good show of tunnel vision is an asset to their work. So I don't know. But, whichever it is, you must stop and ask yourself: How do you feel letting the senator get his rocks off at the expense of women, in the name of his wife? It's all women, one way or another, that he's talking about. I.e., his own attitude that makes us exactly what we are and then gripes about it forever more. And with senatorial immunity. BMOC. I remember them. He knows he's got us, because to print this would be spitting into a high wind, and it's a safe guess that nobody in the *Femme* building would so endanger her makeup.

Here's the question in its most localized form: Do we print the routine advertisement for MY WIFE as Cook, Secretary, and General Directress of Ass-Wiping Operations (not to mention Ass-Kissing, the chief means thereof) or do we really intend to anatomize the situation that makes wives like his, and absolute strangers like ourselves, the victims of such contempt.

What will the honesty cost us, Harriette? A little discomfort with ourselves and our inconsistencies? I know, when it comes to this kind of thing, you have all the same domino-theory terrors of (pardon me) a segregationist: if they all sit in the same kindergarten class my grandchildren will have nappy hair. Only you say, if we try to tell the truth about wo/men, our grandchildren will be born from the mouths of test tubes. Well, you don't like my language either but even you were thinking BULLSHIT when you read that man's diatribe.

If you can admit that, then you are on your way to rethinking the whole "Beyond Liberation" issue. (I will leave your life out of this.) Let's for once take ourselves seriously as a magazine created by real people, not artifacts, for the women whose 75 cents we pocket, or who read us in 120° heat under the everlasting dryer they're spending their best years sitting under. Let us expose men like Joseph Tender and give their wives fresh ideals to pursue *by themselves*. Let us move toward new ends.

Or shall we hang a collar around the long curvy neck of our January cover girl that says what, who was it, Pope? (see, my English major wasn't wasted) suggested for the king's dog?

> I am my master's dog, at Kew.
> Pray tell me, m'am, whose dog are you?
> Cathy

FROM THE DESK OF:

Cathy. We all have problems reconciling ourselves to our images. Have you asked yourself recently why you go on working for *Femme*? I am, we are dedicated—unfashionable as it is becoming—to making girls into women and making women more desirable, yes, to our men and not ashamed of it. If that aim is so insidious, why do you continue your association w/ us? I hope there is more than a paycheck involved here.

By the way, what specifically do you suggest abt. this Tender business? What "choice" are you referring to?

H.

To: H.M.

From: C.K.

This is only partly a question of images. But I'm not surprised at the way you put it, you are so dedicated to image, illusion, trick, impersonation.

I came to *Femme* after college because I thought it was a job I could use for serious ends. E.g., you publish good unfrivolous fiction. Now I have to ask why? For whom? The list does look good with those Nobel winners every couple of years, but what is it really for, Borges in the beauty parlor, Kawabata in the kitchen, Beckett in the bathroom? (Well, he'd be amused at that, actually.) And I thought you—I no longer say we—were serving a purpose assisting women in defining themselves, improving themselves. Well suh, we am the ladies' Booker T. We are helping them, by the thousands, toward the *wrong* definition of themselves and what we call improvement just digs a deeper grave for their best possibilities.

Now, Harriette, if you must know, I stay on here: (1) for the pay-check, which is at least—I'll grant this—the equivalent of a man's salary on a male-dominated staff; (2) because I can try to work from within. Just as I believe men can do more in the army than in jail as draft resisters. That's really how I see *Femme*, as a kind of women's army barracks where we shine up the equivalent of our belt buckles, learn to use a great array of light and heavy weapons against both enemies, ourselves and "our men," and generally protect the status quo as if it were a country. Decayed though it may be. And I will stay here until I am asked to leave. Maybe, in fact, since you continue to tolerate my vision of things, I'm not doing a very good job. . . .

Harriette, bas, although you have never allowed your age to be so much as guessed at in public, I am twenty years younger than you are. I don't say that to be bitchy. I mean first that you have a hell of a lot you can teach me. If you could ever admit to the things you've witnessed in your twenty-five years here climbing this greased totem pole you could give a black-belt course in The Ultimate Feminism. Second, the twenty years between us make it impossible for me to share your theatrical view of femininity. You've devoted the best part of your working life to making these pages as slick and shiny as the nose you teach little girls to dread. The deepest dream your ideal reader indulges is to be stripped to the bone by a man made helpless by *Femme*'s First Aid Beauty Tips, user-tested, utterly disapproved by *Good Housekeeping*. But can she, i.e., have you ever been *naked*? Or are you never ever seen out of your basic black? Your taupetone, your honeyglo, your silversheen? You see—twenty years between us means that you enjoy Broadway, literally I mean, you go to those overripe openings and to Sardi's afterward, while I want the actors in front of me, maybe in my lap, so that everyone and no one makes the illusions. I want to go naked and sweat and not taste of raspberries until I'm reborn a raspberry. I want my mind as well as my body to be weight-bearing.

Cathy

FROM THE DESK OF:

Asses are weight-bearing too, my dear.

You may save the sociology. It is stale. Even the Sunday *Times* can make the distinctions you've found and lost again in your purple haze. (If Personnel had known you were capable of writing like that you would have been spared your present identity crisis, too busy clearing counters at Nedick's.) And lest you think my pique is a sign you've drawn blood, let me say that your polemics are not challenging but irritating. You girls are forever harping and harridaning and ignoring the business at hand, which makes you all too guilty of what you call "unfairly stereotyped feminine behavior." I can't accuse you of dereliction of duty but of slapdash work now that you're forever flying off to organize your little cadres in the lounge, and of having a generally demoralizing effect on a staff of women *who do not share your spleen*. Nor want to learn to. You may have your little victories when they're in line with our policies anyway—like the expansion of our Women in the Headlines into a monthly feature—fine—but do not presume to teach us to despise ourselves.

You are right when you say I have a lot to share with you, and if you ever had the openness to hear it, you might learn that life lived under a bare bulb, on a dirty narrow mattress on the floor, no raspberries in sight, is a sin against both spirit and body. I am on somewhat better terms with both—my age notwithstanding—than you might guess.

Cathy, your party-line devotion is doing a disservice to your talents. Isn't that an irony you girls could deal with at your next consciousness meeting or whatever you call them? How a talented and competent junior editor can destroy her powers of observation and analysis by selling herself to this year's—oh yes, my love—fashion. Ideas may not be born on Seventh Avenue, but they might as well be, the way they come and go. If you want women's minds maligned, indulge your irrationalities this way and men will be only too happy to call you all the names you hate. As for Sisterhood, how could anything as contemptuous as your note invite confidences from anyone who lives and likes a way of life blessedly different from yours?

Incidentally, I would have to be led to Sardi's on a leash, if anyone were mad enough to think I had any business there. Apparently such petty distinctions are beneath you. But at least you owe it to yourself and your little counterinsurgency—your boutique guerrillas—to reconnoiter accurately. The enemy, apparently, is all around you. You had better know where and why, uptown or downtown, eastside or westside, if you're going to subvert us.

About the Tender letter, you were saying . . . ?

H.

Inter-office
To: H.M.
From: C.K.

I do not sleep on a bare mattress on the floor. Is that all you can say? That is so *cheap* of you.

May I go to Washington to interview her? Try to find out what she's really like? Please.

FROM THE DESK OF:

Not on our money you can't. I am not as interested in this woman as you are, be she maligned or otherwise. You are assuming, of course, that she is very different from the Senator's characterization and that this would be evident to your oh-so-naked eye. Or perhaps she is kept at home in chains and you could free her. But then I would have to buy *your* distortions in setting the record straight. You may mutiny to your heart's content, but don't beg for the help of this captain.

H.

Inter-office
To: H.M.
From: C.K.

I am writing to her, more or less our standard preinterview questionnaire. OK? Relax, the response will probably be very dull.

FROM THE DESK OF:

Anything you wish, since this is your baby. Just, please, don't involve the name of this magazine in any unseemly questions about the gentleman's selfishness in bed. You would like to discover that she bears whip marks on her shoulders, but I doubt you will. (And you needn't worry, I am nothing if not relaxed about the outcome.)

Still awaiting completion of two overdue features from you. What about "The Hamptons in Winter" and the (January) Fireside Booklist? When will I have them?

H.

Inter-Office
To: H.M.
From: C.K.

Do you enjoy sounding like the mother of us all? ("Don't talk to me now about where it hurts, I have to wash the kitchen floor.")

FROM THE DESK OF:

Cathy. Please. Desist. It takes a child to make a woman a mother. Now let this be the end of it.

H.

Dear Cathy Klein:

How nice of you to suggest an interview. Thanks. But it seems unnecessary to me. Perhaps you can understand: this particular lionized wife is just a little tired of having the whip cracked over her head when she doesn't even have the privilege of being the lion. I have been giving some thought to it recently: did you ever wonder what it feels like to be the moon—stone-cold except for the light it reflects because it happens to lie in light's path? If you follow.

Yours,
(Mrs.) Mary Margaret Tender

Dear Miss Klein:

You ask if I will elucidate. Why not? You've sent a sweet little list of sample questions (at least that's what I take it to be?). I'll answer that much and add a few of my own, and then I'll send you something I'm working on; writing, that is. If you like that you may use it for your magazine. Make it, say, an anonymous airmail letter from the moon. I'm not ready yet for stage center in my real name.

—What I have always wanted to be. Besides who I am, you mean. A football wife, a knight's wife, a movie actress (pardon, film star for your columns), the President's wife. Finally, I'm beginning to think, a wife in plastic curlers and a pink Orlon sweater cheating on her diet, putting a dime in the Coke machine near the A & P checkout counter. Now, after all those years of fruitless dreaming, I might even like to try being a husband for a change. (Being alone, of course, is beside the point: no contest. Running unopposed in the third district. You can expect to learn nothing useful that way, except emotional sloth, which is not useful.)

—Childhood influences. Dear me, this is one that needs a Buckley or someone with that kind of gemmy heirloom of a family to answer it. One thing, though, that is worth noting if only because I haven't quite figured out yet what to do with it myself. A live charge.

My father was a minister. This meant nothing in actual terms—we were no more moral or genuinely God-fearing than your garden-variety Southern family, squabbling endlessly as chickens in our raucous drawls. But since my daddy was a minister of the First Methodist-Accommodationist Church (or so I called it) there was a lot of obligatory frowning on just about everything we did. Few outright prohibitions: I could go to dances and wear lipstick, but there was an edgy sense that a lot of things were right on the borderline of immorality. But he was not a particularly authoritative man. We were suburban rather than plantation Southern, you see, with a kind of shoddy genealogy, which matters to Southerners almost as much as it does to the British (maybe more). Half the families in the country claim they're out on a distant twig of Charlemagne's family tree, but we couldn't quite pull it off. This may have something to do with my father's slackness; if his want of a pedigree didn't explain anything, it did present a ready enough excuse. "You either learn at home or you never learn," he would tell us when we were recalcitrant.

Rather unhopeful of redemption for a man of his calling. When I was very young I remember seeing, I think it was in a doctor's office, a matched set of those huge dark portraits hanging, slightly tipped forward, from the upper molding. After that, whenever my father tried to beleaguer us into doing or not doing something, I could see what he was up to. He was impersonating one of those stern ancestors he too had never had. He would stiffen and use his Sunday voice on us, propping himself, inside, against a dark background that implied velvet and heavy wood and unquestioned absolutes.

But he had to stoop pretty low for his results. He offered my brothers a hundred dollars each if they reached their twenty-first birthdays never having succumbed to the evils of smoking, drinking, or fornication, or having joined a secret society. That he forked over to both of them, crisp new bills, I realized only later was not a tribute to the truth, or to his trust in their honorable representation of themselves, but to the fact that he had painted himself into a corner. A minister could hardly trumpet forth across the land the joint realities that he had made an inane commitment, and/or that his sons had failed to honor it.

When I told him I was marrying a (would-be) politician, I was made, by the expression on his mouth, to feel as though I had broken one of the easier of the ten commandments. Furthermore, the wd.-be politician came from a dirt farm in a town called Marigold—no oil to be seen up there—which was of about the same magnitude and finality as introducing a darker shade of skin to the family gene pool. He is over that now, of course, utterly. He has become a professional father-in-law. That keeps him busier than being an alumnus ever could, borrowing quarters out of the collection box to send to us in campaign years.

I recall the presence of my father, clothed in black but bearing none of the black smell of brimstone in the folds of his suit, to ask myself if my own very different obeisances to the look of things, the hang, the drape, of appearances might have begun there.

It might not have. ("You either learn at home or you don't learn." That echoes, disappears into its own sententiousness, then echoes.)

If you wonder at the absence of my mother from this brief report, you may be onto something, too. Perhaps as a girl she envisioned herself a minister's wife.

—How I keep busy (and off the streets). Well. I would like to have been a writer, at least a real Lois Lane, girl reporter. (Note reference: Who is L.L. without Clark Kent/Superman? I give myself away at every turn.) But I was too easily persuaded that my bust was the bust of a natural-born homecoming queen. And so, being the dutiful daughter that I was when the occasion suited, I took those measurements and this face (that face—I'm afraid they're no longer quite identical) as a judgment and a path and told myself that professional sorority sisters, even if they get A's in cow college frosh comp., are made for handling, for turning this way and that so they can be seen even unto the last row of the stadium. And not for much else. This, of course, seemed a more than adequate fate as far as my father was concerned. He may have been a man of the cloth but he never missed a football game. Therefore it was only consistent that he honored as well that tradition that respects and reproduces the woman whose brains have all gone to her tits.

I tended to talk back, however, to certain of the young men who fingered the goods too avidly, and so Mary Margaret Armstrong was not infrequently called Strong Arm. That was an easy trick—pictures of Indian arm wrestlers flashed on and off in my defenseless head and there I was with my sleeves rolled up over muscles, trying to flatten some Kappa Phi's wrist to the table. But I persevered; I walked like so many of the girls you see in the deep South, knees padlocked and the key mislaid.

I write about college because nothing has happened to me since then. My last year in school I met Joe Tender, put on a few Southern airs (you can imagine!) that didn't work this one time, subdued my strong arm, or had it subdued forcibly by a certain innocent tenaciousness that I persuaded myself grew, like the sweetest corn, only in the country. Married him and graduated from cheerleader servicing the vagrant needs of crewcut linebackers to private groupie for a Public Man.

—What do I think about Washington? Do I like it?

This is a very strange place, you know, and this is our twelfth year here. It is a deep crevice between the public and the private where a great many bright and skillful people live wedged together hand to ass and ass to mouth. There are too many temptations—to action, to inaction, mostly to seduction by television lights and 8-point type. I see it as a place where a man or woman can get any kind of contact lenses, to look better at diplomatic clambakes: blue, green, brown, hazel, mirror. Half the town is in mirrors this year; you ought to do a story on it. You can knock over your best friend and not say hello if your eyes are coated with quicksilver.

In this crevice, from which I'm writing you, I should add, live a great many uninvited types not known for their ability to get invited anywhere. Migrant farm children. Vietnamese grandmas with their ears shot off, South Bronx junkies with perforated arms ready to be torn off on the dotted line and mailed to their congressman. I am sentimental, I have been told, a real goddamn bleeding heart who lacks respect for problem solving and phasing into, over and out, who is in short a woman (bleeding everywhere) in the men's washroom. The men's graveyard. I try to let it be.

Parties here are parties everywhere and they are just like our lives: between the men and the women drifts a kind of scrim, a curtain made of printed forms (IRB 322 Short Form D), luncheon programs, committee agendas, the scrawled messages of legislative assistants, and it is all held together with a neat glue, compliments of the ladies, made of contraceptive foam laced with equal parts of Ma Griffe, Palmolive dishwashing liquid, and fine Jamaican rum. This is what we go out to have an evening of, and come home to when we're finished. Our homes are on the annual Georgetown house tour, our heads hang from the Christmas tree in season, we thank our constituents for remembering our birthdays, we visit orphanages, stepping through their cinder-block halls like minor goddesses bestowing our presence like a box of chocolates. We spend what passion is left making small dolls and fashioning cunning silver pins to stick in them according to our husbands' or the majority whip's or the straw poll's specifications. Our thoughtful husbands bring home the printout from election-time computers and we make clothes out of it, we cut strips and braid them into rugs, and once in a while around October, those of us who don't employ cooks boil it up and slather it with spaghetti sauce or maybe a nice remoulade. Then, if we have to eat it on election day, we'll know what to expect. When we fill out forms, where there is a blank next to "religious preference" we write—candid before our God—"Influence."

—How do I feel about "the new feminism?" I am not entitled to a vote, being one of the victims it has come too late to save. I understand it with my heartbeat. I send up bubbles of assent from my hollow stem that burst when they hit the surface.

Now I get to ask my own questions.

—What is the myth you've found most dangerous (since your baptism)?

The idea that a little arsenic every day makes you immune to large doses. Also that you marry what you need.

—What is the myth you've found most useful?

That a woman's little noises of duty and devotion, forthcoming at strategic and expected times, betoken satisfaction. Men are easily assured on this score. The more indifferent the more readily assured.

—What is the rock upon which the nation's capital was builded?

Cheaters never prosper.

—Why don't you change your life?

I have joined forces with the sharkskin and silk shoulders of the nation to keep power out of little hands (my own foremost and representative). I shill for the carnival owners. If you can't beat 'em, you're lucky if they'll let you come along for the ride. I am speaking next week at a high-school graduation in Maryland on the topic of "Law and the Younger Generation." I will not, if I am sober, tell them that from the evidence a distressingly large sample of cheaters appear to be prospering. I am always sober. And I don't know why I am going to find myself behind that microphone lying to children except that my husband regretfully declined, and turned to me smiling: Here, this is for you. Let's pretend we speak a common tongue; then you say these words for me.

—What is there about your husband that keeps you?

A vivid tongue.

An extra ball.

Candor.

Strong hands.

Good arches.

A calm that surpasseth any intrusion.

A comprehension of seven different influences on the GNP.

Fidelity. If not to me, then to what he takes to be me.

A long shadow, good to walk in: like a slicker in the rain when it's really coming down.

His wife's matched set of perversions (with bone handles, to be carried anywhere, on planes, in taxis): tongue lashing and interior flagellation. If he will commit these atrocities upon her, or assist her in committing them upon herself, she will bare her wolfish teeth, which, reciprocally, moves him. She sucks blood from his neck and attacks him with her nail file but he is victorious. His cloak of self-regard, all self-woven, spun of the thread of congressional immunity and contempt for all noncoms on deck, keeps him safe. Were it not for him, he reminds her. She shields her teeth. Were it not for him.

Here is the first graffito I will be guilty of one day. It will be the handwriting on the wall of, say, the ladies lounge in the Capitol building. The man who first wrote it resided (as we say in polite society) for many years in D.C. himself, behind the very real bars of St. Elizabeths (as we say in impolite society) Asylum.

I will write it just above

PLEASE DEPOSIT SANITARY NAPKINS IN RECEPTACLE

A slave is one who waits for someone else to free him.

Inter-office
To: H.M.
From: C.K.

Just received enclosed, to which Mrs. Tender alluded early in her second letter.

We are, even the most sensitive of us, caught in a riptide of habit and smallness that keeps our eyes off the real pain of the truth: that we live in caves.

If you answer this with a "distinction" between kinds of caves, Harriette, I am packing up my desk and turning in my gold key to the john. Does anything get through your firmed, smoothed, rosewater-sweetened, smoked, horned, thorny skin?

Your sister,
Cathy

Untitled piece by M. M. Tender, rec'd 7/9 (acknowledged 7/13)

I have left him, finally I have left him. I am standing on a rock looking out to sea and the sea is purple: red blood and blue water make purple, that is elementary. I knew it in the second grade. There isn't much I know these days that I didn't know in the second grade but there are a lot of things I don't know anymore.

One of them is how to talk to people like him, how to get my mouth right up close next to the horned armadillo scales that guard the ear and talk into it without getting scratched like the rabbit in the briar patch. He is somewhere else all the time, doing the things I went away with him because he could do. When he comes back at night or on Sunday or on the 31st of a long month, he is too tired to tell me. Anything at all. He is like the wives who turn over (and the springs throb wearily like bells) and say, apologetic because duty insists they be humble, "I'm sorry, darling, you can't imagine what a hard day it's been." Kind men pretend they don't know the best balm for a hard day. As kind women try not to remember how talk is the place where everything without words begins. No, they can't imagine how hard a day.

I have left him. I turn away slowly from the empty horizon and there is the most astonishing man I have ever seen, staring back at me. He is bearded, all in red, with yellow patches on his coat in wild designs. He is wearing a top hat and when he takes it off his head a bouquet of violets falls out of it and he hands it to me with a flourish. He is a magician and I go with him falling on the rocks. Scrambling, my knees are bloodied, but I will not complain or he may leave me there.

My new life begins. In a short fluffy skirt I stand at his side and I am privy to all the secrets of his magic. I hand him everything he needs: the eggs, the scarves, the scissors, the bananas. He pulls daffodils from my nose and pennies from my ears. Once he pushed at my navel where it peeked out above the tiny skirt; he rang it like a door chime and when he opened his hand he had gathered two tangerines and a purie marble. The marble was like a clear sky, as cloudless as my joy, and I carried it with me for luck until I lost it. In the spotlights I help him with everything he does and the audience cheers for us both. And in the dark, far from the crowd, he touches my breasts and they turn to buds and then they flower for him. Where I was once a cactus he turns me to a desert spring.

There is only one job I don't like to do but I submit because I love him. In this trick I must lie down in a clever box with special compartments and let him take a saw to me—at least the audience thinks that. I do lie in it but I hold my breath and listen to the even in-out of the saw as if it were his own breath answering mine. Of course his saw, the blunt-edged prop, never comes near me. I lie curled like a silkworm behind my special shield, spinning songs in an in-out rhythm.

One day I am almost asleep in my secret half of the box. The saw is breathing steadily and the audience is hushed with fear. I feel a pin prick in my side and then a real, prodding pain. He is sawing me in half. There is no hidden compartment. I begin to scream. My own real blood is welling under me and the saw is hot as a torch as it slices neatly toward the bone. Frail smoke is rising from my ragged skin. Just before the darkness slams down on me like a coffin lid I see him lunge at my side with his finger pointing. Then he reaches into the wound that is flaming with my blood and pulls from it a giant red scarf. It is long and longer and longer, endless, I am unraveling, I am a single silken thread, and he is waving it above his head. The audience whistles through its teeth for more.

Means and Ends

THIS IS Mrs. Winston's daughter. What is her name? Hattie, Hennie, Hettie?

She faces the narrow world head-on, like someone posing for a portrait angrily, trying to shame the photographer by shaming herself. Here, she likes herself at the greatest possible disadvantage: she is eleven, maybe ten, all bust, all waist, all hips. Already her blouses part between buttons, her lap is rumpled with fault lines. She has a wrinkled neck, like a grandfather turtle's, made for drawing in. Sometimes she strokes it with disgust as if it were a foreign limb.

When she was a baby Hattie-Hennie-Hettie seemed to put out her right hand and catch every sickness that blew by, seemed to stuff her mouth with it the way some children eat dirt. She would swallow it down and the next day there would come hives or scarlet fever, blisters or the asthma that made her roll her round eyes back in her head as if she were a slot machine. Oh Luvester, Mrs. Winston would say to her silent husband, all my beautiful babies and then her. She didn't care about the beauty much—not the actual facts of feature and proportion, she herself was all nursing woman's bust and sitting woman's butt and dark, dark as polished black walnut. It was a question of spirit, high or low. This girl seemed born defeated and Mrs. Winston couldn't say why. Last babies ought to have high blood and a carefree nature, all those others to love her and carry her around, do the work, and she beloved sitting in the dirt making sand babies and nobody minded. Maybe, she told Luvester, I was wore out inside when she come on and she couldn't find a good rich place to grip on to. Maybe she was just born hungry. They would have taken a good look at her thumb if they'd suspected, to see if she'd been wearing it down the whole nine months.

There had been a lot of Winstons growing up tight in the house—

we a pack of Winstons, they liked to say, only ain't none of us white or filter tip. There were six or seven children and a premature set of grandchildren and then Mrs. Winston was one of the famous providers of sustenance, physical and psychological, to everyone from sweet mama's girls to the Movement desperadoes who lived in Yazoo City, camped there, perched or passed on through. This is the 60s we're talking about: early 60s. She was one of those women, still called Negro and never did mind, who wanted to give a son or a daughter to Freedom the way Catholic families hope for a nun or a priest to dedicate, even if that means they are lost to daily affection. Even a child in jail for the right reasons would do.

Now they were down to Hattie-Hettie-Hennie who slept, or these days could not sleep, in the back room with Cliantha and her baby. Cliantha was fourteen and had no visible figure yet—she was long and flat and rudder-footed—but apparently someone had wanted her even without visibly enticing parts, someone had known what to do. Absent from sixth or seventh grade, she had spent all her time getting her baby boy and then noisily delivering it, shouting for Mama like a five-year-old with her hand caught in a door, and now having it around to keep her younger sister awake. (Or so the sister claimed, as if insuring her discomfort might be sufficient motivation for months of Cliantha's morning sickness and assorted asymmetrical miseries from toothache to ankle bloat. "Think I gave up my belly button just for you?" Cliantha would say into her sister's face. "Don't strike me so unlikely," the younger one would answer, scowling, her lips pulled out toward a smile.) But she liked the baby, called Willie, in spite of its mother. It wanted to be held against her pillows of bosom and Cliantha let it be so she could get some time cut free from him.

One time Hattie-Hettie-Hennie even seemed to run off with the baby. It looked like she had kidnapped him (with no diapers, as far as Cliantha could see, and only the bottle he had lying beside him for his morning sleep.) Jack Cuff, neighbor, had been driving his pickup to Jackson to price a new transmission and, seeing Hattie-Hettie-Hennie coming down the steps on her way to school, had asked if she'd keep him company; he'd had to sell his radio to pay a bill and keep the sheriff from his door.

It happened that Jack Cuff was one of the few people in Yazoo City that she managed to like: an old man working on his third family and waiting for his third set of teeth, two things you could apparently do with no loss to either, since they each took a different kind of concentration. Something about him always seemed to be patient and contented, waiting for whatever might happen. Her mother made everything happen and her father's teeth stayed clenched to resist them, but Jack Cuff was more like an amiable old dog, color of a beagle, who might be bigger than you but had no plans to overpower you. She said "Sure I'll come"—the fact that this was a school day made it the best idea she'd heard in a month—and just as she was going down to his truck she said "Can I bring Willie? He never been nowhere."

"Sure, bring Willie," Jack Cuff said. "He don't take no room, and if things get too quiet we can always make him sing."

So she appropriated the baby in his diaper and his short-sleeved undershirt, both of them pinned together for some reason with tabs—to keep his stomach in, she supposed, though what would be the matter with a baby with his stomach out? He wasn't any barrel-shaped ten-year-old.

And they went down the highway. As they approached the city they passed the motels and the shopping centers and Willie slept on her knees against the bolster of her chest so quietly he didn't seem to be there at all; he cried from hunger all the way back. Hattie-Hettie-Hennie hoped, without giving it much head-on thought, that Cliantha had come looking for her baby and figured they were only out for the longest walk ever. Another part of her hoped her sister had fainted flat-out with terror, maybe even hit her head on some furniture, and called the police. She personally was convinced that she loved the baby more than its mother, who yielded to an alarming temptation to get out of its sight every chance she got. (She was still going down to see its father and they had plans that didn't include a reminder of what could always happen again, what might even be happening already.) She couldn't wait to have her own Willie, although she wished she could fix it so she wouldn't have to touch anybody to get it.

"All you want is attention!" Cliantha shouted when her sister got out of Jack Cuff's truck and handed her son back to her, sopping and starving. "Just like to make trouble, get everybody worked up!"

"I'm not worked up," Hattie-Hettie-Hennie said. "That's you

you're talking about. I baby-sitted your baby and this is my thanks. You was just hoping I run off with him for good and now I can see you're sorry I brought him back."

Cliantha clutched her howling baby against where her breast should be and tried out various styles of revenge in her mind. But she couldn't think of a single thing her sister loved too much to have broken, or wanted too much to be kept from it. For a split second, until the baby's yiping distracted her, Cliantha saw her little sister with a nearly restraining sympathy: cheeks like a groundhog, shape of a groundhog, plus that waddle, all alone at the bottom end of the family, and look, having to take Willie, stinking Willie, for a friend. No boy would ever walk her into the dark and start a Willie in her. Stay with Mama forever, that was what her sister was going to do.

The other Winston children had failed their mother too, one after another like leaves detaching themselves from a tree, falling in a desultory pile, and blowing away. They all left Mississippi behind. Every one had a double name—Lotha Lu and Danda Marie, Torrence Tee, Luvester Junior called Lutie, Cliantha Joy, Hattie-Hettie-Hennie Ann, and Johnnie G. who was on the wrong side of the law in Sarasota. Each did a zealous job of keeping in touch with their mother, sending the bad news on down. They also sent their children and then took them back without much warning and wrenched her heart each time she lost one. She was right to think they'd have been remarkable freedom-fighters because they all seemed unshakeably bent on assertion. But freedom, or the organized fight for it, had come too late and all of them, the three boys and the two departed girls, seemed to be embroiled in seamy enterprises and doomed love affairs far from home, each more desperate than the next, when voter registration came to convert their mother.

Mr. Luvester Winston was neither pro it nor con it: he was strongarmed from his work, which was loading and unloading the big colored wagons down at the gin, and silent about most other things, a born-steady man where steadiness was an amazing grace. When he drank he only got more silent, which could be irritating but—praise the Lord! said Mrs. Winston and looked at heaven with smart shining eyes—not about to be dangerous.

Mrs. Henrietta Winston was a serious woman and she never took scared. Up in church, up at meetings, her knees forgot how to bend to get her in her seat again. She got three fireballs through her window for thanks, firebombs that somehow failed. They rolled skidding across her living room linoleum and then probably they sank back in sparks because of the way she scowled at them, like dust devils. "Luvester!" she shouted. "Come douse some water over here on these." There had been a sound like a car door slamming out front but no lights, no sound of feet coming closer. Cowards threw them like a paper boy tossing the *Evening Bulletin* in the general direction of the house.

She went on every march after that; she took a clipboard and knocked on doors and used herself as the model of a brand-new voter who wasn't born thinking on Freedom. (Don't need schooling or money or friends in high places, just the itch to be a first-class citizen.) She spoke whatever language she had to and passed no judgments on the fearful.

How bout a bulletproof vest? some of her neighbors asked her. Better get you one of them, size double X and a half.

You gon die anyway, why not go out like a hero, she liked to say cheerfully. Either way the Lord be waiting on you with wide-open arms. Then she would lean forward—this got to be a polished performance with nuances cut to fit the listener—and whisper some vile gossip about the town government, the justice of peace at his games, the council at its pleasure. People struck from the commodity food lists, women sterilized when they were still under, families sent north, banished like criminals with barely any time to pack. Some true, some not so true, but all of it, from her point of view, moral. Every abomination was true in essence; what hadn't happened simply hadn't been thought of yet, or dared. Ends and means was a new phrase to her and it made a lot of sense because we all know already everyone lives like that: ends are what you want to and means are what you got to. Men, children, employers—everybody plays means and ends every day, you learn it the way you learn about money: there's giving, taking, waiting, and saving up. A kind of life and death economy. The means is now and the end comes later.

So she was famous in Yazoo City and Mrs. Winston, energy unflagging, was truly happy. Probably it was the first time in her life every part of her was occupied, more than one at a time, not just the cooking or the nursing, the gardening or the loving side. She was good at tactics, going a long day without sitting down or eating anything to speak of, remembering names, convincing the preacher, healing rifts.

She was taken to Washington once to see the Poverty People and when the Big Cheese (the only thing she ever called him, unless it was to mispronounce his name deliberately) took off into his hind-most office to wait for her and her contingent to leave, and told his receptionist to say he wasn't in, she was sick to her stomach. Did he not want to make them less poor because he might lose his job if that worked too well? Why not if it didn't work at all? Their arrival in the moneyed class didn't feel to her like an immediate problem. She sat down in a swivel chair outside his office door and told the pale secretaries she would wait. To keep busy she studied the bunch of them: they all had red nails sprouting from their fingertips like roses. They looked impatient and panicked at the same time. Even Luvester had more guts than that. If somebody came to his door to settle something, he never would take off out the back window. She was tired of having the power to scare people but not to change them. That was the power of weakness without shame, it made your enemies nervous but it wouldn't butter your parsnips or keep your toes warm into January.

But this is what happened near the end of summer and how it changed some things, if not others. They were all sitting on the little porch of their house just as the sun was dropping down, draining off the light. Hattie-Hettie-Hennie was up top on a cane chair and Cliantha sat on a step with the baby in her lap. She was sitting a little longer than she ought to, putting off changing him well past the point of common decency, even all in the family. Luvester Winston was there with his mind somewhere else and Mrs. Winston was tell-ing a story on Mrs. Verney Tuttle, the voting registrar who had more trouble reading the written word than any three sharecroppers come in to fail their test. She sat in her office and listened to her radio dialed to the Daily Ministry of Souls that was sponsored by a major feed company that talked about making cattle healthy for God and man.

If there had been someone there to take their picture this would have made a good one to remember, they looked gathered together for some purpose beyond the passing of time: it looked like it might be a family reunion. Everybody was benefitting these days from Mrs. Winston's mood of absorbed energy. There was less of it to spend forcing the girls to make up their quarrels or Luvester, slouched, to take an interest. No grandchildren as far as she knew were set to arrive (and then, inevitably, leave and rip another layer off her skin).

Suddenly there came a flash, exactly as if that photograph had been taken by an old-fashioned camera with its explosion of phosphorus that parted the dark for a split second. Everybody's voice seemed to rise in a great "Aah!" of bewilderment and surprise and one of the chairs went down with a crack of its own, but no one knew what had happened. They all turned and shouted "What? What?" and the baby, startled by the commotion, set up the only cry that sounded indisputably angry. A car took off in dust that obliterated every detail, only the tip of its roof visible like a piece of something solid hurtling up out of a smoky fire.

It was then that they saw the younger sister, Hattie-Hettie-Hennie, running around in a circle down on the ground in front of the porch where her chair lay with its legs up like an overturned animal too clumsy to right itself. She was making a strange small noise in her throat, a gull's or a pigeon's, and holding her hands to her eyes. Even in the dark, which had thickened, it was easy to see something black washing over her fisted hands and raining on the ground where she scuffled it under. Square and solid as a woman in a ritual dance she traced the same steps around and around, bobbing her head. When Mrs. Winston caught her they collided with a damp resounding smack. She held her daughter's strong shoulders as if the girl were going to break and run off into the evening. She might have been.

Luvester couldn't start his car, whose battery was suspect, and no one had a working phone, so Mrs. Winston raced down the street trying to hold her daughter up by clutching her under her far arm. They zigzagged across littered lots until someone she knew finally picked them up as they rounded a corner still a mile from the fluorescent-lit grounds of the County Hospital.

The hurrying didn't help because, of course, the eye was already gone, splintered along with a bit of bone and a handful of flesh into shards, like a smashed glass. There were twelve pellets in the eye socket alone. The girl, silent, blamed no one but her mother. Mrs. Winston, who could get a distance back from herself, was contemptuous, among other things. It was like the time of the bomb— why were these boys such cowards? I dare go sit with my family out on the porch right there for anybody to see who don't mind driving down such a raggedy street and they come sniffing around at night and their hand quiver so much they can't barely get their aim.

Who say they didn't take good aim? protested Mrs. Winston's detractors, who had always thought she was asking for what she got if it was bad enough. Everybody know you make a dent in someone like her by shooting one across instead and getting a dear one. She don't matter for herself, she got a hide like a hippo. And if they get the baby right in the diaper, better still. They probably gunning for Willie.

Maybe so. But who they got was Hattie-Hettie-Hennie, who was identified for the news people (with their notebooks and their microphones and even their panel truck full of shiny heavy equipment, cameras that young white boys hoisted on their T-shirt shoulders) as Henrietta Winston, Jr. It galled the County Hospital to have these crews of insolent young media people prowling around; it further irritated them that there was a pile of mail for this child and flowers arriving as fast as the florist truck could get into reverse and come back again. To look at the return addresses it was clear that this was nationwide sympathy coming in. It was easier to love this child from far away, the admissions nurse (deliverer of the daily mail) was heard to say: she's round and she's sour and she's the exact color of mop water. And now to make her perfect, she's missing an eye and going to have to get it plugged.

But Henrietta, Jr., was making a turn around, even while she lay in bed with her face in gauze, like a caterpillar wrapped in a chrysalis. They poked a microphone under her nose and wondered if she had given any thought to Freedom since she had given an eye up for it. (Nobody had asked, of course, but she guessed she had, if that was the answer they wanted.) Did Henrietta, Sr., tell Henrietta, Jr., about her plans for opposition and disruption? (She supposed she did, they were all one family, even she who was the last of them.)

These answers seemed to please everyone who heard them. Her lawyer—she had one now, though it wasn't clear they were going to find anyone to prosecute for the shooting—clipped an article out of the New York *Times* and glued it to red cardboard so that she could prop it up on her dresser. She memorized it hungrily with her one eye. It was about heinous acts and cowardly spite and was called And A Little Child Shall Judge Them. Although they didn't call her name, she was certainly the child so biblically and respectfully referred to in two sizes of print. Cliantha and all her school friends were made to read it. She hoped they envied her.

Mrs. Winston was very gentle with her for a while, not so much from guilt as from pity: she did not like pain and she didn't think you should have to pay for being right and doing right. But she told her daughter she was a means now, and that was where the pain and sorrow tended to puddle up. When they got closer to the end, which she was helping them toward, she would see what the purpose had been; right now it was still a long way out of sight.

Some of the sourness cleared off her face when Henrietta, Jr., discovered how much of the world she couldn't see even from Jackson, and how strange it was that a lot of people who weren't even related could love her for her loss. She didn't miss her eye much—people overdid the sympathy on that but she wasn't about to say so. There was a fund for her College Education and another for Hospital Expenses, which would include a black patch now and later a brand-new eye: she thought she might try a different color. Cliantha gagged but Henrietta, Jr., said Why not? More people ought to get into the line of fire, she thought (but kept it to herself) as long as they're left with one of everything. It was better than selling off your radio and having to listen to the road.

ESSAYS

Don't Just Sit There: Writing as a Polymorphous Perverse Pleasure

S O M E T I M E S it's a good thing—like reflecting on the kind of adult you thought you'd become when you were a child, when thinking wasn't yet complicated by knowledge—for a writer to remember what writing felt like back at the beginning.

This is probably most useful to those who were, as I was, resolved to be writers at an early age. I was nine when words began to serve their extraordinary purposes for me: I was lonely and they kept me company, they materialized whenever and wherever I called on them, without an argument or a competitive leer. No one knew or judged how well I did them. This was not jumping in as the two ropes turned and came whipping down like a great moving parenthesis around me and slapped the ground and snarled my feet. This was not trying to connect the broad side of the bat with a ball that got miraculously smaller as it approached the scuff of dirt we called the plate. The words were purely mine at first, a secret transaction between inner and outer, between silence and speech, between what I knew—or *knew* that I knew—and what I didn't recognize as knowing, but that I could bring up like a brimming pail from a deep unlighted well.

What I wrote as a child I wrote for comfort, for invisible power, for the astonished pleasure of the *feel* of the letters—for their look, which was shape and color: every letter had a color for me, *E* yellow-orange and *K* and *P* blue and purple, like shadows on snow, *W* brown, *I* transparent as ice. There was a private ad hoc physics at work in the form those letters took; and sound, the fricatives and glottals and aspirates as satisfying to move around, for me, as tin soldiers or matchbox cars for someone who liked to wage different kinds of fantasy wars. This was a time of polymorphous perverse pleasure in language, with no end outside the moment, no end outside myself.

So I wrote murder mysteries: my first, the plot (because even then

I was no good at plotting) lifted in part from a Sherlock Holmes Classic Comic, was called "Murder Stalks at Midnight," which I thought marvelously original until my brother, a musician, showed me a record—Ray McKinley or Lionel Hampton, I can't remember whose—called "Celery Stalks at Midnight." I enacted dreams beyond achieving, namely ownership of a black horse with a perfect white star on its forehead, and a stint at boarding school with girls whose names—Ashley du Lac and Cynthia Weatheringham—came from the trickle-down of debutante lists I'd seen in the newspaper and English gothic novels I hadn't read. I wrote rhyming doggerel— "In the wonderful land of Rin-tin-tin." We lived in Los Angeles at the time, just up the block from Hollywood, but I had never gotten the word that Rin-tin-tin was a *dog*: the sound of the name, its syllables that drummed like rain on the roof, conjured up a misty fantasy kingdom to me, and reality was nothing but intrusion.

But I had entered phase two of the writer's life by then—the power of words deployed on the page for my own delight had inevitably asserted itself in public, in school. Like a talent for numbers, only more ubiquitous, a talent for words will eventually come to someone's attention, and then, having blown your cover you find you have happened upon a skill that is, as they say, marketable; that can serve to disarm, to amuse, to make itself pragmatically useful in the communal intercourse of children: *you're* the one who does slogans, news stories, yearbook jingles, class shows, petitions—you're available and you're unbeatable at all the odd lots of verbal communication most people lack the grace to execute easily or well. It is, in fact, the area in which, quite possibly, all your panache puddles, and your élan, and whatever other French nouns have never been used in your direction. You've got rhythm, you've got dash and dazzle, you've got a voice that cuts like a sharp beam through the fogs of verbal confusion, you've got something almost like a sixth sense about organization and metaphor that operates somewhere between your tongue and your hand, that is not quite art, not yet, but (unless you abandon it, and even then it's persistent) will someday perhaps *become* art.

I was recently reading a 1934 essay by E. B. White about the St. Nicholas League, a group of children across America "who wrote poems and prose, took snapshots with box cameras, drew pictures at random and solved puzzles." They submitted the results of their fer-

218

vor, White wrote, to the League, which was a permanent competition sponsored by *St. Nicholas Magazine*, and the lucky winners pocketed the Gold or the Silver Badge of extreme merit: this was clearly the point at which the young artists-in-potentia had reached phase two, the moment at which they realized their secret ardor could buy them respect or even local fame. "We were an industrious and fiendishly competitive band of tots," White says. "And if some of us, in the intervening years of careless living, have lost or mislaid our silver badge, we still remember the day it came in the mail: the intensity of victory, the sweetness of young fame. . . ." In the first few years of this century Edna St. Vincent Millay won all the trophies the judges had to give; Robert Benchley and Elinor Wylie excelled at drawing. Conrad Aiken and Babette Deutsch wrote poems. Ring Lardner won his laurels for verse and puzzles. Cornelia Otis Skinner wrote a poem; Janet Flanner, famous later for her essays dispatched from Paris, won for a drawing; and Vita Sackville-West sent a rather immodest, though matter-of-fact, little essay about the house she lived in, which had once belonged to Queen Elizabeth—that's the first Queen Elizabeth—and possessed 365 rooms, fifty-two staircases and an altar in the chapel that was given by Mary Queen of Scots before she was executed. A huge number of the contributors to the magazine have familiar names, though they may not be so to this generation of readers. Most of them put those as-yet-unnotable names on record in the great access of nonspecific energy of creative children—they were talented at just about everything solitary and crafty and made of ink, undoubtedly the kinds of children whose mothers tried to get them outside on sunny days to play with the kids on the block. Half a century later I recognized the loose rules of the club: had it still been around, surely I'd have wanted to join it.

But to return to ourselves. Phase three in the life of the young writer-to-be commences when your academic essays begin to bring home superlatives. Your teacher has her eye on you. You write without outlines, your ideas just line up in neat formation, at times the elegance of your style is a camouflage under which huddle insufficiencies of fact and comprehension and you write a paper on an economic theory you don't understand or an analysis of *The Golden Bowl* which you actually didn't finish reading *but it doesn't show*, and you get an A, and then you do a book report that debones an inferior author and holds his little spine up before the class to be laughed at for its puniness and insufficiency and you realize, a little sheepishly, that this thing you drive has a lot more power than the family car you're not yet allowed to take out alone and, if you're decent and honest, you'd better be careful with it.

Unless you are unnaturally shy and not academically and personally ambitious and you keep this skill hidden like a weapon, then you become the quasi-public commodity called the Class Writer. Your secret pleasure, like a terrific voice or face or even body, has become negotiable currency.

There is one thing I want to say about all this writing, the small child's innocent self-delighting scrawl and the cynical college student's paper on the Regressive Tax and Its Effects on the National Debt: they were committed to paper, all of them, but especially the child's, when as a writer walking among ideas and stories and characters and themes, you would take all comers. You had no commitment to a style, to an attitude and—least of all—to a genre. At nine, like the versatile members of the St. Nicholas League, I was not a poet or a short story writer or, God forbid, a novelist. (Though at twelve I admit I delivered up in three secretarial notebooks a huge opus about Mickey Mantle, in which Mickey was Mickey but I was his preliberation love, a pony-tailed, saddle-shoed fan who had broken through the membrane of his fame like a girl leaping out of a cake and, having brought myself flamboyantly to his attention, now reaped the reward of his grateful love. "With you I can be just plain *me* again," he said as he took me in his muscular arms. I repeat, this writing business brought a lot of power in its wake. Illusory power but satisfying nonetheless.)

One of the things that separates the child writer, whose only interest is in pleasurable discovery, from the adult, aside from our entry into the lists of competition, of the need for mastery, for patience and energy and for an outside source of income, is that most writers have, like kids on the ball field, chosen up sides. Give or take a shockingly small number of writers, most of us are poets or fiction writers, subspecies short story writers or novelists or playwrights. With the hard-won expertise that allows us to do only one thing well, and that if we're lucky, has come a sort of tightness of the muscles that makes it hard and maybe even makes it feel unnecessary to adapt from one form to another, and I think it's a shame and a loss.

Because with versatility come a lot of benefits, chief of which is a constant openness to possibility and its sister, serendipity. To revert to my first love, Mickey Mantle, you can face a lot more pitchers comfortably and go for a lot more kinds of pitches if you can swing from both sides. You stay closer to a memory of the sources of your writing, the sheer improvisatory joy of it, if you can remember that first you were writing the way you swam or sang or roller-skated, just because it felt good to do so.

Let me assume some of you know all this and are now, or are getting ready to be, working in more than one genre. Let me assume the rest of you have to be coerced. Here is a miscellany of observations, caveats, threats, promises and speculations arranged for you by the writer who made the list of the best and worst post-office kissers in fifth grade, the official grievances of a seventh grade class abused by a malicious teacher, and, latterly, of questions I *really* wanted to see answered by my college class for our thirtieth reunion. I have never given up my love of lists: I even published a story called "All This" that dumps out the contents of a particular woman's mind as if it were her purse overturned on a desktop. I recommend the form to you. Here are the confessions and caveats of a switch-hitter.

1. Steal from yourself. Cannibalize your own work. Handel stole from himself constantly: you aren't given so many terrific melodies that you can afford to waste any. If you have been writing out of an obsessive interest in something, say in the form of poems—I remember, for example, a spell of guilty motherhood, full of fears and doubts—do not hesitate to use those poems somewhat but not wholly altered in a prose piece, in a story or a *pastiche* of prose and poetry that makes its own rules. My own witch-mother poems surfaced, revised, in a story about a hyperactive child who was nothing like my own; thus they were considerably distanced by the time they found their most effective setting. But their rhythm was compact, their imagery arresting. Their intensity, in other words, was a poet's, not a prose writer's, and what they enriched was not story but an interior landscape. It is a fact that sounds more cynical than it is that a so-so-line of poetry, journeyman stuff, can make a lovely line of prose. It is a fact, however sad, that readers do not expect prose to be "written"—by which I mean *wrought*, with an attention to sound, to syllabic weight and echo, to varying sentence-length and phrase-length which are the fundamentals in the armament of poetry. You also have at your disposal, as a poet, an appreciation for silences,

ellipses, leaps in the narrative, and a talent for compression that can make an interestingly spare superstructure for certain kinds of prose. E. L. Doctorow, discussing his impatience with the realistic novel, quotes Marcel Duchamp at a point when he seemed to have given up painting. "Someone said, 'Marcel, why have you stopped painting?' and he said 'Because too much of it was 'filling in.'" If you can play fast and loose with the rhythms and strategies of another genre you will be that much less likely to spend your time filling in or, as Virginia Woolf called it, padding out your work with the "cotton-batting" of everyday activity.

I recently came upon two references in Raymond Carver's miscellany *Fires* to the basic situation in his well-known story "Why Won't You Dance?" That story begins: "In the kitchen, he poured another drink and looked at the bedroom suite in his front yard. The mattress was stripped and the candy-striped sheets lay beside two pillows on the chiffonier. Except for that, things looked much the way they had in the bedroom—nightstand and reading lamp on his side of the bed, nightstand and reading lamp on her side." In *Fires*, there is a poem called "Distress Sale":

> Early one Saturday morning everything outside—
> the child's canopy bed and vanity table,
> the sofa, end tables and lamps, boxes
> of assorted books and records. We carried out
> kitchen items, a clock radio, hanging
> clothes, a big easy chair
> with them from the beginning
> and which they called Uncle.
> Lastly, we brought out the kitchen table itself
> and they set up around that to do business . . .
> I slept on that canopy bed last night. . . .

In the same book, in his interview with the *Paris Review*, Carver tells this story, or rather anecdote: "I was visiting some writer friends in Missoula back in the mid-1970s. We were all sitting around drinking and someone told a story about a barmaid named Linda who got drunk with her boyfriend one night and decided to move all of her bedroom furnishings into the backyard. They did it, too, right down to the carpet and the bedroom lamp, the bed, the nightstand, everything. There were about four or five writers in the room, and after the guy finished telling the story, someone said, "Well, who's going to write it?' I don't know who else might have written it, but I wrote it. Not then, but later. About four or five years later, I think." And wrote it, apparently—this is me, not Carver—as a poem, not a particularly noteworthy one but as evidence of the idea in process, working at him, before it became one of his most characteristic stories of suppressed hostility and loss, the kind that is almost a play, all that furniture on the sidewalk a little clot of props, oddly, almost luridly back-lit, set up in isolation on what feels like a stage facing an audience of tranced onlookers.

Writers are, as this might illustrate, a peculiar hybrid: we are half obsessives who can't get those melodies out of our heads, and half—to change the metaphor midsentence—half frugal housewives, practical cooks, and seamstresses who will find a way to use a turnip or carrot or leftover end of meat to make a stew or cotton to sew a pillow-cover rather than let it go to waste. Just as every experience is useful to a writer, joy and misery included, so is every intuition of a useable situation if you've got the craft to bend it to your will. It's worth checking our pockets from time to time to see what's lurking in the corners, still to be aired and used. And it's necessary to be comfortable in many genres so that we don't have to pass on it, let it go, or give it away to someone else.

I remember when I was a young writer, a poet and nothing but a poet, and I lived in Mississippi in the mid-6os—exciting times. Quite frequently something fascinating would happen, either violent or contradictory or otherwise too complex for the kind of poetry I knew how to write. And I would utter, without recognizing its stupidity and lack of resourcefulness, the most helpless of all sentences: "If only I knew how to write stories"—and sigh and pass up a priceless opportunity because I thought I had a license that limited me to poetry, like the code on my driver's license that allowed me a car but specifically forbade me to drive a motorcycle.

2. If you have written something you like and it doesn't work in its original form, you are hereby enjoined to borrow or invent a form to contain it. Play fast and loose with definitions and categories. We write in an age that has lost a lot of the old comforts and courtesies of form but what we have in their place is a wonderfully fluid, fanciful sense of form that makes few rigid demands of us. Consider books like Bruce Chatwin's *Songlines*, poetry like Frank Bidart's monologues, Phillip Lopate's personal essays that read like fiction,

Max Frisch's unique series of notations in *Man in the Holocene*, including many from the encyclopedia, pseudo-historical fiction like Doctorow's *Ragtime* or *Billy Bathgate*. The list of works that use old forms with new license is endless. My own first book of prose, the stories in *Street Games*, began as a set of vignettes which I published as what I thought of as an essay called "Mainlanders." The magazine in which the essay appeared forgot, that quarter, to differentiate in their index between fiction and essays, and the story won third in the *O. Henry Prize Stories for 1973*. I didn't argue. Instead I went on to take apart the pieces of "Mainlanders" and make them into fuller, more conventional stories; add new ones to the mix, and there was a whole book of interrelated narratives. Back to my first rule: steal from yourself relentlessly.

Another time I sent around a story I was calling "Justice of the Peace" that concerned a woman I knew in Mississippi in the mid-60s who had tried to become the first black justice of the peace of her little Delta town. (This is a woman—my daughter's godmother, in fact—who makes appearances, though in different situations and different language, in a poem I wrote in the 60s and a novel I wrote in the 80s.) But in the case of the story, it was not being published and, I suspected, it was not being read with an appreciation for its tone, which, though it wasn't exactly didactic, might have been called exemplary: it was an angry little tale about small town politics, jealousy, vote-buying, and the defeat of modest ideals—half politics, half art. In frustration, to clarify its intent, I renamed it (re-aimed it, in a sense) "Justice of the Peace: An Essay in the Form of a Story" and immediately sold it to a good little magazine. I could almost hear *those* readers saying "Ohh, in *that* case. . . ."

3. Ask yourself nervy questions, such as: Must I really use this hunk of subject matter, or this intriguing character, or this haunting atmosphere or glimmer of emotional insight *whole*, or might I use a slice or a chip of it, cast it in a form that can absorb it or enlarge it, shrink it, spaces, blanks, unknowns and all? Let me give you some examples by way of elucidation. One is the suite of poems. Take Margaret Atwood's *Journals of Susannah Moodie* or Ruth Whitman's *A Woman's Journey*, her poems about Tamsen Donner and the Donner party, or her recent book of poems about the World War II resistance martyr Hannah Senesh. Or Carole Oles's book-length poem *Nightwatches*, which introduces us to the astronomer Maria Mitchell.

What is gained and what lost that these are not full prose biographies? That, of course, is not where their authors' talents or interests lie, they aren't researchers or scholars. Whitman, I know, actually travelled the path of the Donner party to its ill-fated end of the road en route to California, and she went to Israel and to Hungary to meet the family of Senesh: treated her subject, in other words, with the fullness of attention that might have issued in a factual book. But she wanted to distill an essence other than factual from all that study, and especially in the Tamsen Donner poems she has made a moving elegy, part specific, part generic, to a woman who, in a very different time in America, did what she had to do, and died of it.

I have two instances of my own which I think are instructive for those who are saying, But why? If you write prose, why turn to poetry? For the first few years after I moved to New Hampshire I had promised myself that I'd write about a neighbor born and raised right on our small town road. She was a good friend who fascinated me partly for her differentness from anyone I'd known growing up, and I thought I'd write something about the two of us, contrasting neighbors. But, blessedly, I had to come to terms with how little I really knew about her life—knew of its dark close-up places—and, lacking a story I wanted to tell, how little I could find to say about that life. What I really wanted was not exhaustive but rather a glancing impression. Not a superficial one but not a fully circumstantial one either. My friend was worth more than a single glimpse to me. Thus *Cora Fry*, eighty-four spare little syllabic poems that work like a mosaic to compose a modest life out of tiny pieces of experience. There is as much missing here as there is present, as much empty space as there is speech. But a picture emerges and even a bit of a story that illuminates the character. My challenge, especially because it came after I'd finished my first very wordy novel, was to see how few words I could use in the composition of that face and figure, town and time. I could not have done that in any prose I know.

A corollary to command 3: Find a form to contain the little you know without lying. Prose fiction, especially the novel, but even the story, is an accretion of fact, knowledge, insight, observation. Poetry can be a quick hit, a fast high, a light touch. I was in the Soviet Union for a short while a few years ago; I wouldn't have *dared* make fiction or even an essay out of that trip, but ah, my pathetic pallet of a bed in a once-grand hotel in Leningrad yielded a poem, and so did my confrontation with the ghost of Anna Karenina beside the train track, and so did dozens of other small moments, experiences, visions, and the dreams they engendered. Taken together they work like mirrors to expand and reflect an experience too meager and, really, too incoherent to make lucid statements, let alone characters.

If you, a fiction writer, are not prepared to make a set of poems out of your stalled novel, have you considered any of the other "odd lots and broken sizes" of form that are, these days, so enticingly available to you? In his small book *Little Lives*, Richard Elman, writing under the name Spuyker, composed a whole small town, like a prose-bound Edgar Lee Masters, as a cemetery full of ghosts speaking their audacious headstones. In *Flaubert's Parrot*, the British novelist Julian Barnes creates a character, a doctor named Geoffrey Braithwaite, who deconstructs Flaubert's life with an attention to fact and probability so obsessive and inventive that he traces every clue *ad absurdum*—for one example, the effect of railway travel on Flaubert's affair with Louise Colet. Braithwaite includes a short Dictionary of Accepted Ideas to parallel Flaubert's own, thus reminding us that the "father of Realism" had a few playful bones in his own staid body. Barnes has invented, or at least made use of, a form halfway between biography and anti-biography—if there's such a thing as the anti-novel there ought to be anti-biography—that reminds us in turn of Nabokov's *Pale Fire*, which played fast and loose with poetic form as serio-comic case history.

A second corollary: If it begins to feel too easy to do something, change forms. Make yourself an amateur in a new genre. Professionalism is something we want in airplane pilots and plumbers. But writers should always be doing something new and therefore dangerous, putting their feet down carefully the first time, feeling themselves walking over an abyss, or leaping into space without any idea where they'll come down.

A few years ago I ran headlong into a story—I should say a plot—that was so perfect I felt as if I'd already written the novel about it. So I'm writing a play to surprise myself. Half the play—the only half I've written—was performed in Houston. There was an audience there right before my eyes. There were actors who couldn't say certain lines and sound human. There was a whole new conception of acceptable, not to say engaging, action. The old virtues would not serve. Good conversation wasn't enough, in fact it was a blight because, contrary to a lot of people's understanding, conversation is not what theater is about. I learned so much so fast about play-making my teeth ached. I may turn out a good play, more likely I'll turn out a bad one, but I won't feel that I've danced the same old steps, which would have been the novel, which was coming to me preshrunk to fit the idea, and prematurely softened up, like stone-washed jeans.

4. When you've worked for a long time in a long form, your stomach will stretch, or your muscles, or whatever part of your body you care to locate the hard work in. When I'm caught in the intricate and slow-grinding machinery of a novel I begin to long, understandably, for the speed with which a story can be written, the fact that it can be finished during the same calendar year in which I began it. For its streamlined elegance, its canny capacity to do so many things at once. Just before I'd got sprung from my newest novel I looked at a list of Pushcart Prize winners, for which I hadn't been eligible because I'd published nothing that year while the large and deformed body of my novel hulked over me like Quasimodo's shadow, and, deprived of the pleasures of variety and visibility, murmured to myself self-pityingly, "I used to be a writer but now I'm a *novelist.*"

But when I was set free to return to those lost lamented forms, I remembered from the last time: they feel puny. They feel inadequate. Eventually, if you blow on them long enough, or read enough good ones by other people, they take on size and vitality again. But it's always hard and you have to expect that. You get used to the slow cumulative movement of the novel, the way your effects gather at their leisure from all the words you've laid down; the structure is broad and carefully articulated; you have flow-charts that tell you how recently certain characters have been heard from and which chapters hang together to make part I or part IV. But the story is bare and time in it rushes by with a hummingbird flash. The play, after a novel, snaps like new elastic—wham. So few words. Nothing on the page, but on the stage space filled with tension, potentiality. You can write four scenes in a morning, a whole act on a good day. Then you can revise on another morning. And when you get onto the stage itself you can wipe another quarter of the words away—superfluous. It isn't any easier to write a play, not one bit, but it certainly is quicker.

Consider, though, how great the odds that as a fiction writer, especially a novelist, plump with narrative flab, you'll never write a really good play: almost none have ever done so. Henry James and Thomas Wolfe wanted more than anything to write plays. Using those two baggy monsters as examples you might say ruins my argument that we should be conversant with all the available use of words, but in fact it doesn't. It only underlines the fact that, without free movement across the borders of genres, all of us could be stuck where we accidentally began. The Israeli novelist A.B. Yehoshua began as a playwright and somewhere along the way realized that he could take the form of the dramatic monologue into the novel with him: thus his two spectacularly interesting books, *The Lover* and *A Late Divorce*, which are almost all confidences, speech to an audience. ("It was the *stage* through which I moved from short stories to the novel," he said in an interview. "I wanted to get out from under the first person, the 'I,' the one character who dominated the short story and move to other characters without putting all the extra stuff around them. I just let them speak, as in a play, and eventually from these speeches came the novel.") Once inside the capacious house of the novel, Yehoshua says it occurred to him that there were other rooms as well. His newest novel, *Molkho*, called *The Fifth Season* in English, is a more formally conventional book. He has walked through a door I am trying to walk out of, each of us in search of the right size and shape of vessel, not so much to contain new matter as to make the old new, thus transforming it for ourselves.

5. In the eyes of others you have something called a Career. Certain people, should you be lucky enough to have them, like your agent or your editor, will hasten to tell you that what you need now for that career is another novel, or another book of the same kind of poems that everyone loved last time. It is very difficult to ignore the practical exhortations of such parental figures in your life, but if you can afford to, you ought to ignore them with a gleeful sense of relief. The voice of responsibility can all too easily shout down the small shaky voice of your originality and your need to find another way, a road you, at least, have not yet travelled. And your need, if necessary, to fail at it.

It doesn't need saying that the world is not set up to honor your as-yet-unfulfilled hopes. It tends to reward what is called a track record, implying that it is all a footrace with winners, losers, and also-rans, and a race with a clock, a race around a narrow unchanging track. Not only is your reputation at stake when you walk off attending to a distant voice, like Ferdinand the Bull who wanted to sit pacifically under a cork tree rather than fight, but every time you ask some foundation or writer's colony or whatever to buy into your uncertain future, of course all they can expect to go on is past work and project description. To answer truthfully at a moment of change would be like a suitor for someone's hand in marriage answering the inevitable question about career prospects by saying "I think I'm going to walk barefoot across America" or "I'm going to spend my time developing a blue rose." We shouldn't be surprised if our patrons are too dismayed simply to hand over the purse full of cash—we are declaring ourselves subject to a master other than nurturance of career, following a vagrant singer into the wild. Sometimes it leads us out the other side resplendent, sometimes we're never heard from again. And so we tend to perjure ourselves and say "More of the same."

Needless to say your internal doubts are by far the hardest to deal with: To make yourself an amateur is painful, it is like hitting the keyboard with gloves on. Why abandon what you do well? Why allow a long interruption in your visible output? Why take the chance, perhaps a long chance, that you'll *become* a good poet or whatever is the new skill needed? Why all this uncertainty? Each writer has to answer the question for herself, himself. But the writing child I was never thought much about habit or ease, and certainly not about career. She thought about how to use the word *cascade* as often as possible, or to find a place for *halcyon*, or wondered why there was no English rhyme for "orange."

6. Have a bag of miscellaneous stop-gap ideas for the days when nothing "important" will come, or when there isn't time for a project with much heft to it. Retell old stories, fairy tales, myths, in new forms. Translate; translate from a language you don't know—I've seen fantastic poems bloom from intentional mistranslation. Make a list of all the things you know: how to make fudge, how to give the Heimlich maneuver, how to get from N.Y. to Miami on five dollars. You will have a new respect for all you have mastered and all you might write out of. Make a list of all the things you'd like to know: How many of them can you learn, how many might you fake with a book or two and an on-site visit or a consultation with an expert?

Read Jamaica Kincaid's marvelous little story "Girl," which is essentially a list of the wisdom her mother passed on to her, cynical and insulting, loving and necessary. Can you do the same? Better, can you adapt the idea of the list, with its secret order and shapeliness, to your own obsessions? Write a scene for impossible characters: Biblical. Comic strip. TV anchorpeople. Government officials. Recast one of your stories as a play. Eavesdrop and write it down from memory. Lorrie Moore wrote her wonderful book *Self-Help* as if she were constructing a manual for the proper use of the machinery of our emotions. Lydia Davis, in her odd and beguiling book *Break It Down*, demonstrates how you can create something as unlikely as a murder mystery in the form of a French lesson, in which the newly mastered but rudimentary words end up describing a scene of carnage.

Walk through a graveyard, meeting the people beneath the stones. I did a project with a photographer in which I wrote alternative stories, two apiece, for every suggestive gravestone he had photographed. Collaborate. The most pleasure I've ever had from my writing was a musical I wrote from a children's book. It made writing alone, after all those people who had shared my passion (director, actors, set and costume and lighting designers) the loneliest thing I had ever done.

Take a written line you love or a line you don't understand, someone else's, and write from it. Take a minimalist poem or story and convert it to maximalism, at least in style; fill in the blanks, like a detail of a painting enlarged. Find something old and terrible that you abandoned without hope. Recast it, preferably in a different genre. If you've never written a poem, take a list of interesting words—wildflowers, car parts, names of cities in Albania—and arrange them in their best-sounding order, listening to them in juxtaposition. If you've never written a novel, think about it. What would it demand of you to take your favorite, or your least favorite, story and make it into a two-hundred-page book? Would you kill it or cure it?

Unless you are in desperate need of a fallow period, a period of passivity, don't just sit there. Think of your words as molecules in constant movement, hot to cold, cold to hot. Religious Jews on the sabbath, when they, and presumably the whole universe, are enjoined from doing work, do nothing that will encourage anything to change form. They are not to use hard soap because it becomes bubbles, they are not to make steam or tear paper, any kind, not even toilet paper. They recognize that a change of form entails an exchange of energy. It is work.

But it is also play. It is the best exercise to forestall the hardening postures of middle-age. It raises the adrenalin level. Gabriel García Márquez is possibly the world's most stunning proponent of change and flexibility at the moment. He has just, for example, written six screenplays from his own stories; he likens the imagination to a car battery: "When you leave it inactive," he says, "is when it runs down." One of his directors calls him "an amphibian" who moves easily between the written story and the film. "I have a lot of stories that occur to me," he says casually, "but when I am in the middle of working on them, I realize that they are not suited to literature, that they are more visual. So I have to tell myself that this one is good for a novel, this one for a story, this for a movie and this for television. . . . I'm a story-teller," García Márquez concludes. "It doesn't matter to me if the stories are written, shown on a screen, over television, or passed from mouth to mouth. The important thing is that they be told."

I, who can't tell his kind of story for love or money but who can tell my own kind, agree. Whether essence precedes existence or the other way around I surely can't say. But I know that *words precede the form that contains them*, and all of us, if we want to, can reach elbow-deep into the world of syllables and syntax and pull up a generous handful and arrange it to satisfy ourselves. We can do so exactly as we did when we first learned how to write words down and, in the silence of our own concentration, read them back to ourselves.

Notes on This Issue's Issue: Women on Men/Men on Women

I was going round Manhattan . . . and I noticed a girl sitting all by herself on the other side of the deck—a girl of about thirty, wearing a shabby skirt. She was enjoying herself. A nice expression, with a wrinkled forehead, a good many wrinkles. I said to my friend, 'I could write about that girl—what do you think she is?' Elizabeth said that she might be a schoolteacher taking a holiday, and asked me why I wanted to write about her. I said I really didn't know—I imagined her as sensitive and intelligent, and up against it. Having a hard life but making something of it, too. In such a case I often make a note . . . About three weeks later I woke up . . . with a story in my head. I sketched the story at once—it was about an English girl in England, a purely English tale . . . [When] I began to work it over, clean it up . . . I thought, Why all these wrinkles? that's the third time they come in. And I suddenly realized that my English heroine was the girl on the Manhattan boat. Somehow she had gone down into my subconscious, and come up again with a full-sized story. And I imagine that has happened before. I notice some person because he or she exemplifies some part of my feeling about things. The Manhattan girl was a motive. And she brought up a little piece of counterpoint.

That is Joyce Cary, speaking in a *Paris Review* interview. It's a routine sounding quotation, no prescription for How To Do It, nor a revolutionary statement. Cary's is a modest illumination of a process familiar to any writer, a day in the life; aroused curiosity; a hint of possibilities, unspecific; a note made on the endless journal tape of the memory. What made me look twice at it—right now, my elbows hidden in piles of read and unread manuscripts for this issue of *Ploughshares*—is its enviable *casualness*. Cary is able to note and then pass on from this scene on the ferry in the unquestioned faith that he can, if he wants to, make a story of any character that interests him. That the gender of his character is only one of a number of significant facts to be approached and accounted for. This is a freedom, few would disagree, that has only recently begun to be available to women, whose "working (i.e., writing) knowledge" of the world has

232

suffered the same constrictions as their lives, our lives. It is a sort of "freedom of assembly" within the mind: a fiction writer's First Amendment.

I think I tend to trust most those writers who have taken what they've needed—taken *on* a voice or a point of view they've needed —not as an end but as a means to an end. (Cary: "She exemplifies some part of my feeling about things.") "Oh," say the skeptical voices—these days, women's voices—who feel wronged by certain masculine simplifications of our lives. "Then *that* explains the inaccuracy of so much of that writing about us. If they're serving *their* feelings about things . . ."
But there is no other self for a writer to serve.

"The poet is capable of every form of conceit but that of the social worker: 'We are all here on earth to help others; what on earth the others are here for I don't know.' " That's Auden on Responsibility.

The irreducible in a story is the part without a gender. Too few stories have anything irreducible in them, any editor or teacher, any reader, knows that. It seems to be the writer who's the last to know.

Where the story fails its protagonists, male or female, it fails as art. Is that too facile? Let's come back to it.

Flaubert, saying something that is astonishing at first, and then perfectly plausible: "The story, the plot of a novel is of no interest to me. When I write a novel I aim at rendering a color, a shade. For instance, in my Carthaginian novel, I want to do something purple. The rest, the characters, the plot, is a mere detail. In *Madame Bovary*, all I wanted to do was to render a gray color, the moldy color of a wood louse's existence. The story of the novel mattered so little to me that a few days before starting on it I still had in mind a very different Madame Bovary from the one I created: the setting and the overall tone were the same, but she was to have been a chaste and devout old maid. And then I realized that she would have been an impossible character."

Consider Doris Lessing's novella, *The Temptation of Jack Orkney*, a story about a journalist past the halfway point in a life committed to politics, a man coming to the end of his belief in the efficacy of his work. The story is, variously, about dying, about each generation's doomed repetition of the futile gestures of the last, about an aging rationalist's compromising brush with religion. It is clear from the start that Lessing wasn't trying to "do" a portrait of a man as a *tour de force*, or as a form of retaliation. Only, knowing what we do of the lives of men and women—not liking it necessarily but knowing it—this story would have been impossible if it had been about a woman. The woman in whose life politics could have played this particular role—not *a* role but *this* role—would have been a unique woman; Jack Orkney is meant to be a rather ordinary man, and on that assumption the weight of the story rests.

Everyone has a list of successful transformations—as good a word as any—of male to female/ female to male perspective. Mine would include Zane Kotker's wonderful and neglected novel, *A Certain Man*, which is about a small-town minister, in the literal sense of the word "to minister." Amos Oz's *My Michael*, which is about the condition of marriage and about Jerusalem, as the Song of Songs is about woman and God. Larry Woiwode's Alpha sections in *Beyond the Bedroom Wall*, Jean Stafford's boy, Ralph, in *The Mountain Lion*, some of Nadine Gordimer's earnest political victims. And Toni Morrison's Macon Dead and his son Milkman in *Song of Solomon*. These and everyone else's dozens of examples begin wherever they have to; they don't necessarily constitute the whole point of view in a novel. The switched sexual perspective is fairly incidental, I am sure these authors would agree. "You have to get it *all* right. If it takes speaking in an unlikely voice, then that's what you've got to be able to do."

Question to myself, no longer elbow-deep but knee-deep in manuscripts. What are we proving here? Anatole Broyard says that anthologies with a thesis remind him of expressions like "flea circus" or "elephant ballet." I'll be the first to admit that the limitations one imposes on contributors when they are asked to send one-tenth of one percent of their work can be deadly. Surely there are more important rows to be ploughed. At a time when women, especially, are toiling for their own sex. . . . But this is a time of apparent openness when few overt barriers of experience and "appropriateness" are left standing between the sexes. The question is irresistible: Are there many writers who seem to be taking advantage of this freedom? Is there, for example, a preponderance of women whose stories are taking them far from the domestic, in which so many have been mired in the past if only for lack of familiarity with any other frontier?

But that's two-sided, isn't it? At the same time that women are feeling free to explore whatever they choose to, many are single-mindedly concerned with getting their own stories told, not with telling anyone else's. Every time a man writes—sensitively, accurately—from a woman's point of view, or the reverse, might we not say that we're seeing a triumph of the possibilities for understanding between the sexes? Wanting the empathy of the opposite sex, ought we not to welcome the writer's single form of it: identification?

When we don't like the results, we call it colonialism.

Even when we do like the results, the reason this identification has so little to do with life, the artist's or the reader's life as lived (aside from the general inapplicability of art to life) is that for a serious artist the sexual ventriloquism is incidental; for an unserious artist it is The Whole Point and therefore even more incidental.

George Gissing wrote a novel in the 1890s called *The Odd Women*. It doesn't mind being sociology, this book; it is a brave presentation of a number of arguments in behalf of a woman's right, often her responsibility to herself, to remain unmarried. *New Grub Street* was Gissing's book "about" journalism; this is his book "about" the situation of women. Contrast that to, say, *The Lonely Passion of Judith Hearne*, Brian Moore's agon of an Irish spinster who stands alone on one dry spot that narrows treacherously before our eyes until there is no place she can, with any dignity, rest; or look at Evan Connell's *Mrs. Bridge*, that carrier of our cultural inhibitions as though they were an inherited disease. In the end, the distinction between these classic novels and a journeyman's job like *The Odd Women* rests in that cliché I threatened to come back to: that most disingenuous question of artistic depth, or emotional scope, of the resonance these lives are given, so that the vulnerabilities of Judith Hearne and India Bridge must strike responses in any reader and not be seen merely as artifacts of class and contemptible prejudice, encapsulated, unique. These books are about life forces failing, struggling against entropy. The throbbing of amputated limbs—of hope and adventurousness and some undefined sweetness, wildness, passion, simple comfort—is neither a male prerogative nor a "female problem" in a writer of any size. But the specifics of situation are not interchangeable. However irreducible that part of a story that has no gender, the characters need one, and a great deal of accurate detail to support it.

Whatever I may have found in the stories that came to *Ploughshares* from men—these imagined lives of women—I certainly found very little joy. Is that a problem of flawed psychological perception or flawed artistic perception? (Women are, after all, currently said to be suffering Affliction.) Think, though: How many writers can render joy, satisfaction, tenderness, sex of character notwithstanding, sufficiently well to do it often in the ordinary course of things?

When I was fifteen I wrote a scathing review of a book for an English class. (It was about George Gershwin and I remember calling it "puerile," flaunting a brand-new word, thus, I was sure, putting myself safely beyond its reach.) I still haven't forgotten the dangerous flush of adrenalin that accompanied the discovery: it is so much easier to be convincing about what's wrong than about what's right—not because we have so little experience of bliss, not because happy families are alike; only because it embarrasses us to say out loud what makes us happy, and because it threatens our membership in the Unflinching Club.

What a delight to double-cross the simplifiers, though. Talking with Tillie Olsen, whose feeling for those who are trapped in their working lives is as boundless as Agee's, and who might be thought to believe there's not enough satisfaction to go around. What, I asked, did you think of *Working*? (Studs Terkel's book of interviews.) Whatever I may have expected her to say—one expects with Tillie at peril to one's preconceptions, always—she answered "But where was the *joy*? Where was the pride in their work? And you know how many people breathe a sigh of relief when they get to their jobs, which are so much more manageable than the rest of their lives!" A hedged kind of joy, maybe, but she has a point. Which I extend to the fiction that's lying in piles (yes, no, maybe) all around me here: The men have much anxious concern for women's angst—the bleeding of the soul, the suppressions and oppressions and depressions—which I think has come to these writers somewhat the way that adrenalin flush took me, as a teenager: so *that's* the way to touch the power of real life, real pain, real complexity! Only it has come to them benignly and with the best of intentions. I think it will be a while before men dare to propose a moment of real satisfaction for their female characters for fear of offending with facile "solutions" or with what might look like a suggestion that women take the moment and run, be happy, shut up, lie down, and roll over: the old game again, rules by Lawrence or Hemingway or Mailer.

Of the four stories by men in this issue, only one (Fred Busch's) makes a stab, and a desperate and doomed one at that, at a "positive" ending. (Which caught me off balance. How amazingly like Mrs. Ramsay it sounds, too, thinking about Lily Briscoe and Mr. Bankes: "They must marry!")

Which is to say that men are as frightened of suggesting women's comfort as white folks have been, in the last few years, of suggesting black folks' comfort.

And of the women's stories—two are, in fact, rapt contemplations of women and what might make them happy, the men bewildered at the women's dissatisfactions! Another view of the Problem. There were close to *no* stories submitted for the magazine that saw either men or women engaged in work or play or other pastime except as it related to a sexual relationship. Two stories about children, safely prepubescent, thus concerned with their own still singular lives. Are our days and nights so wholly obsessed with sex as all that, or are our writers pulled, again, toward one of the obvious sources of power, for lack of the subtlety to locate, amid the intricacies of our social lives, nonsocial forces of self? Moments of real solitude, for example—Ivan Ilyich's, Kurtz's, Meursault's, Miranda's, in *Pale Horse, Pale Rider*, when she chooses life—one has to search hard through Western literature to find much convincing interest in nonsexual relationships as primary subject matter. (And all four of those characters are about to die!) This is no modern tendency, but it is no less a limitation for its being perennial.

As much damage can be done our comprehension of "the other" in the writing of men in the voices of men and of women in the voices of women as by any appropriation of the "opposite" voice or point of view. And the third person omniscient author hath dominion over all and causeth much havoc and despair by suggesting anonymity and then, consciously or not, plumping for its particular interpretation. But why not, to be positive, take it the other way around? No woman's polemic against the exploitation of women as sex objects could be as convincing or poignant or funny as Andre Dubus's "If They Knew Yvonne," which is, on the surface, a young man's story (and as such would not, had it appeared in our mail this month, have been eligible for this issue of *Ploughshares*!). Dubus's "They" are the priests who get their hands on his Harry early and make him crawl for every sign of life he gives: for masturbation; not for making love but for using a contraceptive; for looking skeptically at such moral instruction as "masturbation is worse than rape, because at least rape [is] the carrying out of a natural instinct." When finally Harry comes to understand how preoccupied with himself his rebelliousness has made him, and how little with the girl who loves him, he confesses to the first priest wise enough to appreciate him. "Then for your penance," the priest tells him, "say alleluia three times." No story with resonance is a "young man's" or a "young woman's" story. Achieving resonance, a human sympathy, is the only hard part.

"Imaginary interviewer: . . . could you explain why you are writing about women?"
Mary Ellman (this is from *Thinking About Women*, still the most brilliant analysis of women's place in literature): "I didn't want to overreach. Right from the start I thought . . . you must limit yourself to *half* of the human race."

When you know yourself, when you have toiled through 'the contours of emotional life' where are you, what is it that you know, how far can it take you? Self-consciousness—narcissism, solipsism—is small nourishment for a writer. Literature is hungrier than that: a writer with an ambitious imagination needs an appetite beyond the self.

Cynthia Ozick, writing in *Ms.* and agitating a good many readers who consider her a traitor for insisting that there is no such thing as a woman writer. Theirs is the kind of semantic infighting that makes me wish writers were not allowed to talk, only to write.

Narcissism, solipsism—when I was tired of those I decided it was time to put aside poetry and write fiction!

Janet Burroway, also in *Ms.* I should think these comments would place her beyond controversy. (Naive to the end.)

In *The Buzzards* I had used five radically different viewpoints, all of them imperfect and in dissonance, each illuminating the others by its misunder-standings. . . . Now, with *Raw Silk*, I was as frustrated by the first person voice of Virginia Marbalestier as I had been by the male narrator of *The Dancer From the Dance*. . . . I could not, through her voice, convey it all . . . Her husband remains to some extent for me, as he does for her, a cartoon.

This is a moral choice-point, the most significant in any story or novel, this one of breadth of perspective masquerading as an aesthetic question. Some writers never think to ask it.

Writers who feel an animus against the opposite sex will deal harshly or defensively no matter how those characters appear: as lead in the drama or as walk-on. "Bech could only say, 'Kate, you've never read my books. They're *all* about women.' 'Yes,' she said, 'but coldly observed. As if extraterrestrial life.' "—Updike. The stifling of a fully developed sexual arrogance is about as futile these days as trying to smuggle a dog under a raincoat so that you can get on an airplane with it: somewhere in midflight that dog is going to get out from under, and barking will probably be the least of what it wants to do.

Androgyny? Yes, but there are so many other kinds of understanding and versatility a writer needs as well, so many oppositions and possibilities within ourselves out of which we must write. Which, I wonder, was harder for Alan Broughton to imagine for his story, a woman's life or a person's dying? For myself, having just finished writing a novel which is told from the perspective of the husband of a woman who is a quadriplegic, I can testify that the familiar terri-tory for me was the man's, who could come and go and move at will. Moored in one spot, her hands in her lap forever, the woman and her vision of her life took all my energy and courage: speculation, all of it. Negative capability is the pretentious term for that leap. (Pre-tentious, when one uses it for himself, herself.) In the end it is more like acting, I think, than anything: there are those who play character parts—you will never know their real faces. There are those who play themselves, and you will never know any other's when they play but theirs. The majority do their turns, effectively or not, somewhere in between. All of them act within their natural range, or ought to: "no irritable reaching after" uncomfortable styles just to show they can do it. There is no *intrinsic* virtue in speaking in borrowed voices.

Donald Barthelme:
A Preliminary Account

I T W A S the summer of '90 and the minor writer was still thinking about the major writer. This was the season of twelve million dollars to Ken Follett and twenty million to Jeffrey Archer (or was it the other way around?), but she persisted in thinking of major and minor in less remunerative terms. She had a soft spot for the kind of fiction that operated as a low-volume, high-integrity mom-and-pop store in the publishing economy. She liked loss leaders. The real thing, the seminal figure, the snazzy world-class muck of mucks, modest but confident "leading edge of the trash phenomenon," was dead a year and the implausibility factor was finally dwindling, but only a little. The more she reread him, the less it dwindled. But a bad year had passed in which his perfect formal accentless enunciation had not been heard, nor even the challenging bracketed silences at which he excelled. It seemed he was going to stay dead.

Henceforth and hereafter the major writer will be known as D. B., the minor as R. B. They were not related except by propinquity, collegiality, a profession in common, and some affection that ebbed and flowed as such things do. Also, they shared Houston, a fate many would not have welcomed. Most often he called her "my dove," and planted a socially appropriate kiss on her farther cheek. She has washed the cheek since, routinely, but with regret. He was a famous man and his dry, collegial, vaguely wine-tinged kiss was probably worth a lot more than she realized at the time. Surely, she thinks, a year after his disappearance, his friendship was.

He, aware of the power of his role as living legend, the Moby Dick of the third coast, had sent her a letter first, before she ever met him. She was dickering with taking on Houston, known at a distance as a city of dreck (a word he loved)—should she, shouldn't she, why jump off the edge of the world she knew into the substanceless sky of Texas, and to teach, to teach those Texans? But although he taught there, she didn't meet him when she went to interview Houston; he was in New York—which seemed only natural for the man who played so much footsie with the *New Yorker*. When he wrote her, she recognized that she hadn't been sufficiently mindful of a line in a story of his called "The School": "I said that the children shouldn't be frightened (although I am often frightened) and that there was value everywhere." Along those lines, soothingly, he wrote her a letter in the style of High Recruitment for the university he had attended, had quit ("too busy to graduate"), and to which he was now devoted, with an unironic passion, the enthusiasm of a salesman of cars he genuinely believed in. He said—this is the melody, the words are gone—Come. Chance it. Civilization looms here, high and low. Sometimes I live on West 11th Street in the Village but I take to it, that gigantic jiveass jigsaw puzzle city. You will take to it too. Signed, D. B. R. B. remembered the story of his in which he, or rather someone living in his name, bought Galveston, that nice little city, a neighbor of Houston's. Partway through he mentioned the misery of democracy, to which he subscribed. R. B. decided she could live with it. She thanked him sometimes, later, for having put his considerable thumb on the scales of High and successful Recruitment.

Thereafter she ran into him in the most democratic places: skulking in the parking lot of the discount dress store to which he had delivered his daughter, who was tracking the spoor of a good sale. Driving his powder-blue pickup. At the Safeway, packing his basket with necessaries and unnecessaries. For a book party in honor of R. B.'s book *Civil Wars* and her friend Max Apple's *Free Agents*— an evening that would seem to have been devoted to the popular American sports of war and baseball, though neither in fact entered in much. D. B. put together a rock, or rather rocky, band of graduate students which he led from behind the drums. They were called "Moist and the Towelettes," a special Houston blend of sog and gutbucket, and they played in the bookstore parking lot, where a few hundred readers came out of the closet to dance about books in public and to eat nachos and drink Dos Equis, the native water. The *Texas Monthly* celebrated D. B.'s band as the worst thing to have happened to Houston since the oil business went belly-up.

When she was in Poland lecturing in universities, in departments where they sort of spoke English, R. B. kept coming upon D. B. His picture decorated walls in American literature offices in Cracow; young professors in Wroclaw and Poznan, with goatees, furtive and dead-earnest in black turtlenecks, had written monographs about his work—he and the other absurdists whose tradition was all literal to them. Story of their lives, city life in the zany spirit-shaking capitals of the world, and didn't they know it when they saw it.

There are less legendary Houstonians, not to mention writers anywhere, who live far higher off the hog than D. B. lived in his rented second-floor apartment, where he was surrounded by his wife and grown daughter and young daughter, some handsome plants, and a very small cairn terrier, a dog he insisted, like said wife, and carefully trained by her, was Presbyterian.

Sometimes he and the child could be seen in the school yard across the street from their apartment "romping"—his word, made apposite only by irony; he was too self-conscious for a good romp. In a scene from a late story, "Chablis," he sees himself looking like any ordinary father running while his little daughter teeters after him. But after a couple of paragraphs of more-or-less engaged romping, he is back at his window, moodily sipping his wine, pondering what is wrong with him. "Why," he asks, "am I not a more natural person, like my wife wants me to be?" Autobiography has claimed him, with some exaggeration, in this story: no polyphony of disembodied voices, no metaphysics or wild collage. He is a human father in real time this time, a downright loving man, buck-naked where sophisticated pretense has always held mock-court, and vulnerable.

D. B. could have lived higher off that Houston hog. Although he went to public high school—the same one R. B.'s plebeian daughter attended, implausibly called, like something in a D. B. story, Mirabeau Bonaparte Lamar High School—and then to a public university, he was the son of an architect and a professor of high sophistication, who built the family house to resemble a famous building by Mies van der Rohe. "It was wonderful to live in," D. B. later said to someone who wrote it down, "but strange to see on the Texas prairie. On Sundays people used to park their cars out on the street and stare. We had a routine, the family, on Sundays. We used to get up from Sunday dinner, if enough cars had parked, and run out in front of the house in a sort of chorus line, doing high kicks." The peculiar pathology of this family of Rockettes yielded four novelists among its five children: D. B., F. B., and S. B. (Donald, Frederick, and Steve) whose melancholy stories engage the world with varying degrees of irony, flatness, sweetness, or acerbity, depending on which is writing, and P. B. (Peter) who does mysteries.

The house was full of books and, thinks R. B., amused, while some of us credit our fathers with teaching us fly-fishing or an abiding love (or hatred) of the Yankees, D. B.'s dad put into his hands an anthology of modern French poetry, which the son said was influential in his life, though not as much as his father's own interest in artistic modernism. For influences such as that—modernism and Baudelaire, jazz and drinking and refinement and doubt and how to smoke too many cigarettes—D. B.'s cronies in *The Dead Father* kill off a patriarch five meters tall, who *looms*, in the habit of fathers, "teachers of the true and the not-true." "Fathers have voices," he tells us, "and each voice has a terribilittà of its own. The sound of a father's voice is various: like film burning, like marble being pulled screaming from the face of a quarry, like the clash of paper clips by night, lime seething in a lime pit, or batsong. The voice of a father can shatter your glasses."

A view of D. B. taunting his father: as bad boy, all in black. He liked to call himself a sort of delinquent. There is no evidence he was anything but a smart boy in a fast car. Texas provides the roads for everything from speeding to suicide. He told about running off to Mexico once, but not for long enough: "Ah, we came back all too soon." At the end of "Chablis," which has been entirely true in the parts visible to a naked searching eye like R. B.'s, there is a final paragraph that presents D. B. in full nondelinquent danger: "I remember the time, thirty years ago, when I put Herman's mother's Buick into a cornfield, on the Beaumont highway. There was another car in my lane, and I didn't hit it, and it didn't hit me. I remember veering to the right and down into the ditch and up through the fence and coming to rest in the cornfield and then getting out to wake Herman and the two of us going to see what the happy drunks in the other car had come to, in the ditch on the other side of the road. That was when I was a black sheep, years and years ago."

When he gave up physical for psychic danger to attend the university, D. B. wrote under the name Bardley, a knockoff of the Bard's name, maybe, with a little wimp thrown in, dressed up in a Prufrock coat. One essay that attracted some attention was "A Modest Proposal for Short Tables" in which "he answered the complaint that the cafeteria tables were too short for the sororities by proposing sororities small enough for the tables." It was only a little leap before D. B., full-grown, was threatening a character with "You may not be interested in absurdity, but absurdity is interested in you."

He worked for the *Houston Post*, which he later claimed mournfully to have been written by literate people, a tribe long since gone obsolete. "The earlier newspaper culture, which once dealt in a certain amount of nuance and zestful, highly literate hurly-burly, has deteriorated shockingly," he wrote with a wishful earnestness not so long ago, and seemed to be saying that you couldn't get much of an education at one anymore. "Where once we could put spurious quotes in the paper and attribute them to Ambrose Bierce and be fairly sure that enough readers would get the joke to make the joke worthwhile, from the point of view of both reader and writer, no such common ground now exists." He wrote speeches for the university president, a fact almost impossible to associate with the later man, obsessed as he was with the integrity of language and the power of the fragment to supplant the spurious connection. He was known, at least to R. B.'s satisfaction, to have written the sharpest and most passionate words since Orwell on statespeak and expedient euphemism: "Quickly now, quickly—when you hear the phrase 'our vital interests' do you stop to wonder whether you were invited to the den, Zen Klan, or coven meeting at which these were defined? Did you speak?" But, having himself undergone the ignominious experience of writing the president's luncheon toasts and fund-raising songs, he has one of his characters engage in a similarly smarmy venture and call the speeches "poppycock" and sometimes "cockypap." For sure.

For a while he was director of the Contemporary Arts Museum in Houston, which looks like a triangle made of the silver foil that lines gum wrappers. That was one job he liked. D. B. knew a lot about art and inevitably, when it was over, when he left Houston for the blare and tang and ineffable redundancy of Manhattan, no one thought he'd ever come back. He threw in his lot with the likes of Frank O'Hara, who smiled as he and his friends dismantled the modernist tradition; he edited a magazine of art and words started by Harold Rosenberg, called *Location*, where he published Gass and Bellow, McLuhan and Kenneth Koch. He wrote a lot, to not much avail, and then in his thirties produced a story called "L'Lapse," unfindable, perhaps suppressed by main force, that he published in the *New Yorker*. Presumably D. B. had finally passed the National Writers' Examination, a five-hour and fifty-minute test that he describes in "The Dolt." ("The written part is where I fall down," his character Edgar says morosely—he has taken it twice before "with evil results." "The oral part is where I do best.")

But better, D. B. seemed to have discovered the most important thing, which was that if you make up a character to be your surrogate, someone to take the place of yourself, you will think about him rather than about you. "I was thinking," his character says, "but I was thinking about the wrong things." "Does it work?" he is asked, this creator of others to stand in for himself. "I have not," the writer answers, "had a thought about myself in seven days." "The self cannot be escaped," he says, earnestly, at the conclusion of "Daumier," "but it can be, with ingenuity and hard work, distracted. There are always openings, if you can find them, there is always something to do."

Thus—a word for which, R. B. suspects, though she never discussed it with him, her friend had little use, since it so strongly implies causation, sequence, certainty, and he had little faith in those—he spent the next thirty years and fifteen books courting verbal serendipity, looking for the perfect cross, and a non-Christian one at that, to hold up to chaos. His friend Kirkpatrick Sale suggested to him once that it seemed as if he'd like to get it all done in a single sentence. " 'Yes,' he said, 'I think I just might stop writing if I could get the exactly right words in the right single sentence.' He paused, and there was that little smile at the edges of his upper lip. 'Or maybe,' he said, 'a single word.' We didn't name the word that night, to be sure," Sale continues, "or ever, but I thought about it a lot after that. I would try various suggestions on him as we would pass in the hallway over the years—*celestial, oaktree, bumfodder, rotomontade*— but he would always give just a faraway smile and shake his head and not say anything."

D. B., still rooting around in the whole hectic mess of the language, found the world to be a most plunderable junk shop, a trove of treasure 'n trash, of slogans, public announcements, question and answer sessions, warning signs, news reports, psychobabble, spurious legalese, come-ons from the back of breakfast cereal boxes—all the noise that annihilates sense. The proposal had been submitted by others, of course, far earlier: that the project of the contemporary imagination was to be redone. Anaïs Nin had put it plainly, nicely, but without rhythm: "It is a curious anomaly," she said, straightening up more than Anaïs usually straightened, "that we listen to jazz, we look at modern paintings, we live in modern houses of modern design, we travel in jet planes, yet we continue to read novels written in a tempo and style which is not of our time and not related to any of these influences. The new swift novel could match our modern life in speed, rhythms, condensation, abstraction, miniaturization, X-rays of our secrets, a subjective gauge of external events. It could be born of Freud, Einstein, jazz and science." Thus D. B.'s passion for jamming high and low into a single sentence, King Kong and Captain Blood, or a gila monster, run over by an Exxon tank truck, that is reincarnated as Dumas *père*. This clangorous clash of tones, the sly manipulation of scale, the magniloquent and the puny wantonly juxtaposed, is a trick Woody Allen may have learned from him, snatched from the same reality that's to be sniffed out there, Sacher torte and cuchifritos, curry and day-old smoke and Nathan's kosher.

D. B. improved on Nin's plan by adding his own nervy syncopation—the King of Jazz, whose "few but perfectly selected notes have the real epiphanic glow." "The what?" "The real epiphanic glow." "You mean that sound that sounds like the cutting edge of life? That sounds like polar bears crossing Arctic ice pans? That sounds like a herd of musk ox in full flight? That sounds like male walruses diving to the bottom of the sea? That sounds like prairie dogs kissing?" That glow, D. B., that's the glow we heard with our ears, the just-submerged glint of longing and genuine-always-surprising sadness that surfaces in your very best moments. In *Snow White*, the wickedest retelling that tale will ever have, especially if Jesse Helms gets it his way, he says: "After a life rich in emotional defeats, I have looked around for other modes of misery, other roads to destruction. Now I limit myself to listening to what people say, and thinking what pamby it is, what they say. My nourishment is refined from the on-going circus of the mind in motion. Give me the odd linguistic trip, stutter and fall, and I will be content."

The trip, stutter, and fall. Pratfalls, in fact, Beckettian blind alleys, the voices of Lucky and Estragon alive in the land, and always with a perfect ear cocked to the music. The interviewer for the *Paris Review* asked him why he wrote comedy, not tragedy. "I'm fated to deal in mixtures," he said, this double-minded man, "slumgulleons which preclude tragedy, which requires a pure line. It's a habit of mine, a perversity."

For those who think it's easy—who matriculate in the well-attended school of "Jackson Pollack? Cat scratches. My *kid* can do that!"—D. B. cautioned, "There are rules." "Writing is a process of dealing with not-knowing, a forcing of what and how. . . . The not-knowing is not simple, because it's hedged about with prohibitions, roads that may not be taken. The more serious the artist, the more problems he takes into account and the more considerations limit his possible initiatives." He goes on with a gusto that hits us high and low:

Well, where are we? Surrealism gone, got a little sweet toward the end, you could watch the wine of life turning into Gatorade. Sticky. Altar poems—those constructed in the shape of an altar for the greater honor and glory of God—have not been seen much lately: missing and presumed dead. The Anti-Novel is dead; I read it in the *Times*. The Anti-Hero and the Anti-Heroine had a thing going which resulted in three Anti-Children, all of them now at M.I.T. The Novel of the Soil is dead, as are Expressionism, Impressionism, Futurism, Imagism, Vorticism, Regionalism, Realism, the Kitchen Sink School of Drama, the Theatre of the Absurd, the Theatre of Cruelty, Black Humor, and Gongorism. You know all this; I'm just totting up. To be a Pre-Raphaelite in the present era is to be somewhat out of touch. And, of course, Concrete Poetry—sank like a stone. So we have a difficulty. What shall we call the new Thing, which I haven't encountered yet but which is bound to be out there somewhere? Post-Postmodernism sounds, to me, a little lumpy. . . . If we're going to slap a saddle on this rough beast, we've got to get moving.

"First," he says, not fooling, not even knocking it around like a cat with a ball of knitting, "there is art's own project, since Mallarmé, of restoring freshness to a much-handled language, essentially an effort toward finding a language in which making art is possible at all." D. B.'s solution, or at least his stab at one, his effort to find a "clean language," drags us through the corrupting experience of cultural glut back into an innocence that seems to register everything, that includes Mowgli, Hokie Mokie, pop-top beer cans, Buck Rogers, and Kierkegaard unfair to Schlegel. "Capitalism arose and took off its pajamas. Another day, another dollar." "He that hath not love," he pronounces both ponderously and not, "is a sad cookie." His friend William Gass spoke of his "dizzying series of swift, smooth modulations, a harmony of discords." Dizzying maybe. Confusing, but not obfuscatory. D. B.'s human is a large, verbivorous animal, helplessly gorging on words, on lists, on names, and identifying details, the fingerprints of all existence, and their trademarks. When it comes time to define nothing, he can't do it, though in "Nothing: A Preliminary Report," his narrator keeps whipping us on to hurry, reminding us that there's not much time to complete the inventory of what is not. He can name a great many things but they keep adding up to something. At nothing he fails. "What a wonderful list!" he concludes like Sisyphus turned inside-out. "How joyous the notion that, try as we may, we cannot do other than fail and fail absolutely and that the task will remain always before us, like a meaning for our lives."

"Art is not difficult," D. B. wrote in a formulation of exalting simplicity, "because it wishes to be difficult, but because it wishes to be art. However much the writer might long to be, in his work, simple, honest, and straightforward, these virtues are no longer available to him. He discovers that in being simple, honest, and straightforward, nothing much happens: he speaks the speakable, whereas what we are looking for is the as-yet unspeakable, the as-yet unspoken." Not a modest proposal, not so modest as Bardley on sororities back under the Texas sky.

R. B. would not like to be a daily-grind critic or, worse, a thesis-maker, a tinkerer with scholarly scraps, saying resounding nothings in D. B.'s neighborhood. He is one of those icons of complexity and arrow-to-the-fundus honesty that bends back his hunters' weapons hideously, so that they fall to the ground when they hit his hide. John Gardner, author of *On Moral Fiction*, a work that obdurately misunderstood and misrepresented its times, in dispraise: "Fiction as pure language is in. . . . At bottom the mistake is a matter of morality, at least in the sense that it shows, on the writer's part, a lack of concern. To people who care about events and ideas and thus, necessarily, about the clear and efficient statement of both, linguistic opacity suggests indifference to the needs and wishes of the reader and to whatever ideas may be buried under all that brush." One man's sludge is another man's Windex. Gardner would not see what a profoundly ethical, even political, writer D. B. was, what a

sad and disappointed social critic under and through and by way of
our very own impure language.

But praise sounds just as sticky, like a parody by our main man
himself: "The main thrust of the story is that conventional episto-
mology fades." "This is a tour de force of spatial dislocations, reflec-
tive of our dislocated sense of direction in life and our inability to
connect experience with meaning, the word with feeling or event."
"The constant experimentation with styles . . . function[s] to call at-
tention to the fact of writing (or *écriture*, as we are learning to say) to
the medium in which B. and his perceptual field intersect." To which
R. B. would answer, "Speak for yourself, baby. *I* ain't learning to say
no *écriture*." And D. B., with a little beat, "As Goethe said, theory
is grey, but the golden tree of life is green." Or, "Truth is a locked
room we knock the lock off from time to time, and then board up
again." Save your breath, analysts of this dance, you only flatten the
movement, square the circle. His tish is better than your tosh. Relax.

D. B. speaks of the aggressiveness of scholarship: "A couple of
years ago I received a letter from a critic requesting permission to
reprint a story of mine as an addendum to the piece he had written
about it. He attached the copy of my story he proposed to repro-
duce, and I was amazed to find that my poor story had sprouted
a set of tiny numbers—one to eighty-eight, as I recall—an army of
tiny numbers marching over the surface of my poor distracted text.
Resisting the temptation to tell him that all the tiny numbers were in
the wrong places, I gave him permission to do what he wished, but I
did notice that by a species of literary judo the status of my text had
been reduced to that of a footnote."

Picture of D. B. teaching. For a man who saw so many complicat-
ing corners and seemed to judge so much, so hard, who found most
writing either lackluster or, as his daughter said of Versailles, "over-
decorated," he was an astonishingly active and generous member
of the Union of Concerned and Committed Teachers, who answer
cries in the night and sometimes even make housecalls. He sat in ad-
ministrative offices shaming or reasoning the bureaucrats into giving
what was needed to move the half-starved caravan of student writers
along. He gave his own money to build oases where he could. He
loved typesetting and graphics—they are everywhere in his stories,
funky architectural vistas and baroque statuary staring into our eyes,

like Uncle Sam who *wants* us—and he designed the witty brochures for his program himself. He patiently puffed and chablised himself through endless lunchtime meetings, for all his listening sometimes bringing forth as many as half a dozen words in an hour, sometimes fewer, none of them wasted.

As for the teaching itself. How many kinds of mentors we writers bend to, are made and unmade by. Rumor has it that one celebrated editor-of-the-moment listens to a line of a story and stops the proceedings if it is not the shocker of a line he's listening for. Humiliation, the more public the merrier, is the stick he beats his students with, and the exhortation to make it snappy. Another, R. B. has just confronted in an interview, one of her favorite poets, says that in a workshop, when the group has finished talking about a poem, giving some terrible advice, "and the right things haven't been said yet . . . I don't say them, I just go on anyway. Because if I entered in then, saying, 'This is the way it ought to be,' I'd spoil all the other group engagements.'" So his way is open-handed silence.

D. B. would have been appalled. He'd have felt underemployed and the writer ill-served. He was a man of profound and often terrifying silences, but they were not the silences of opting out, of passively waiting for the airs of receptivity to set in. He was fairly tall, the wearer of an ascetic, Amish-style beard, the kind that refused a face-softening mustache, and he seemed to list a bit back and to the side, appraising with the faintest incipient amusement, though not mockery. He was a reactor—his stories are, in fact, the stories of a responder, not an initiator. They are all the questions he asks of others, and finally of himself; a bemused arrangement, as if for study, of words and behavior that seem simply to be in the air, waiting to be seized, not to be originated but to be captured and wrestled to the ground before they overcome him. He made himself seem to be a helpless receiver of the Babel although, in fact, he was the fiercest of its sorters and organizers.

If you met D. B. at a party he would stand beside you in sometimes companionable, more often uncomfortable silence until *you* said something interesting. He rarely bestirred himself to speak first. Then he'd bring forth a response, sometimes a dazzler. A first word that was a last word. It could be unsettling, unilluminating, uninviting to stand there in the cool wash of his silence; he could not pass himself off as a man who wasn't thinking *something*. It was unsettling to stand beside D. B. at a party of his, or yours, or any-one's making, and know that he knew that you knew that he knew. Usually both of you smiled.

In class he did the same with his verbal minimalism, and he scared the hell out of everyone. Here is one of his best students, Glenn Blake: "I can remember my first writing class with D. B. A friend of mine walked to the front of the room and started reading this forty-five page story about basketball. . . . I mean, there wasn't so much as a dribble until about the tenth page. Somewhere about halfway down the third page, D. stopped him and said, 'Rick, does it get any better?' 'Yes,' Rick said. 'Oh yes,' Rick said. 'Oh hell yes, D. It gets a *whole* lot better. Just wait.' D. just looked at him and said, 'I think not. Have a seat.' I remember this vividly because I was the next student to have to walk to the front of the room, shaking so badly I could not read my own prose. And I proceeded to read a fifteen-page story in about forty-five seconds. The man was not going to stop me."

And Beverly Lowry, who became a very good friend after this initiation, and a widely published novelist: " 'Cut this,' he said, pen dancing through my pages. 'Change that. Don't explain. Cut this. Switch these around. New paragraph here. Change his name. Don't use Bruce.' What was wrong with Bruce? (I had changed that name twenty-seven times already.) My instructor frowned, sighed. (D. had a star quality sigh, awash in perplexity and general world weari-ness.) 'It's a terrible name,' he explained, 'unless you use it with irony. Plus in certain circles it has . . . connotations.' I didn't know which circles, I wasn't sure what connotations, but I got what he meant. Circles weren't the point. What mattered was the *care*. The pickiness. The art of tireless selectivity, which he practiced, I swear, on every word he ever wrote. . . . He ran his pen down a page to these sentences: 'I never said a word, never asked, never complained. I did the dishes.' He peered down his eyebones. 'You don't have to do this of course.' And he made the one substantial change he was to suggest that day. 'I never said a word, never asked, never com-plained.' Period, new paragraph. 'What I did was the dishes.' In low comedy, I'd have slapped my forehead with the heel of my hand. It was like jokes, after all; you had to set up the punch line, same as Henny Youngman. I had always admired Gertrude Stein's dictum,

'Paragraphs are emotional, sentences are not.' With one swift jiggle of his pen, D. had demonstrated what Ms. Stein meant."

D. B. did not waste the fierceness of his response on unpromising students; he knew that by now, a few years down the Boulevard of Real Life, Rick would be otherwise employed. He was coolly dismissive of them without animosity, simply by inattention. The ones he believed in got rich and compassionate and exacting assistance, sometimes line editing, just as often a single scrawled word: MORE, or LESS. When he believed in a work or a student, his loyalty ran deep—he made marriages with agents and editors and labored in the atrocious, tangled literary vineyards like a man who did not routinely see over, under, and beyond. This was in the nature of an existential commitment for someone like D. B., that double-minded man, who had his own fish to fry. He could have gotten an exemption like so many dreamy incompetents, draft dodgers who won't fight the daily wars of politics and institutions. But D. B. lived in the real world in spite of its poppycock and cockypap. He was I-A and however much it pained him, he marched.

When he was on his deathbed—and the terrible irony at the end was that his consciousness was the thing insulted; that this unconfused man lost his clarity for a cruel little while—the doctor reportedly said to him, as they so often do, "Mr. B, do you know where you are?" And D. B. answered, all clarity restored, "At the gates of heaven."

Later, after his grieving friends had savored this extraordinarily sweet and clear-eyed response—this from the man, the lapsed Catholic, who had written, "The death of God left the angels in a strange position"—someone who had heard a revision brought it to us in the name of accuracy. D. B. had said "in the *antechamber* of heaven." The music was off a beat, but D. B. would have found gates a bit familiar, perhaps even grimy with overuse.

R. B., in the year since then, has wished to file a complaint protesting his premature disappearance from all our lives as a gross miscarriage of justice; she has wanted to share the blame between the naked drafts of the universe and D. B. himself, whose fidelity to smoke and alcohol were his unsubtle and unresisted contribution to his own undoing. At the death of God, D. B. wrote in better times,

"New to questioning, unaccustomed to terror, unskilled in aloneness, the angels (we assume) fell into despair." Here is where R. B. and the angels part company, and for all his comic jamming she knows D. B. did too—he was no angel. He was nothing if not an old hand at questioning, accustomed to terror, and quite skilled in aloneness.

His memorial service, in September of 1989, was alive with his own prose voice, the best argument R. B. has heard for writing as well as we can—so that our mourners will be happy even while they're sad. He had said he wanted to place his scuffed cowboy boots on high ground. High enough, D. B., as they say up here in New England.

Lest she too simply blame that chablis, those Marlboros, which appear to have been the proximate causes of D. B.'s removal, R. B. forces herself to remember other friends plucked from her midst by bad drivers, bad genes, bad hearts, and even by bad feelings about their own worthiness. Blame is difficult to assign. D. B.'s St. Anthony lived with the ineffable, and D. B. himself with what he called mystery. Called Not-Knowing and praised.

And fear. He spoke of fear a lot more openly than most, and more frequently than someone we call a comic writer. In a time when centrifugal forces seem to splinter everything to bits, fragments were the only form he trusted. Cosmic fear and an unfulfillable wish for comfort was the dark familiar ground against which he spread out the broken shards for viewing:

> "Say you're frightened. Admit it."
> "—In Colorado, by the mountains. In California, by the
>   sea. Everywhere, by breaking glass."
> "—Say you're frightened. Confess."
> "—Timid as a stag."

> > "I said the children shouldn't be
> > frightened (although I am often
> > frightened) and that there is value
> > everywhere."

> "Smoke, rain, abulia."

> > "Zest is not fun for everybody."

> "I walked to the end of my rope, discovered I was tied, tethered."

"I'll dream the life you are most afraid of."

"The center will not hold if it has been spotwelded by an operator whose deepest concern is not with the weld but with his lottery ticket."

"I like people better than plants, plants better than
    animals, and music better than animals."
"And another thing. The human voice."
"Then there are the bad things. Cancer."
"Bitter with the sweet."

"One should never cease considering human love, which remains as grisly and golden as ever, no matter what is tattooed upon the warm tympanic page."

"Grace to all of God's creatures at the end of the mechanical age."

Ground Rights

Y O U C A N N O T love an invulnerable city. In that, I suppose,
cities are only like people. They may dazzle or intrigue us, com-
mand or buy our respect with their power, their accumulation of
talent, the sheer weight of their money and our acknowledgment of
the cunning it takes to amass it, but those are not lovable qualities:
they are functional, and spiritually off-putting. They are meant to be
so. Every new monolith hoisted against Houston's skyline is only
another strong-arm tactic to me—a permanent pitch to my vision
that says, A profitable package has been born; air rights, frontage
rights, sewer rights, and setbacks.

But even Houston has a humble center, easily glimpsed when the
eye accustoms itself to looking down, not up, at ground rights, not
air rights. Having quite accidentally found the vulnerable place, the
still point of this crazily turning world, I have had a good many
hours in which I have forgotten, and then remembered, jolted back
astonished, where I was.

I am sitting now, writing this, under an unfriendly sky, color of
cold granite, on a black iron bench meant to resemble a bower of
ferns. I am in a crook in the elbow of the Allen Parkway and Mon-
trose, where it is perpetually noisy—I imagine that at three in the
morning cars still pour by with the distant sound of fast running
water. The American General building rises on one side and, further
up, the America Tower. Behind me, outside the stone wall that is just
high enough to repel curiosity at 50 miles per hour, the long block
of rice silos looms, hectored and patrolled by a thousand officious
blackbirds as if it were the Galleria. There is nothing remarkable
about such a confluence of rivers of traffic overseen by complacent
industrial guardians in their glass and fluorescent aeries, except that
I sit in an oasis, sweet and calm, whose obliviousness transcends,

even mocks, all urgency. From here, Houston is only a small dog barking at my heels. This is Magnolia Cemetery, where live oaks and gray rock and hunched mounds of flowers hold back the ravening city without ostentation, with only shade and silence.

There is no jostling for space here: this is not even one of the huge cities of the dead, those enterprises outside of which monument makers and florists set up their wares like food vendors around a stadium. Those are intimidating as the cities of the live to me; this is a modest, orderly park whose intimacy makes street signs and row numbers unnecessary. Office workers from the neighborhood skyscrapers stroll through at lunch; occasionally someone jogs past or brings a dog to let him run across the low stones as if he were in a rocky Vermont field.

At the south end are what in Texas must be called, by way of differentiation, Anglo graves. Instantly they take me into their mystery. Which of these is the name of a good man, which of a scoundrel, who is truly beloved of the survivors, who's "Gone but not forgotten" leaves a hundred bitter ironies in its wake? Why did J. H. Fry die in Houston in 1892, having been born in 1861 in Dunville, Ontario? The game is irresistible—perhaps because I'm a fiction writer, perhaps only because I'm human, and it's both a profound and titillating game. What did J. H. Fry see in 1892 in a city only sixty years old, and thriving?

In another cemetery, in a rather grand tomb, I will come upon Araminta M. Noble Wettermark—I have my favorites, whose fates I ponder with all the delicious sentiment of a reader of Dickens's weekly installment concerning Little Nell. Mrs. Wettermark's daughter and son, age nine and two, born here, died in Sweden two days apart, in 1868. On each side of the tomb is the inscription: *Buried apart, they are now together*. Whatever the cause of the tragedy—I imagine them visiting their grandparents in Stockholm and encountering some epidemic we are safely delivered of in our day—I note that their mother, however bereft, survived her grief and separation and outlived them by seventeen years. One takes out one's stereotypes to air, given such stingy facts and such an ultimate as a broad stone inscribed with flourished serifs, a dignity implying wealth and ceremony. The Mrs. Wettermark I see is probably too much like Liv Ullman in a Bergman movie, weeping in her high-necked dress, in Texas, in a hot September 1868: fans would have been moved by hand; she probably had servants to keep her tolerably cool; children dead in a foreign country would have to stay there forever.

Down at this end of Magnolia Cemetery, near my bench, on both sides of the single stylish mausoleum that draws the eye like a centerpiece, are the Hispanic graves, cleaving to each other without a lot of room to spare. They are brilliant concoctions, many of them, of colored tiles inlaid in stone, of wooden crosses and handmade markers, shakily handcarved inscriptions, some with their "n" reversed. Discernibly unskilled hands chiseled many of these headstones, amateurs at carving but probably all too experienced at the grief of untimely partings. I stare and stare. There is nothing morbid about relishing hints of deep feeling and hidden drama. The numbers on the Mexican-American graves seem to me, though this is unscientific, to chronicle earlier deaths than the Anglo-American. No surprise in that: the families are poorer. I can see, without trying, the chiseler of the stone gouging the name of the twenty-year-old girl who died in childbirth, as the Mexican phrase has it, "with a prisoner in her womb"; of the baby who was just learning to walk, the mother *recuerdo de sus hijos y su esposo*. There are few family plots among them; these are piecemeal death, bitter purchases eked out one by one. Where did the rest of the family go when their time came?

In another cemetery I will find that the Hispanic names adorn stones interchangeable now with anyone else's, those uniformly polished granite hulks, the graceless contemporary sign of assimilation: a triumph of demographic equality over the charm and harsh economic necessities of folk art. In yet another old cemetery, there is a broad hill, a new section, much of it as expectantly empty as good building land, devoted to those flat markers that look like bronzed calling cards and cast no shadows. A sign on the hillside brusquely and explicitly forbids handmade markers, ornaments or crosses: if death is a leveller, let it obliterate the celebration of mourning as well. I know there are excesses of imagination here and there—a friend in Tennessee told me he saw a gravestone with a telephone planted beside it, receiver off the hook, with the inscription, *Jesus called*. But why uniformity is preferable to the individual gesture I can't imagine. Isn't it enough that the flesh falls from the bone, that no one is getting up from these graves at midnight to dance? Apparently it is not enough. But from the road I can see a brave resistance to the imposition of such anonymity: a field of red and yellow and bright baby blue plastic flowers, heaped shiny and unchanging against the brownish grass, some of them huge constructions—crosses and floral gushers that fill and bedazzle the eye like Rose Bowl floats.

It is another day and I have just come from a nearly invisible cemetery whose existence I quite literally stumbled on, out walking one morning. It is not a place to sit in comfortably; I find myself looking over my shoulder constantly as I heave myself through the weeds— one could hide or be hidden all too easily in this jungle of neglect. This is the College Park Cemetery, just outside the fourth ward on West Dallas, an inadvertent monument to impersonal change and the splintering of community. What was the college celebrated here? Where is the park? There is the plastic lozenge of a metro stop in front of the wrought iron gate; from the street this is only an un-claimed lot, an eyesore, a dumping ground.

It is, in fact, an old Black graveyard. The college, long gone, was the Houston Central College for Negroes; it is only one of many Black institutions ploughed under by a city some of whose citizens held better cards than others. Somewhere, I am sure, there are pic-tures of serious-faced young men and women in stiff clean collars, posing for their graduation picture in front of this or that build-ing whose solid bricks have gone the way of the students' flesh, to nothing.

Near the entrance to the cemetery stand three matte and shiny marble stones erected in the late sixties by optimists who presum-ably trusted that this yard would provide some dignity in perpetuity. Farther in, though, I am lost in a field whose graves are hidden like mines; they appear in the midst of gnarled and splaying under-growth, overgrowth far taller than I am, nettles and weeds. It hurts to walk here, assaults both eyes and bare legs. From time to time there comes a clearing, and here and there, blooming in the shade of cedar and high grass, white lilies spring into view, gone wild on thick succulent stems. Out of the insistent groundcover and broken and toppled stones, sudden open gashes in the soil can only be graves falling in. Under a low tree, heaped purposefully as any authorized dump, there lie a Greensheet turned a urinous yellow, paint cans rotted to rusty lace, flower pots, a plastic cup with the Astros' logo on its bashed side, an electrician's cap, mud-splattered; then in a ten-der bald opening, just beyond, pale narcissus blooming for no living eye. *Our Mother Asleep in Jesus, Oh How Sweet. Abraham Thomas, born 1860* when there were slaves, whose 1930 stone is snapped off jaggedly, like something done in anger.

Every time I think I have found the last grave I look farther through yet another species of bramble and there is a small stone or a platform bearing a fine weighty monument, a sign of pride: *The Holtz Family Asleep. Mother Fry, 1881–1925*, the familiar reclining lamb that marks the grave of *"our Viola V. Hart, 1899–1900."* My father was born in 1899: I cannot therefore fail to see the Hart baby grown into a destiny at least as fortunate as his: she is sitting on her porch, leaning on the rail, smiling at what her life might have held.

This cemetery pits two emotions against each other, fiercely: nostalgia, like an itch that can't be reached to be assuaged, for a glimpse of West Dallas thronged with horses and wagons, when exslaves and the children of slaves were put to rest in this modest yard under trees much smaller but undoubtedly more numerous. (Horses make fertilizer, not air pollution.) Against this I lay my anger that such hideous neglect has denied these graves their peace. But families scatter, and the last of some are buried here themselves. I was told that once the old and devoted sexton of the cemetery died sometime in the 1960s, there was no one to gather the upkeep fees that had kept the graveyard presentable. Once upon a time, the keeper of these grounds went knocking on doors, such was the intact community fifty years ago, and with the piecemeal revenues he hired help in the summer to keep the field clear. Growth is virulent in this climate: it takes no time for nature to reclaim the neatest plot. (Yet, when my egalitarian blood begins to boil on behalf of the distressed black survivors, I remind myself: I have seen a scrapbook from the thirties that showed Founders' Cemetery, farther toward downtown on Dallas and full of "important" graves of Texas heroes, so badly tended there were scandalized letters to the newspapers, wherein people remembered when the only keepers of the grass were the cows that loped and lounged over the graves. Now, in a sort of backlash of care, the cemetery is patrolled by guard dogs, according to its signs, and inhospitably locked against vandals and benign visitors alike.)

There are plans to make College Park a perpetual care cemetery. That is an official designation that acknowledges that we no longer can expect grave-clearing parties on spring Sundays, not with the children living in Minneapolis and the grandchildren in Miami. At that point there enter trusts and legal covenants; the Banking Commission regulates the whole, and one more family and village function falls to strangers and the courts. This is not a bad solution, this legal protection of the defenseless dead; it is only sad, a makeshift efficiency, with a hint of profit perhaps attached; a symptom.

Every cemetery I visit forces me into sociology, yet tugs me back to an enjoyment of pathos without analysis. One sunny Saturday I visit a metropolis of graves. Inside the Loop, still this one is distinctly suburban in feeling. It is laid out in subdivisions with an occasional reminder of where I really am: Catacombs Terrace would doubtless not appeal to developer Harold Farb. This cemetery has a Babyland that seems not much used these days, with a giant granite heart in the center. The acres and acres of graves face out, like houses, toward the grid of streets. Nothing random about them, they are oriented to the driver, not the walker.

And there are the efficient communal mausoleums, like apartment houses, in which neighbors sleep side by side in the ultimate anonymity. This is, of course, an old European tradition, the stacking of name upon silent name, with a little cuff on the sheer front to hold a bouquet; and in New Orleans, whose water table is more disastrous than Houston's, above-ground burial is as necessary and routine as the stacking of shoeboxes in a stockroom. But these are exceedingly neat, these walls of recent ancestors: they are the generic "deceased," as nearly shorn of visible inflection—of public eccentricity and private emotion—as they can be. I think, as I approach them across a vast lawn, that in this kind of giant wall of the dead, there is a monumental equalizing implied, as if this were the mass of names of the Vietnam dead in Washington, whose remains are elsewhere. (In recoil I see the poor, pure gestures of affection on the graves of deep country cemeteries across Texas; the designs made of shells, the empty dishes, the chairs and toys and marbles of the children pressed into the dirt right about where their crossed hands must be.)

No one dare criticize the mortuary customs of another, there are too many variations in taste and economics to presume judgment. But differences in practice come whole out of our lives. I assume that the uniformity and neatness of such a resting place is appropriate for the families who have chosen it. Monuments, unique or not, are made out of the style of the survivors.

Still, it may be only the taste borne of economic power that could create and tenderly nurture such gardens as the River Oaks of cemeteries. High bushes along Memorial Drive make it invisible, I have discovered when I've mentioned it to people who drive past it daily. This is Glenwood, which has a large country mailbox at its Washington Street entrance, and where I have never been without hearing birds at song. Since Houston likes to call attention to its growing list of world-class attributes—artistic, architectural, culinary—let me call Glenwood a world-class cemetery: not that it contains the owners of half the street names in Houston (which it does), or that they rest at the feet of a downtown horizon many of them helped to create. But it has, among its beautifully landscaped acres, its trees hung with Spanish moss, its various levels and terrains, the only real statuary in the city, in some cases quite genuinely moving: a woman, or perhaps an angel, prostrate on a tomb; bas relief faces of mother and son; a modern, semiabstract figure doubled over itself like a pained animal, or a god not yet awake—these are worthy of the French and Italian cemeteries that encourage artistic flowering alongside the natural.

Glenwood is the only cemetery where I saw visitors, not joggers, not mourners: people out for a Sunday drive, who came looking at Houston's silent history sleeping with its stories out of sight. What a history class could be taught beginning in any of these places—textbooks, every one, to testify to the various and conflicting lives Houstonians have always led.

There is Holy Cross, with its old stones still visited by the faithful who leave bouquets behind fifty years after a death; its Italian and Slavic families nearly side by side, photographs on so many stones that stop the heart at such ordinariness, such innocence in the face of what was soon to happen. Hollywood Cemetery, where I saw the first of a number of stones inscribed not FATHER but DADDY, and remembered where I was, and in what tone that DADDY would be said. Adath Israel, stunningly situated on the crest of the bayou, nearly grassless, pebbled, positively urban in its tight massing of stones, no more quarter given grass and weeds than in the so-called scraped graveyards of east Texas, whose owners attack any green excrescence as if it might shelter snakes or poison ivy. And there is Glendale, high above the junction of Braes and Buffalo Bayous, a tiny clenched fist of fenced land, first in the city, where the dominion of death and silence seems in danger of extinction by the extraordinary clamor of train, barge, smokestack, garbage scow, that hem it on all sides; where scummy water bleeds beneath sheer cliffs of tangled vine. These banks are rumored to have been lush and green in another century, and this as lovely a scene as anyone could have found putting up any river looking for a likely place to gamble on a future and start a settlement. On a barge below me someone has scrawled ALAMO in white paint on a steel bulkhead door. When John Harris in 1828, before the Allen brothers, discovered this spot where he is commemorated, the ALAMO was long years from its moment of glorious ignominy.

There are stories I can't begin to dream of in these places and stories I have been told, in turn, by friends, many of them political in nature: There was a woman who could not get into such and such cemetery, as if it were a sorority, but never you fear, her ashes are sprinkled across it; she is laughing last. There is a cemetery stubbornly holding on inside a picket fence in the middle of a Safeway parking lot, and a set of family graves under this famous building or that. Howard Hughes is buried so modestly you will walk right past him. And Indians, Indians lie very possibly everywhere.

I have achieved no greater concentration in this city than I have as I've tiptoed around the curbing of these plots, imagining, being amused, doing calculations. No psychiatrist or religious pleader can dispense the existential perspective lying at our feet. But lest I sound too Pollyannaish about the distilled and distant sorrow I am suggesting everyone come close and touch, let me finish with this footnote.

I was walking, satisfied with a few hours' dramatic and historical reconstruction of the world of passing time—when, walking toward my car, I saw, startled, what I thought was a rat lying on the grass near the path. It was gray and rumpled, rained-upon, a thick animal hunched on its side with its head out of sight from where I stood. I took myself close enough to see, by tails and ears, that it was no rat, it was only a cat, but by then the distinction barely mattered. What stunned me—knocked the breath out of me, literally—was its simple stillness. It was unmoving with the immobility, the mineral stationaryness, of a thing—a stone, a wall, a building, something that had never moved. Its stillness nearly made a sound, I imagined, feeling myself shrieked at. It was a different element, in short, from anything it resembled.

I thought, watching it hard, finally acknowledging that it would not suddenly rise the way sleeping cats do, and streak away: *This is what you are seeing here. You the living fix on life, you see the young mothers moving between their children, the old men whose gravestones say* FATHER *or* HUSBAND *as if that is all they ever were, and the babies on the day before they sickened, and in your imagination they are always on your side of the divide. But they are not, and that is the only thing you see here that is not your fiction.*

This was the only moment in all this cemetery-gathering when I did not feel welcome, when I felt as if I presumed to know things which I could not know. The train on the far side of Memorial came clamoring through then, bleating out its high note that we always call sad, and I felt the windy volume of cars and trucks turn up again. And then, to defend myself against the fear that I was being ousted from this place I had thought peaceful, whose eternal stillness I had tried to sip and swallow, I reminded myself that dying is the least of what living's for, the only incidental, the part that every family tries to put aside when it remembers whom it's lost. These are still the inhabitants of Houston and I have reason to want to visit them. Having lived here, many in unimaginable times—summer of 1827, September of 1900 when news of the hurricane at Galveston swept in, spring of 1912, the year of the end of the great war to end all wars, the year the St. Louis Browns won the pennant, two years ago Christmas—they are still here in the city's daily changing shadow. There would be no Houston on this day, March 21, 1985, without them.

Fingerprints

T H E   A S H A N T I, before any tale:
"We do not really mean, we do not really mean, that what we are
going to say is true."

nearness	:	words
words	:	weapon
weapon	:	pain
pain	:	distance
distance	:	silence
silence	:	peace
peace	:	distance
distance	:	pain
pain	:	nearness
nearness	:	words
words	:	peace

Having words: a paradigm of consequences. The crux lies between
those two vectors of dependency: pain distance / / distance pain.
What inescapable change occurs right there? How many years fall
into the space between those lines, into that inexplicable souring
(sweetening?) of sufficiency into need?

> "(He) was furious at me for 'the crime
> Of abandoning your first wife.'
> He asked, 'Why did you abandon her?'
> I replied, smashing the desk with my fist,
> 'That woman abandoned herself.'"
>
> (Nicanor Parra, "What the Deceased
> Had to Say About Himself")

Noises at the window
Animal ears,
spring flies tipping across the glass

careless
caught in the glare of anger

this side of the window.
A pair of something—
furless, damp—
prowl cages of voice, of smoke,

paper and stuck stones;
fleeing, with thick cries,
leave footprints
at the throat.

I compose myself. Both meanings of the word run dangerous. Never trust poise, unless it dares to invite its own collapse. I told you that once, or words to that effect, a challenge, but you were watching me cross my legs.

What was I doing as a child, I want to know, while you were becoming formed and fixed, full of yourself? I thought children became what they had to and then, at some unmarked majority, discovered what had overtaken them. Unwound the mysteries, like bandages, that had bound them, the forces that had prodded and poked a day, an hour, at a time. Settled down either to live with or to fight with themselves but weren't consulted about who they were until it was a hard walk back to the beginning. A place where you begin and end, visible edges. Though you try desperately to change those boundaries, if you know what you don't want to be, then you must know what you are. Can you guess what queasiness one feels (I feel) with no opinion of oneself? Hung jury: too much evidence, pro and con, badly organized. But for every hung jury there is a truth that is close to acknowledgment . . .

What rejoicing at my first definitive, unmistakeable enemy, who came quite late to me. Not quite a scalp for my belt but a simple confirmation of my existence. An imprint on the hard surface of the world, a nasty reflection, but one to reckon with, in the mirror of my peers. All the people who'd disliked me before—I assume there had been some—cared so little they ignored me, and therefore did me no good. How much more constructive to be so despised that my First (Loud-mouthed) Enemy could not constrain himself to let me pass by without hearing from him!

My own fingerprints, something of mine, a consolation and the measure of unbroachable distances. I can only visualize my face head-on as I see it in the mirror. If I had no mirror, as many don't, would I know myself differently? I am my body, the folds where my wrist bends—embedded in my vision is the space between the three creases at each wrist, which I know without a caliper—the moles on my arms, lines I've grown up with, belly, knee, neck. I know your body too, but not those unnoteworthy places, though we are at home with each other, with all we hardly know of our own warm places, hidden folds and invisible slopes. And we have made another body, our daughter's, which she uses now with all the oblivious arrogance of its health and newness, her own to learn. She will be the one to know just that angle where her right arm bends, fine small uneven creases, a brown contained freckle to the left of the middle (as seen from her own eyes), the green-blue fork of veins and—if she never loses them, as I in twenty-nine years have not begun to lose them—two shallow folds, one above, one below, the joint, where the first year of baby fat surrounded them. They are the lifelines I am fondest of; no one has ever noticed them.

Often these days, when I'm wheeling the baby in her stroller— pushing her off curbs in front of me, my unwitting scout who would be the one to suffer for some fool rounding a corner against the light—I see quick visions of her catastrophe. (I say *hers*. It is as though she has just been weaned. Finally I know that she has what Catholics call a soul at the instant of conception: I swear it has taken her all these many months and perhaps her first words to grow it.) I picture her astonished, angry, wrecked, bleeding—in her own, her very own death. I can see her wide eyes take it in, or not take it in. She would be no more or less passive about it than any adult. I watch this again and again in my mind before I drive it away. I, spectator, who dare feel such separateness whether I want to or not, who dream it up out of terror because all the love she pays me cannot buy her protection. I find that I rarely call her "the baby" any more, an object in my possession. Why did we name her the instant she breathed our air, have her name waiting, in fact, like her first warm blanket? (To let me know her sex, the doctor, holding her out at the end of the cord for me to see her kicking, said "Adina it is!") But she didn't need that name for more than a year. Now they go together: her name, her separateness, her own star-chart.

Ishi in Two Worlds: Charged with a far-off rumbling excitement I never feel when people speak of the power in names, of Adam seizing the world. But it is here, unexpectedly, in this book of Kroeber's: Ishi will not—cannot—tell his name because it has ceased to exist along with his family and friends. The California Yahi Indians never speak of their own names, certainly would go dumb before they would give their names in answer to a question. So his new friends call him Ishi—man. He leaves behind him even this name which exists only in the mouths of the others. When those others are dead or he is away from them, so is his name absent or gone. How did he ever exist alone? What did he know?

> Love, name me.
> Do you give me my only face?

T. is finally having a Black baby. She has taken her Jewishness headlong into the Black world these six years (never repudiating it; using it as a wedge to open the way, for she too has "suffered" in her people, has had pain for an ancestor.) Now surrendering to the truth that she cannot darken that obstinately fair skin, nor can she hold her lover either with it or in spite of it, she is creating someone blacker than she: she will love her child as she has never loved herself. She will never forgive him.

B., in his drawl, told us how he could always tell a Northerner (deep essences of hardness; chin-jut; shoulder-stance, etc.) It was our description of how we can always tell a Southerner.

> From other battles,
> all those victories, you've come.
> You have arrived from wars that were kind and small,
> and won as gifts are won.
> Wait now. Try to forget, if there still is time,
> how the liars loved you
> and called you beautiful.

I work so hard at absorbing the reality that I am not brilliant and all-deserving that my knuckles bleed and my lips go pale . . . I work so hard at enjoying the reality that I am brilliant and all-deserving that my knuckles bleed and my lips go pale . . . The others tumble by, like clothes in a dryer, randomly getting where they're going, and I watch through the little round steamy window, envious, contemptuous. I keep busy.

I was eighteen. My friend S. and I excused ourselves from our boy-friends at intermission and went to comb our hair. We stood side by side, shoulders touching in the mirror, and S. began to cry. Stupidly I tried to comfort her. I wish I were you, she said. You are everything I would want to be if I could. You . . me . . you . . I wanted to jam the words back in her mouth. No one has ever said anything that fright-ened me so. I wanted her to say them again. I was abject. Euphoric. The only thing that disturbed me was that their truth or falsity was not to be my problem but hers. She could not simply give the words to me as a gift, they were eating at her. The evil eye, still big with tears, stared back at me from the mirror.

It is a sign of vanity that one fails oneself perpetually. (Even greater vanity when it is far from true.)

". . . the simplest division it is possible to make of the human race is into the people who take things hard and the people who take them easy." Henry James.

"Poetry is for me one of the luxuries, like tennis, conversation, good food and drink." Reuel Denney.

Me: Why does Denney make me feel guilty for taking poetry so hard?
You: Why doesn't Denney feel guilty for not being Henry James?

It is so quiet on the lake—only the loon's insane calls, which sound unbearably lonely but must be a form of speech, break the whole silence. For days I have been shaken with guilt for doing so little this peace should set me free to do. I copy Merwin's poem in large letters and tape it to the wall next to the mirror, for once not a public gesture but a note to myself, an acknowledgment of the truth (which I do not understand) that an ache, or its twin, is soothed by the open air. The poem says:

All morning with dry instruments
The field repeats the sound
Of rain
From memory
And in the wall
The dead increase their invisible honey
It is August
The flocks are beginning to form
I will take with me the emptiness of my hands
What you do not have you find everywhere

Again and again I threaten myself that I will not write anything
for a year. It is an interesting habit: I indulge the thought only when
the writing is going terribly, and I do consider it an earnest attempt
at help. Perhaps if all the words are bottled up, they will finally ex-
plode under pressure—an orgy of creativity! But the very idea is a
punishment, never a cure, and it frightens me back to work. I know
that for me writing has something in common with nursing the baby.
I can't do it if I don't do it all the time. Put it aside to build up
strength, the flow will dwindle and finally disappear. When the baby
was at my breast ten times a day, I had the rare secret feeling that we
were violating a law of nature, defying a form of entropy (though of
course we were very close to the center of some other law in a system
I can't dream of naming, a crucial exchange of energy). One cannot
hoard some things. The more I gave the baby, the more I had to give
her, and had I tried to conserve myself, I would have found that I
had conserved nothing. Perhaps love regenerates itself in this same
universe where energy returns to the giver.

An hour ago I was sitting on the side porch, nothing but a little
peaked roof to keep the rain away, going through a ritual of the
blues more regular and self-pitying than anything I ever give in to be-
fore my period. I will never be able to write anything again, good or
bad; L. was speaking at dinner about her prolific friend who tosses
off every form of brilliant work—I despise L. (who doesn't know
how I happen to be feeling today); despise the friend; disparage, thus
discredit, L.'s taste in writing; despise myself (which I should have
begun with); then all around again. I also despise the baby, who has
spent the whole day hanging on me (reluctantly—she too can think
of better fun but she is teething and very sad) so that I couldn't even
read. Why didn't I wait to have a baby till I had *done* something, so

that I wouldn't have to keep doing it when it got so treacherous to be many things on one hot sticky domestic day?

But I stop (sniffling and watching the undramatic drizzle roll off the roof and splatter at my feet). I have just argued convincingly with myself that having written means nothing in itself, that working must exist in the present tense to exist at all. And the baby has nothing to do with it. (Everything else I have in fact done besides writing I never count, thus starting with something of a handicap. I keep this spare part in the back of my mind.) I blow my nose with histrionic vigor, and feel my small self-conscious funk being ignored so loudly by my husband that he is telling me what he thinks of my indulgence without even having to look up from his book (for which he would never forgive me) or stanch the tears that almost always makes him angry. Defeated I stand up, let the screen door slam behind me like a backfire, and—never to write again—sit down in this chair and begin: Again and again I threaten myself . . .

Feeling vaguely dizzy for a few days, I do the inevitable: Cede myself over, without so much as a question, let alone a fight, to a dreadful, gnawing, final disease. That way I begin to mourn each birthday months early, to wear down its capacity to hurt me by surprising me. So I know I am really frightened. I embrace it, plunge my hands in it up to the shoulder bone, no halfways or maybes. Possibly (for example) I need a change of glasses; I have all I can do to ask my husband if he will marry again. Trying to disarm disaster by offering immediate surrender, like a rare kind of trust—again the profound belief in the evil eye, which is a mythic way to admit that good things, good feelings, good health end at last and for no good reason. If you can engage its stare in broad daylight, it will not come for you at night. And these words on paper: an exorcism of secret fears. Kafka said that writing is a form of prayer. I know that he never meant it as literally as I do today, this very instant, writing this.

> The lake is grey.
> Paddles flat on our knees,
> our thoughts make
> concentric circles.

We are on the plane to Washington, to go to a wedding. Suddenly, looking sheepish, you remember that you've left your jacket hanging on the closet door. I am furious. You've done this before, always in the most humiliating circumstances when you will embarrass others besides yourself. I leap at you, thinking of the two dresses in my suitcase, between which I will choose at the proper moment. Perhaps that frivolity makes your negligence even more unthinkable. I sulk; I drag the matter before our friends many times, with unamusing variations, till they warn me to stop being shrill and wifely. After grave consideration I announce, condescending, that I have figured it out. You must prove you are different, that you are less conventional than the assembled mass of senatorial aides, journalists, lawyers, bureaucrats. Your shirt-sleeves proclaim you free. And envying you that freedom, even if your subconscious deals with it (I continue to insist, endearingly) like an adolescent, I punish myself by wasting vitriol on a defense of the conventions. Finally we forgive each other. Far from ever trusting ourselves, we share it all.

> I remember it
> must be a saying
>
> Make love in anger
> you will have a scar
> and many lovers to ask about it

Fighting your way into real married trouble—trouble that resounds, no shrugs and laughter and taking it warmly into the circle of your myth together—that takes a strong and determined will. When Mailer wrote about Floyd Patterson's weakness, it was a moral failure he was sniffing out (or a moral strength, depending on your preferences). You cannot fight, he chided, if you do not want to kill. We fight, call it that, and run to protect each other from the blows. Have we ever listened hungrily to hear soft parts ripping? Only our own, I think, for repentance.

> Elbows on the glass
> I watched till the wings tipped into the sun.
> Then I blinked you gone.
>
> After that last hard talk
> like work we'd done
>
> you leave me in a fit of calm,
> an ice-burn cool,

easy in our distances.
Look, they are only miles.
Measurable.

and all around us
signs of imminent laughter

INTERVIEW

An Interview with Rosellen Brown
by Tom LeClair

1981

Where did you grow up, and what effect did it have on your writing?

BROWN: That's one of my favorite questions because, in fact, I didn't grow up anywhere. We lived in a great number of places for no particular reason, chance included. We left Philadelphia when I was ten weeks old, went to Allentown and Reading, Pennsylvania; then to Mt. Vernon, New York, and to Los Angeles, and back to New York, where I was a teenager in Queens. I've always thought a major determinant of my personality was my forever having to begin again. The influence on my writing is that I'm very preoccupied with *place*. That was not at first conscious, but now it has recurred enough times for me to see it. Not just locale, but characters of, from, and made by the place they live in. My first book of poems, *Some Deaths in the Delta*, was set in—that is, the poems were palpably *about*—Mississippi and New York City.

Did your three books of fiction begin with place, or was this something you worked toward?

BROWN: My first fiction, *Street Games*, is a linked series of stories that takes place on one block in Brooklyn. Not all the characters are natives, but they are the kinds of people one would find in that neighborhood. In these stories place is almost like a character. I had written about half the stories that appeared in *Street Games* randomly, with no larger scheme in mind; some, but not all, of them had their seeds in the lives of my neighbors in Brooklyn. I had also written a series of vignettes that was published under the title "Mainlanders" and, parenthetically, went into the O. Henry Prize Stories as a story only because the magazine which published it had neglected in that issue to differentiate between fiction and essays! I hadn't

277

thought of it as fiction and I don't think they did, either. So much for form in our day! But when I had the idea that these stories could hold together as a set of variations on—well, not so much a theme as a vantage point, a specific place and time; when I discovered that the marvelously mixed neighborhood was a phenomenon in itself—I cannibalized "Mainlanders" (as I often do: my words are my words) and made four stories out of my sketchy little essays. Then I found another half-dozen probable voices—I could have kept going indefinitely—for neighbors, some of whom I'd never spoken to, some of whom didn't exist.

The Autobiography of My Mother is about the sense of exile. A character in that novel recites a long list of places where she has lived, then says, essentially, "After the first move, there is no other. That is what made me an exile." *The Autobiography* is less fixed on the place of its action (New York City) than either of the other books of fiction. That's probably because a lot of my energy went into a short (but to me satisfying) recreation of Gerda's childhood in Alsace-Lorraine, where I once found myself accidentally for two days, just enough time to be intrigued, to feel an itch of curiosity but not to linger long enough to scratch it. That may be as good a motive for writing something as the typical one, which is a deep familiarity. That's writing as investigation, filling in the blanks by intuition and guesswork, not making a sure likeness.

I think I may be eager to write about people who have roots, to use the currently popular word, that I don't have. Both *Cora Fry* and *Tender Mercies* are about people who understand a place deeply, something I've worked toward. Not too surprisingly, my husband and I have managed to bring our sense of unrootedness to our children. Although my daughters have spent some of their childhoods here in Peterborough, they feel not entirely of this place. They are small-town girls; I was a no-town girl; and the sum for them is that they will never naturally and unselfconsciously "belong" here.

As a Vermonter, I wonder how you dared to write Cora Fry *without living here in New Hampshire for sixty years or so.*

BROWN: I said when we first moved to New Hampshire that it would be a long time before I would write about its people. The only reason I did was that I had a good friend who lived nearby who allowed me to see into her life in a way that ten years of superficial neighborliness would not have accomplished. I began by writing about her and me, country woman and city woman, but along the way I dropped out. If I made it a poem of fragments, with lots of space between, I thought I could manage it. I never would have dreamed of writing a novel about Cora. I wasn't sufficiently steeped in the kind of life she lived. *Tender Mercies* is set in a town "coincidentally like" Peterborough. I believe that took some nerve because the novel is about a subculture—someone I know calls it "the chainsaw set"—that I didn't know very well. I worried more about getting the men wrong in *Tender Mercies* than I did about Cora because she was an individual, perhaps idiosyncratic. One editor who read the manuscript said the small-town material ought to go, but what I wanted—and what was published gladly by another house—was the relation between a small town and a flawed family. So the town constitutes half of the drama; the other half is the domestic drama, lived out in all the intimate spaces of home. And for that I used this house. The book is, thank God, not my life, but the beloved house is my house (albeit a rented one, not quite my own). It was a kind of song of praise to the builders who raised these unshakeable posts and beams in 1789. I almost felt I was paying a debt, writing so lovingly about the arch that holds up my own hearthstone.

John Irving has recently observed that, to write, one should get obsessed and stay obsessed. How would you characterize your best creative process?

BROWN: I'm not sure I can characterize my "best creative process," but I will say that whatever the quality of concentration is that lets me do my work, obsessive or not, keeps me—quite inconveniently—from doing anything else while I'm in the middle of something. No stories, no poems while this damn novel is gestating. Sometimes it's enough to make me feel buried alive.

I will say that I sail a lot by the vaguest of markers, discovering as I go just what it is that I am traveling toward. It's not automatic writing, not with my two words forward-three words back attention to the words. But I often feel myself following a step or two behind my characters, full of curiosity about what they're going to do next. I'm afraid that when I fall into a pit of uncertainty—I'm in one now, for example—I have nothing to blame but that "nondirective" method in which I trust that, if I have posited a plausible character, he or she will emerge in some recognizable place having resolved something of at least modest significance. At the same time, the obsessions, if such they are, tend to puddle up without the restraints of logic and that "irritable reaching after fact and reason" that Keats deplored.

You write about people quite different from you. Do you feel it your responsibility . . .

BROWN: Yes, I admit with both pride and embarrassment to a political passion that could never find its expression in activism. I've never been able to commit myself wholly to an ideology or a movement, nor am I very good at activist "business," so writing about people with whom I deeply empathize is a way for me to try to give them voice when they are inarticulate or kept from speaking for themselves. If you can't *do* anything particularly useful, I thought in the mid-'60s when I was in Mississippi, you can at least make a kind of imaginary record. Not in the naive sense of a tape recording, but when I was feeling guilty in Mississippi about staying home and writing poetry while others were venturing their heads and their limbs, I would justify my poetry by trying to get down what certain lives in that time might have felt like. I thought such poems were more "useful" than love songs or lyrics about the sun rising. Of course, I'm suspicious of utility as a motive for writing. I'm not suggesting the morally pragmatic, the edifying, the work as an invention of object lessons or heroes-in-action. But I did, at that time, cast my lot, in a sense, with the *other*, rather than with *myself* as subject, almost as an act, however futile, however arrogant, of solidarity.

I get very tired of reading about writers. I don't even understand why people want to read novels about them. There's apparently some glamour, but I'll be damned if I can see it. I would much rather try to understand the lives of people who don't write letters to the *New York Review of Books*. I admire Updike, for example, for writing about Rabbit. A book I like very much for the same reason is Ernest Hebert's *Dogs of March*, about a man in a sour little armpit of a town outside of Keene, New Hampshire, whose beached cars on his lawn make him the outrage of the neighborhood. Hebert comprehends his characters' passions and gives them a language that is not stripped down, flat. He doesn't elevate the man, but he does assume there are complex thoughts taking place in there, even if the character might not articulate them aloud. I, too, want to hear and say what such a person might have said had he had the so-called advantages of the writer.

Is "Sally and Me," the story in Street Games *about an outsider and a young woman who speaks for him, an analogue for the role you choose as a writer? Is there any fear combined with the sympathy you feel for the people you write about?*

BROWN: I don't know. That's an interesting question I never thought of asking myself. If so, and probably quite realistically, the writer takes one hell of a beating at the hands of the "outsider," whose life, in so many ways, goes on resisting her good offices. As for the "fear" I might feel—I'm not sure that I truly ever do know how my characters are going to comport themselves ultimately, and so I worry as I would over the behavior of real friends, as if they were flesh-and-blood people I love. You commented once that I—my characters—ask a lot of questions in my books, literally ask them in question form. The questions are real and open-ended for me, and I need to hear them asked outright and earnestly. (Because that is the voice in my novels, isn't it? Earnest.) Such answers as I arrive at are fairly inconclusive because, *pace* John Gardner, I don't believe we should be looking at novelists, head-on, as our moral guidance counselors. But that means I am liable to end up disappointed by my characters, or sorry to see what they've let befall them: fear for them, in other words. They are nominally within my control, but their autonomy, if they are honestly conceived, gives them the power to represent all the hazards and foolishness of "real," and therefore frail, men and women.

Is it possible that you choose characters for their language, for words that are not naturally your own?

BROWN: Much more interesting than my own. I loved writing in the voice of Luis Beech-Nut, for instance, in *Street Games*. I've always been bored with my own autobiography, and I feel I have no accent anyone can identify—another effect of dislocation. So I am engaged by others' voices. In fact, I've promised myself that the next time anyone interviews me, I am going to give only false—imaginary—answers. *Autobiography of My Mother* is written in an accent almost wholly borrowed and fabricated. Even the epigraph on the first page is from a nonexistent source, in a pseudo-real voice. *Cora*

Fry perhaps not quite so much, because the necessities of poetry changed some of the tonalities of Cora's voice. A language with its own color is much more engaging for me than transparent language. Neutral third-person is difficult because I continually find myself falling off the ridge of consistency. Assuming the voice of someone else, which readers think is difficult, is infinitely easier for me. The parameters of someone else's voice are clear to me; my own are not. I know just how far Luis Beech-Nut would go in analyzing the world, for example, and know what he wouldn't say. Third-person is also unrewarding because I feel that passing overt, or even tacit, judgment on the lives of characters in the voice of this faceless narrator is somehow arrogant, a lordly dictation. In making statements about my characters, I feel I'm sermonizing, which embarrasses me. Perhaps this abnegation of the authority of third-person could be a failure of nerve, a frailty of ego masquerading as a becoming modesty. Anyway, it's convenient for me that this narrative diffidence intersects with my delight in the language of others. My father, who paints, once did a ballerina with dreadful hands. He couldn't get them right; so he put them in an ermine muff and called this method the "Brown Muff Principle." Perhaps my speaking in others' voices is my Muff Principle.

Do you think this is an influence of the nonimperial self of the '60s?

BROWN: Yes, I often wonder what I would be like had I come of age in the '40s or '50s. As a person who matured in the '60s, I dislike the cloak of Authority. SNCC used to say, "Anybody can do it." Of course, that wasn't true: everybody couldn't speak. But there was a certain kind of validity in anyone's testimony in his own words, or hers, to how something looked from *there*; a relative (not an absolute) authority, and surely not an official one. Third-person fakes a neutrality and posits a single truth. It seems more honest for me to say, "I'm Rosellen Brown writing in the voice of a sharecropper," because the reader knows, after all, that it's me, the writer as ventriloquist. And if I get the sharecropper's sound, then that's *one* voice, not the only one to comment on the proceedings. I declare myself as an outsider and try to make the best of it. I suppose I share this sense of limitation with the New Journalism: "I'm Tom Wicker at Attica. I don't know what's going on, maybe I'm just a honkie like they say. Writing for the *Times* doesn't confer a guarantee of truth on these words. But this is what these men are saying, and I am trying to hear them."

Could the self-reflexiveness of experimental writers whom Gardner charges with immorality be moral scrupulosity?

BROWN: I'd like to think that, but I believe often it's a failure of interest in ordinary lives and distrust of the artifice and pleasure of the unsophisticated—that is, the natural—ordinary narrative. Another thing the '60s may have done is make us tired of hearing the insufficient voices of "ordinary people." Many writers have decided to replace those voices with scientific talk or deadened, distant, and consciously unrealistic styles. I continually try to confront and enjoy this shadow of the artist's hand across the page, but I keep coming back to hearing people speak, which is more interesting to me than watching the art of writing unfold. That "otherness" is deep and prevailing, yet I wish to pursue it because I still write for the same reason I wrote when I was nine years old: to speak more perfectly than I really can, to a listener more perfect than any I know.

The problem seems to me to be defamiliarization. How do you solicit interest in your "ordinary people"?

BROWN: When my husband acted in a summer theater, the director would compliment him by saying, "Your character was *big* today." The character was slightly larger than life and could therefore carry across the footlights of the stage. What you're talking about is making language *big*: visible, heightened, capable of revivifying experience. Every day when I get up and look at what I've done the day before, I try to eliminate what I used to call "he said, she said writing." The dead circumstantial. I replace scenes in which things simply happen with language as vivid as I can make it, with ellipsis, metaphor, summary which makes a pattern, something which distinguishes the writing from the plodding prose one often finds in realistic fiction.

Is there a temptation to move away from the ordinary subjects in which you're interested in order to generate the kind of language you've mentioned?

BROWN: I do feel that. One needs to be subtle enough to do what seems to be an ordinary subject—although there are, in fact, no subjects that must stay ordinary in fiction—and yet still light that fire.

While I fear the slough of unimaginative, reportorial writing, when I pick a subject such as the quadriplegic woman in *Tender Mercies*, I do feel farther from the probable than I want to be. Such things happen, and frequently, but I wish I could have written about that marriage without the flamboyant premise, the precipitated crisis.

What about the novel you're working on now, in which you're returning to experiences of yours during the civil rights struggle in Mississippi?

BROWN: It has at its center again an emotionally extravagant occurrence. I was having difficulty writing about a couple of super-annuated civil rights workers trying to deal with the "ordinariness" of their lives after the excitement of their activist youth. Their reduced lives would not take fire on the page, so I introduced an element which I had thought was going to be my next book: the couple finds themselves guardians of two children whose parents were killed in an accident. I bring these kids from a very different life, a segregationist background, into this family to prod them to reflect on their post-movement life and political engagement. The mother remembers being thrown into dirty jail cells and being forced to plunge her dinner dish into boiling water up to her elbow, and she realizes now that in a different way it is more difficult, at least because it is less *satisfying*, to decide what to make for dinner for these new children. As in *Tender Mercies*, I use an extraordinary circumstance to push the characters to remember what their ordinary lives were like before everything was changed by a stroke.

Perhaps because I began as a poet, I make large narrative gestures; they vault me into lives in order to do what I really want: to examine character and write as beautifully as I can. The cataclysmic is reflected on but rarely seen, and it is assimilated, finally almost without motion, in tiny increments. I'm fascinated by the play of scale, large against small, as a painter might be intrigued by composition, placing different masses against one another, different weights of event. My favorite quotation about writing is Flaubert's comment that when he wrote *Madame Bovary* he was really trying to approximate the shade of gray, color of a wood louse, the molelike existence of the dreary town. The details of Emma's life engaged him so little that until the last moment she was going to be a spinster. It was the gray that interested him, and that I understand.

What were you doing before you went to Mississippi in 1965?

BROWN: At Barnard I did almost nothing but write, which I regret because I sort of forgot to get an education. No one could have stopped me from writing at the time, but the history, botany, and all the rest that I missed makes me wince now. I majored in English, and at Barnard at that time one couldn't read anything that wasn't in the language of its composition. So I didn't read the Russians or Mann or . . . All I wanted to do was write. Before that, I had assumed I would go into journalism; I didn't dare anything more "creative." In my freshman English class I was told to write a sonnet. I did one called "On the Ghost of Thomas Wolfe," appropriate to a seventeen-year-old, and sold it to the *New York Times*. (That was when the paper was printing absolutely execrable poetry on the editorial page.) Later I had some good teachers, Robert Pack and George Elliott. I did learn to sit still and revise, but I ignored the substance of every other discipline. Then I went to Brandeis to get a Ph.D. I hated it. In my class, which was full of would-be writers, I was the last to drop out. Graduate school was mutilating. In order to learn method, we were told we should suspend our sentimental interest in the content of the work. I quit when I decided that, if I put the effort and time I would spend on my thesis into my poetry, I might actually be a writer. In those days you could let your husband support you without a great deal of self-consciousness, and that's what I did. It would probably be a lot harder to do that now.

What writers were important to you when you started?

BROWN: That's very hard to answer. I was just doing the best I could. I was reading, amazed to be able to understand poetry at all, Yeats, Stevens, all the lesser models in the Hall-Pack-Simpson anthology, grave and iambic every one. In class we would belabor Empson's *Seven Types of Ambiguity*. I was learning a very self-conscious kind of writing, perhaps best for me at the time. I was a true child of the 1950s—inhibited, self-absorbed, all too analytic. The buttoned-up and buttoned-down poetry I was practicing to write was bad for me in one way—it was overcontrolled—but it did play to my strong points. I had written a lot of jingles when I was a kid, I was famous for my yearbook doggerel, so it was fairly easy for me to work with a formal kind of poetry. I guess I also learned the habit of economy and compression, though, and an interest in the sound and

285

rhythm sentences have, qualities I try to carry over into my prose. But when I was in school, I never thought I'd write fiction. I did love Henry James while I was in graduate school, and I suppose if I really let my prose go now it would come out full of Jamesian elaboration and thoroughly devoid of visible event.

Is this what you meant by the phrase "luxurious suavity of style" in your review of Marilyn French's Bleeding Heart?

BROWN: Yes. I am satisfied to read the serviceable gray gabardine prose of, say, Doris Lessing, for the sake of her ideas and her penetrating vision. But there are so many other modes, so many kinds of sensuous style from Woolf to Updike to Bellow to Gass or Paley or even Edna O'Brien (whom Gass would perhaps not like to stand next to on a list). Or there is the pure and elegant style of, say, Elizabeth Bowen, whom I love, or Paula Fox or Nabokov. How can anyone be less than eclectic in appreciation of such richness and diversity?

Some of my early stories are more verbally playful or resplendent than anything I've done since, when my concentration's been subverted by the structural challenges of putting a novel together. Gerda, in *The Autobiography of My Mother*, was a pleasure to create because, as an emigrée speaker, the language still bristled under her touch. It rolled away from her like mercury, precision always just out of reach: it was still a live medium. In *Tender Mercies*, as in *Cora Fry*, I chastened that language for my four-square New England characters, but I gave Laura her head. If she had no more motion, at least she had extravagance of language, a kind of extension of the senses, for what that was worth, as if in compensation.

Were you an only child?

BROWN: The youngest of three, with two older brothers. Why do you ask?

I'm interested in your repeated concern with accident. It seems to me only children are more anxious about accidents.

BROWN: As an only girl, I may bear some of the characteristics of only children. When I was at the Radcliffe Institute, I did an informal survey of women of some accomplishment and "determined" that high-achievers were usually either the first girl or the only girl. It may mean that some of the weight placed on an only child bears on an only girl. I am interested in accidents, fascinated by how much pure accident is possible, accident in which no component of personality is present. In *Tender Mercies* I wanted to explore how Dan's personality contributes to Laura's accident—not willfully, but as an outgrowth of his particular habits of action and passion. How much is he to blame? And then, if he is, because no one human is without fault, how much ought he to be punished? The same question occurs at the end of *Autobiography of My Mother*: How much are daughter and mother to be held responsible for the accident in which the granddaughter perishes? Our lives are full of accidents of varying kinds, and the discrimination between those kinds engages me.

Does this engagement make you primarily a moralist or metaphysician?

BROWN: I'm most wary of attempting to kick my material a level higher toward abstraction. I don't wish to claim that you can solve a problem by reading fiction, or tell people how to live. I'm interested only in the investigation, not in a fixed set of results.

I have been criticized for not pursuing such issues. Cynthia Ozick was surprised that there was not more of the fist raised at God in *Tender Mercies*: it is a very secular book, which is a reflection not only of my characters' pragmatism but of my own. On the other hand, I got a letter and pamphlets from a woman in the Midwest who said my characters could have been happy had they found Christ. They are poles of the same question: What is the next level of extrapolation? But I'm not the one to move my characters there.

In Autobiography of My Mother *you quote Sartre about how immorality is only the concrete made abstract. You have a large distrust of abstraction?*

BROWN: Huge, huge. And the older I get, the more concrete I am. In *Civil Wars*, my novel in progress, my character contemplates the coffins of her wards' parents and thinks the thoughts those kids must be thinking: Are they buried with their shoes on? . . . She says to herself that finally the difference between useful truth and useless mystery turns out to be specifics. I have a bad head for philosophy; when I read it I tend to be utterly confused or else to simplify it, and then I wonder how this could be what people are spending their lives debating. When I was writing a talk for a local lyceum, I realized that I hate to follow certain kinds of thoughts out to their very logical conclusions, as you do when you're giving a speech with a subject that's gone out to the world on a thousand printed announcements. It made me long to get back to fiction, where logic is not exactly the point. You're following your intuitions out to their ends, where there may yet be a dozen surprises.

You can't leave this in the transcript. It makes you a bad feminist.

BROWN: It certainly seems to. However, the *facts* of the lives of women are such that simply to record them as they are is to do a useful service to feminism. I am committed to being useful, if that's the word, as long as I don't have to compromise my sense of the complexity of an issue or a life.

Is there a way of remaining concrete and expanding material?

BROWN: Metaphor is one way. In *Tender Mercies* that slash of accident cutting across the family's lives opened up possibilities for metaphor and an instant deepening or expansion. It allowed me to write the sections in Laura's voice, which are almost pure metaphor, poetic beyond her realistic capabilities yet still, I think, plausible. Ellipsis is another way. My book of poems, *Cora Fry*, is a fiction writer's poem, strung on a narrative frame, devoted to the construction of a character by an accretion of fragments, tiny increments of daily observation enlarged by imagery. Which means, of course, that all the ellipses of passed time and unremarked-upon action fall in the cracks between the poems. It's a sort of hobby-horse of mine that more prose writers ought to make themselves comfortable with poetry so that they can accommodate a greater range of experience.

What writers who are women do you enjoy reading?

BROWN: Someone I like enormously is Alice Munro, who is Canadian. Her linked stories have the continuity of novels. These books about the lives of girls growing to be women in small Canadian towns are subtle, funny, detached, and thoroughly concrete. Munro brings us evidence of a lived life in a particular place which is illuminating and accurate without ever becoming sociology. By contrast, a book getting a lot of play now, Joyce Maynard's *Baby Love*, renders the lives of small-town women, but the novel has little in it beyond an extremely precise naming of brands, both of things and emotions. Marilyn French is also certainly accurate (if narrow) in her sociology, and useful to many people, but hers is not the kind of writing that interests me. There is not a single interesting sentence in her last book: no pleasure in words, no transformation of passionately held convictions into passionately worked prose.

You said once that the writer you'd respect most is one "who'd make a good gossip, a better small-time con man, a bad rabble-rouser, and a worse debater. And yet still be serious." Who else besides Alice Munro fits that bill?

BROWN: Flannery O'Connor, Stanley Elkin, Margaret Drabble at her best, Anne Tyler when she's not being too ingratiating. Fred Busch, who's a wonderful writer full of deep feeling and care for language, and who's still waiting for the audience he deserves. Diane Johnson, Eudora Welty. Cynthia Ozick, though she has a cold cutting edge—she may be the Jewish sister-under-the-skin of Flannery O'Connor.

Does it bother you that Alice Munro is unknown and Marilyn French is widely read?

BROWN: Yes, of course, but it continues to elude me what makes a popular book. It shouldn't concern me; I should be more noble, beyond such concerns for myself. But it bothers me that so many works of quality never reach the public eye, or don't penetrate the public's fixed gaze. No one seems to know what strange conjunction of writing and public interest makes certain books leap to the forefront. It's not simply quality or lack of quality; it's not subject matter. I don't know what it is. Sometimes good books are undone by lazy marketing, the self-fulfilling defeatism of publishers who don't expect anything of works they call, with a certain vaguely exasperated sigh, "literary" even though, in fact, they are quite accessible to a mass readership. Then every once in a while, one of those breaks through and ruins every theory.

You're familiar with the objections to realism. Do you have a theoretical rationale for your work?

BROWN: No. I'm not abstract, remember? You can't get me to do it. I struggle every time I sit down to write; I fear an unleavened quality in my prose, and I fear the staleness of certain mechanics of narrative. People like you have done this to me. I may try some experiment as an agent for textured prose, but each time I find myself distracted by the method, find I'm not able to represent deeply enough the emotional lives of my characters. I think it took a long time to get *Civil Wars* off the ground because I spent time experimenting with odd perspectives and, after a good bit of wasted time, ended up saying, "Back to the usual." I understand there's a displacement of means in accomplishing an end in fiction. I just want to make sure the end is accomplished. I want to *move* you. I may do some sociological business, a little humor on the side, but I'm happiest when someone says to me, "I was moved by that book" or "I felt for that character." People who tell me they lost sleep, or were reduced to tears, well . . . sadist that I am, those are my dearest readers.

If you really take seriously that quote of Kafka's—"The book must be an ax for the frozen sea within us"—except in a very few cases, with people who have a rarefied sophistication, that frozen sea is not going to be cracked open by a writer who takes such an ironic view of human nature that no real people are allowed to exist or be respected on the page. Simpler means are a surer touch for the purpose that most writers begin with: reaching out to other people, not instructing them in the futility of taking their lives seriously. As I look back at my fiction, I see a movement away from experiment. *Street Games* was occasionally innovative or at least inventive, and the uncollected stories I wrote before those were even more so, I suppose, but I've come to feel that the best way I engage complexities of character is by really quite straightforward means.

For you, then, language is referential?

BROWN: Yes, it is referential. Even when a story has an unconventional structure—a nonlinear narrative or a cryptic style—its intention, if it's going to mean anything to me, is to illuminate the way real lives are lived. I can only keep repeating that. Its language may not be realistic, but its exaggerations or energy do not exist reflexively for their own sake. Why don't we say that language for me is a kind of lens: it may clarify or it may enlarge, it may even distort for effect, but, however it works, it always works as a tool to bring the subject closer to the audience. What the writer whispers up close might be thoroughly subversive, but there is the understanding that real words are being heard, with reference to a real world or to an imagined one that reflects the qualities of this one rearranged. I love stylized or elliptical writing, vivid writing, but for me its ends are really fairly conservative. That is not to say that I think that writing should be anything but (as I think Shirley Hazzard called it) "uncompromised by purpose." Perhaps you shouldn't be talking to me at all!

Do you think other writers in the last five years or so have begun to accept the artifices of fiction and to write again about reality?

BROWN: I never understood who was reading self-conscious fiction in the first place. Maybe it's because I don't live in a university atmosphere. In fact, it's very important for me to live in a place where there are nonliterary people. They may not be the best readers of my work, but they're closer to me than to those who read Barth. Most of the people I know—even most of the writers I know—don't read Pynchon, for example. Maybe fiction *is* changing. I have no theory on the matter. When four other writers and I did a benefit reading in Cambridge not too long ago, people afterward said with some surprise that we were all writing about our families. Retrograde, but true.

Why don't women write like Pynchon or Barth?

BROWN: I don't want to get into the nurture/nature issue, but there is evidence that baby girls—young infants—are already more responsive to people, to faces and smiles, than are boys. That could suggest that women were biologically designed, however they may want to respond to that predisposition, to respond and nurture. All through their lives the emotional attachments of women are more bonded; we deal with separations from loved ones with greater difficulty than men. If all that is true, and I believe that for complex reasons it is, it wouldn't be surprising if women were more concrete, more concerned with audience. Art is an extension, after all, of one's whole emotional constitution. This means, possibly, that women will be more engaged by the social than by the reflexive function of writing.

How do you go about keeping your work your own when there are so many groups of readers willing to employ it for themselves?

BROWN: Some writers would be delighted to think their work is "employable," enrolled in a good cause. They would see my indifference to being useful, or at least the qualifications I feel about fiction as tract, as evidence that I'm a moral laggard and would suggest that I not be proud of my frivolity. In any event, I don't think you "go about" keeping your work your own—either it is appropriated by some group or it is annexable by no one in particular, the way the birds in the air serve no party and accomplish no mission. That comes of hearing your own voice when you write, which respects the distinction between fiction and rhetoric, not those of the many proselytizers for worthy causes who are (except in rare cases, I think) like the Sirens leading one astray. Eudora Welty says somewhere that she doesn't write for friends or even for herself. I write, she says, for *it*, for the pleasure of *it*. Anyone who wants to claim the work when it's finished is free to do so; it's the solicitation of my attention before it's finished that I want to resist. Needless to say there's a fine line, often, between a worthy "relevance" and didactic heavy handedness. Or, on the other side, the desire to cast a story about politics in engaging and illuminating human terms might result in a decline into triviality. I'm working on a novel now that has raised all these questions for me: Writing about characters who live for politics, how do I find a point of entry somewhere between the petty and the grandiloquent or the pedantic?

You want to move readers. How do you make sure you don't cheat, don't write melodrama?

BROWN: I don't know. I do throw out a lot of pages along the way. I felt with *Tender Mercies* that if I took a cool enough tone at the outset and kept to it, I would be able to get through some potentially sentimental moments. What happened, though, was that now and then I've been criticized for not being close enough to the characters, for not allowing the reader to like them better. In that novel I may have gone to such lengths to protect against sentimentality that some readers did not feel invited into the book. It is a "rigorous" book, someone has said. The same thing may be true of *Autobiography of My Mother*: it is about a cold woman, legalistic and detached. I find her a sympathetic character, one capable of evoking emotion, because she is a victim of her own family and past; but she is no more easily "enjoyed" than a lot of real people who challenge our capacities for sympathy.

You mention "victim." Several reviewers have commented on your interest in victims. Do you feel that's true?

BROWN: "Victim" is usually a word used from the outside to pronounce upon another person's life. It's easy for middle-class readers to call the denizens of *Street Games* "victims," but I don't think of them that way and I don't think the characters would see themselves as victims. Everybody suffers from something. "Victim" may be reviewers' shorthand for saying, "They are different from us."

Another theme seems to be recovery, both as a bringing back in memory and as getting well.

BROWN: Only in that I think I see what I'm doing in a book like *Tender Mercies* as telling the ultimate scary story. One critic understood beautifully when he said that, to me, life is "always on the verge of paralysis—about to go still, with worry, guilt, fear and with death in the long run"—and then proving to myself (and anyone else who's still listening) that the really vital lovable parts of ourselves can always, though at great cost, be redeemed. There is no redemption at the end of *Autobiography*, except perhaps that cool, emotionally paralyzed Gerda begins to melt into feelings. I wanted *Tender Mercies* to affirm, against all odds, that our love for each other can exist independent of "function," or household service or physical accomplishment. It *persists*, on the human edge of a kind of purity. And so does memory as a record of a lived life.

As a way of summary, would you discuss the titles of your two published novels and Civil Wars?

BROWN: I had the title for *The Autobiography of My Mother* before I had the book, and I didn't care whether the book fit it when it was finished or not. Or say that, like *Ragtime*, which Doctorow, I think, tells us actually gave him the rhythm of his prose, the Moebius-strip elusiveness of the subject in my title influenced my refusal to decide who was subject and who object in that book. Obviously the title really grew out of my conviction that the "reality" of the reader is relative, a function of vantage point, but I think the title may have helped to keep my intentions clear when I was in danger of forgetting them.

Tender Mercies was a harder title to find than the book was to write. Every day for months another two or three terrible titles went up on my refrigerator in my kids' magnetic letters, to be scrutinized or tasted or whatever you do when you're trying to feel the weight and judge the color and flavor of a title. And finally I came upon "tender mercies," a common enough phrase which is actually from Psalms, when I was reading Beckett!

As for *Civil Wars*, that too is an absolute title for me. It repre-

sents every conceivable rift between intimates that I can imagine—
you understand that this novel is set in Mississippi during and after
the civil rights period—every cross purpose at which friends and
family can move. (Alison Lurie wrote a novel called *The War between
the Tates*; her distance from her characters begins in the mocking
pun of the title. Mine is more straightforward.) I love the feeling—
anyone does—that aspects of writing are what Freud called "over-
determined," that is to say, reiterated in different ways, underlined, as
it were, with a thicker and thicker marking. That's what makes dra-
matic structure work, makes felicitous connections between words,
lines, images in poems or richly written, inwardly allusive prose. So
every time I discover another facet of family battle or struggle be-
tween old friends or allies who find themselves, now, with opposing
ideologies, the more pleasure I take in the title *Civil Wars*. It's as if
I go on justifying it after the fact, like a critic gone sleuthing: "Oh,
that's what she meant!" You can feel a real adrenalin high when you
happen onto the title that ties things together. It releases an energy
greater than that of the sum of the untitled parts.

*Have you been taken to task by any feminist critics for not giving
your female characters better lots?*

BROWN: To my surprise—no. Not for sending Cora Fry home to
a less than sensitive husband; not for the mother in *Autobiography of
My Mother*, a person of great intellectual achievement who doesn't
know how to live a forgiving and flexible life. She's certainly not
much of a role model. What has been said, fortunately not too often,
is that *Tender Mercies* was a long drawn-out metaphor for the anni-
hilation of women at the hands of men. The book, however, while it
is about the body, is not about the body politic. Never was I writing
without compassion for the man who found himself to blame in a
way for the destruction of his wife's body. Never did I feel I was
out to get him or to say to all men, "Here is what you do to your
wives." Vivian Gornick in the *Village Voice* saw the entire novel so
metaphorically that she entirely misrepresented the healing that goes
on at the end. Laura does not walk into the sunset, does not walk
anywhere; but her husband comes to her, and she back to him, with
a very difficult and broad forgiveness. There seems to me a sense of
the amplitude of all that is left to them. The husband who has not
thought much before the accident realizes that he values his wife, not

for the things she did with her body, but for who she was in some amorphous and satisfying way. When I was searching for that title I looked through my thesaurus for synonyms for amplitude, fullness, rightness—that's what I thought the book expressed, the ability of people to restitch the torn fabric and move on.

If I had reviewed Tender Mercies, *I would have said that I distrusted liking it—because the writer seems to be fair to men.*

BROWN: I would have taken that as a compliment, because it's what I'm trying for in my fiction. *Autobiography of My Mother* is a less likable book than *Tender Mercies*—it is full of argument between mother and daughter—but what pleases me about responses to the book is that different readers pick different sides of the argument to support. For me that averages out to fairness and says, "You have done your job well," no simple judgments passed.

I can get as angry as anyone about men. But my sense of the ways lives are lived is that everyone is a product of a childhood, of a set of parents who did not choose their lives because they had a set of parents who did not choose their lives, and so on. This kind of sympathy makes me a poor politician—a bad feminist, a bad activist, a bad any-ist. This is not to say that I forgive what people do, but I have a difficult time in my writing blaming anyone. (I wish I were as even-handed in my life.) In *Tender Mercies* Dan thinks about his father, who is a real bastard, a drunk who beats his wife, that he was a child too. He (the father) dreamed of growing up and having children. He could not have dreamed that he would abuse them the way he did. No one plans such mutilation, although to say that does not absolve anyone of responsibility for his actions. But a book is a good place to try for the whole story, the compassionate history of the interior, the invisible pain of the one who inflicts pain. In my story "A Letter to Ismael in the Grave," a wife forgives, or at least comprehends for a moment, her husband, his life and death, as a victim's victim. That is, it seems to me, what writing is for. You have a better chance of understanding people in your writing than you ever do in your life. You can be fair, more perfect, more forbearing on paper. My real fear as a writer is that some inadequacy of which I am not aware will be projected into the work and will limit its value in the final judgment. Because, ultimately, all of our work will be seen from a distance, like a view of the earth from above, and it will turn out that the shape and size of this or that body of writing will look wholly different from there. Skimpy. Stingy. Uninflected and unshaped. Or uninteresting except in relation to its surroundings. We are unintentionally responsible for the private qualities of these emanations of ourselves, and what they lack will, not coincidentally, be a judgment on our personalities and character in spite of all we try to control in them. Even biographers make statements about themselves, first by their choice of subject, then by the way they organize and interpret the life and work of another. The naked accounting will come later (perhaps too late to embarrass us or make us fall into a shamed silence), when we shall have to recognize in our work our own callowness, and by their absence all the thoughts we haven't thought, the imaginings we haven't dared, and the compassion we have not been able to summon. Some of us might even be proud that we found a way if not to display, then at least to embody, our virtues while our concentration appeared to be elsewhere. No sense thinking about it, though. If our life and work weren't spun of a single thread, where would the intimacy of insights—all those chancy shared secrets—ever come from? And why would anyone want to read them?

Acknowledgments

Most of these stories and essays have been published in a variety of magazines and books. For permission to reprint, I would like to thank:

American Short Fiction
American Poetry Review
American Review
Boston University Journal
Chelsea
Hudson Review
Massachusetts Review
New England Review
New Letters
Ploughshares
Quarterly Review of Literature
South Atlantic Quarterly
Tikkun
TriQuarterly
Witness

Anything Can Happen (University of Illinois Press)
Banquet: Stories by Five Women (Peņmaen Press)
Best American Short Stories (Houghton Mifflin)
Liquid City (Corona Publishers)
PEN/Syndicated Fiction Prizes
Pushcart Prizes (Pushcart Press)

Some Deaths in the Delta, now out of print, was published by the University of Massachusetts Press.

Some of these essays began as lectures: "Don't Just Sit There" and "Donald Barthelme: A Preliminary Account" at the Bread Loaf Writers' Conference; "Displaced Persons" at the Southern Literary Festival in Chattanooga, Tennessee; "The Jewish Writer as Endangered Species" at Congregation KAM Isaiah Israel in Chicago and "The Writer in the Jewish Community" Conference in Berkeley.

UNIVERSITY PRESS OF NEW ENGLAND publishes books under its own imprint and is the publisher for Brandeis University Press, Brown University Press, Clark University Press, University of Connecticut, Dartmouth College, Middlebury College Press, University of New Hampshire, University of Rhode Island, Tufts University, University of Vermont, and Wesleyan University Press.

Library of Congress Cataloging-in-Publication Data

Brown, Rosellen.
  [Selections. 1992]
A Rosellen Brown reader : selected poetry and prose / Rosellen Brown.
    p.   cm. — (The Bread Loaf series of contemporary writers)
ISBN 0-87451-575-0
I. Title.   II. Series.
PS3552.R7A6   1992
813'.54—dc20   91–50808